CREATIVE SCRAPS

QUILTING WITH BITS & PIECES™

HOUSE of
WHITE
BIRCHES

PUBLISHERS
SINCE 1947

Creative Scraps: Quilting With Bits & Pieces

Copyright © 2006 House of White Birches, Berne, Indiana 46711

EDITORS	Jeanne Stauffer, Sandra L. Hatch
ART DIRECTOR	Brad Snow
PUBLISHING SERVICES DIRECTOR	Brenda Gallmeyer
ASSOCIATE EDITOR	Dianne Schmidt
COPY SUPERVISOR	Michelle Beck
COPY EDITORS	Nicki Lehman, Mary O'Donnell
GRAPHIC ARTS SUPERVISOR	Ronda Bechinski
GRAPHIC ARTISTS	Jessi Butler, Vicki Staggs
PRODUCTION ASSISTANTS	Cheryl Kempf, Marj Morgan, Judy Neuenschwander
TECHNICAL ARTISTS	Connie Rand, Leigh Maley
PHOTOGRAPHY	Tammy Christian, Don Clark, Christena Green, Matt Owen
PHOTO STYLIST	Tammy Nussbaum
PUBLISHING DIRECTOR	David J. McKee
MARKETING DIRECTOR	Dan Fink
EDITORIAL DIRECTOR	Gary Richardson

Printed in USA
First Printing: 2006 in China
Library of Congress Number: 2006924141
Hard Cover ISBN: 978-1-59217-135-4
Soft Cover ISBN: 978-1-59217-157-6

Every effort has been made to ensure the accuracy and completeness of the instructions in this book. However, we cannot be responsible for human error or for the results when using materials other than those specified in the instructions, or for variations in individual work.

5 6 7 8 9

INTRODUCTION

This fabulous collection of beautiful quilts is for those people who enjoy looking at quilts and those who love to express their creativity by combining little bits and pieces of fabric to create quilts.

Even in the early days of this American needlecraft, when the fabric choices were very limited and quilts were stitched for the practical purpose of keeping family members warm, quilters used their sense of color and their ingenuity to create quilt blocks that were exquisite. What to these quilters was a work of love and necessity is considered by many of us as a work of art.

Today's quilter has many more options in fabrics, techniques and designs, but she or he follows the same path of selecting the design and fabrics to create a quilt that will become a legacy to future generations.

CONTENTS

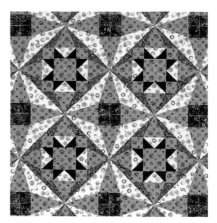

Sunbonnet Sue **6**

Fruit Basket **11**

Eight-Pointed Star **17**

Snowball **20**

Job's Troubles Antique Quilt **24**

Antique Nine-Patch **30**

Connecting Star **35**

Grandmother's
Flower Garden **38**

Chimneys & Cornerstones **43**

Rainbow of Rings **46**

Broken Wheel **51**

Scrappy Stars **56**

Tipsy Trail **60**

Delectable Mountains
Variations **65**

Sunflower Star **69**

Lazy Log Cabin **74**

Harvest Four-Patch Quilt **77**

Kansas Dugout **80**

Nine-Patch &
Four-Patch Stars **83**

Squares & Triangles **89**

Log Cabin
Stars at Midnight **91**

T is for Tulips **97**

Zoi's Violets **101**

Love of Patchwork
Friendship Quilt **107**

Stars & Diamonds **110**

Scrappy Prairie Queen **114**

Stained Glass Diamonds **117**

Peekaboo Yo-Yo Quilt **120**

Winter Snowflake **123**

Winding Ways **129**

Tulips Around the Cabin **132**

Plaid Lap Robe **137**

Turning Leaves **141**

An Autumn Evening **146**

Prairie Lily Wall Quilt **151**

Summer's Dream **155**

Bountiful Baskets **159**

Stars & Stripes **164**

Scrapwork Diamonds **172**

By the Seashore **175**

Bear Paw Jewels **180**

Garden of Eden **184**

Teaberry Twist **188**

Red & White Frustration **193**

Pomegranate Four-Patch **196**

Holly, Wood & Vine **203**

Oh, Christmas Tree **206**

Christmas Puzzle **209**

Christmas Wreaths **212**

Tic-Tac-Toe **216**

Checkerboard Four-Patch **220**

Christmas Counter-Change **224**

Have a Happy Scrappy Christmas **228**

Christmas Log Cabin **231**

Posy Patch **234**

Lollipop Flowers **238**

Crazy Logs Kid's Quilt **245**

Polka-Dot Party **249**

Scrap-Patch Hearts **252**

Butterfly Dance Duo **255**

Patchwork Fun **261**

Stars & Swirls Toddler Quilt **264**

Farm Animal Baby Quilt **268**

Here a Chick, There a Chick **275**

Cartwheel Clowns **278**

Pyramid & Stars Crib Quilt **282**

Mosaic Memories **290**

GENERAL INSTRUCTIONS **293**   SPECIAL THANKS **304**

SUNBONNET SUE

You can make a Sunbonnet Sue quilt that looks like it was made in the 1930s by using reproduction prints of that era.

Sunbonnet Sue
9" x 13½" Block

DESIGN BY CATE TALLMAN-EVANS

Project Specifications
Skill Level: Intermediate
Quilt Size: 58½" x 76½"
Block Size: 9" x 13½" and 4½" x 4½"
Number of Blocks: 16 and 125

Materials
- ⅝ yard pink solid
- 16 (9" squares) assorted prints for dresses—1⅛ yards total
- 1½ yards total assorted printed scraps
- 2⅜ yards green solid
- 3 yards cream solid
- Backing 64" x 83"
- Batting 64" x 83"
- Neutral color all-purpose thread
- Quilting thread
- 12- or 30-weight and 60-weight black cotton thread for machine embroidery
- Black and assorted flower colors 6-strand embroidery floss
- Heat-resistant template plastic (optional)
- Spray starch and paintbrush (optional)
- Freezer paper (optional)
- Fabric glue (optional)
- Basic sewing tools and supplies

Project Note
Several fabric manufacturers include reproduction prints in their collections each year. Look for them at your local quilt shop or online. A search for reproduction fabrics will yield plenty of choices. Have fun making your new quilt look old using this old-time favorite pattern.

Cutting
Step 1. Cut four 15" by fabric width strips cream solid; subcut strips into (16) 10½" x 15" A rectangles. Fold and crease each A to mark the center.
Step 2. Cut (16) 2½" by fabric width strips cream solid; subcut strips into (250) 2½" B squares. Draw a diagonal line from corner to corner on the wrong side of each B square.

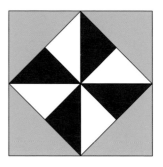

Pinwheel
4½" x 4½" Block

Step 3. Cut (250) 2½" x 2½" C squares from assorted print scraps. **Note:** *Each Pinwheel block requires two same-fabric C squares.*
Step 4. Cut (20) 3⅛" by fabric width strips green solid; subcut strips into (250) 3⅛" D squares. Cut D squares in half on one diagonal to make 500 D triangles.
Step 5. Cut seven 2¼" by fabric width strips green solid for binding.

Completing the Sunbonnet Sue Blocks
Hand Appliqué
Step 1. Make a template for each appliqué shape using full-size pattern given. Trace 16 of each

template on the non-shiny side of freezer paper. **Note:** *The pattern is given in reverse for tracing. To make one or more Sunbonnet Sues face left as in the quilt shown, flip the templates face down on the freezer paper to trace shapes.*

Step 2. Cut out each shape on the traced lines. With a hot, dry iron, press a dress shape onto an assorted print square with the shiny side of the freezer paper on the wrong side of the fabric. Cut out dress, leaving a scant ¼" seam allowance beyond freezer-paper edge.

Step 3. Repeat Step 2 for the remaining appliqué shapes with pink solid.

Step 4. Leave seam allowance at top of the foot, neck of dress and straight edge of hand unfolded. Fold all other seam allowances over the freezer paper and baste in place.

Step 5. After all appliqué shapes are prepared, center motif on a creased A rectangle and baste or pin in place in numerical order; repeat for 16 motifs.

Step 6. Appliqué shapes in place using a buttonhole stitch and 2 strands black embroidery floss. **Note:** *The stitches should be ⅛" wide and ⅛" deep.*

Step 7. Trim background fabric away under appliqué shapes; remove freezer-paper shapes.

Step 8. Trim each completed block to 9½" x 14".

Step 9. Embroider hatband and other designs on hats using embroidery floss colors and stitches of choice.

Machine Appliqué

Step 1. Using heat-resistant template plastic and the patterns given, make a template for all appliqué shapes. **Note:** *Patterns are given in reverse for tracing.*

Step 2. Trace one dress shape onto the wrong side of each assorted print square. **Note:** *For one reverse block, flip templates when tracing.*

Step 3. Trace remaining shapes onto the wrong side of pink solid, leaving at least ½" between shapes for seam allowance. Cut out each shape, leaving a scant ¼" seam allowance around each one.

Step 4. Spray starch into a cup. Using a paintbrush, saturate the seam allowance of one dress with starch.

Step 5. Position the heat-resistant plastic template on the wrong side of one dress so that the template's edges are even with the drawn line.

Step 6. Using a hot, dry iron, press the seam allowance over the edge of the template to the wrong side of the dress. Repeat until each section of the starched seam allowance has been turned and pressed.

Step 7. Remove the plastic template; repeat for all appliqué pieces.

Step 8. Center motif on a creased A rectangle and baste in place in numerical order using pins, fabric glue or thread; repeat for 16 motifs.

Step 9. Use 1 strand of 12-weight black cotton thread or 2 strands of 30-weight black cotton in the top of the machine and 60-weight black cotton thread in the bobbin, buttonhole-stitch around each appliqué shape.

Step 10. Trim each completed block to 9½" x 14".

Step 11. Embroider hatband and other designs on hats using embroidery floss colors and stitches of choice.

Completing the Pinwheel Sashing Blocks

Step 1. Place a B square right sides together with a C square; stitch a ¼" seam on each side of the marked line as shown in Figure 1. Repeat with all B and C squares.

Step 2. Cut a stitched B-C pair apart on the marked line to make two B-C units as shown in Figure 2. Repeat to complete 500 B-C units.

Figure 1   **Figure 2**

Step 3. Join four same-fabric B-C units as shown in Figure 3; repeat to complete 125 B-C squares. Press seams in one direction.

Figure 3

Step 4. Sew a D triangle to each side of a B-C square to complete one Pinwheel block as shown in Figure 4; repeat for 125 blocks. Press seams toward D.

Figure 4

Completing the Top

Step 1. Join three Pinwheel blocks to make a sashing strip as shown in Figure 5; repeat for 20 strips. Press seams in one direction.

Figure 5

Step 2. Join four Sunbonnet Sue blocks with five sashing strips to make a block row as shown in Figure 6: repeat for four block rows. Press seams toward Sunbonnet Sue blocks.

Figure 6

Step 3. Join 13 Pinwheel blocks to make a sashing row as shown in Figure 7: repeat for five sashing rows. Press seams in one direction.

Step 4. Join the block rows with the sashing rows to complete the top; press seams toward block rows.

Finishing the Quilt

Step 1. Sandwich the batting between the completed top and prepared backing; pin or baste layers together to hold.

Step 2. Quilt as desired by hand or machine; remove pins or basting. Trim excess backing and batting even with quilt top.

Step 3. Join binding strips on short ends to make one long strip. Fold the strip in half along length with wrong sides together; press.

Step 4. Sew binding to quilt edges, mitering corners and overlapping ends. Fold binding to the back side and stitch in place to finish. ◆

Figure 7

Sunbonnet Sue
Placement Diagram
58½" x 76½"

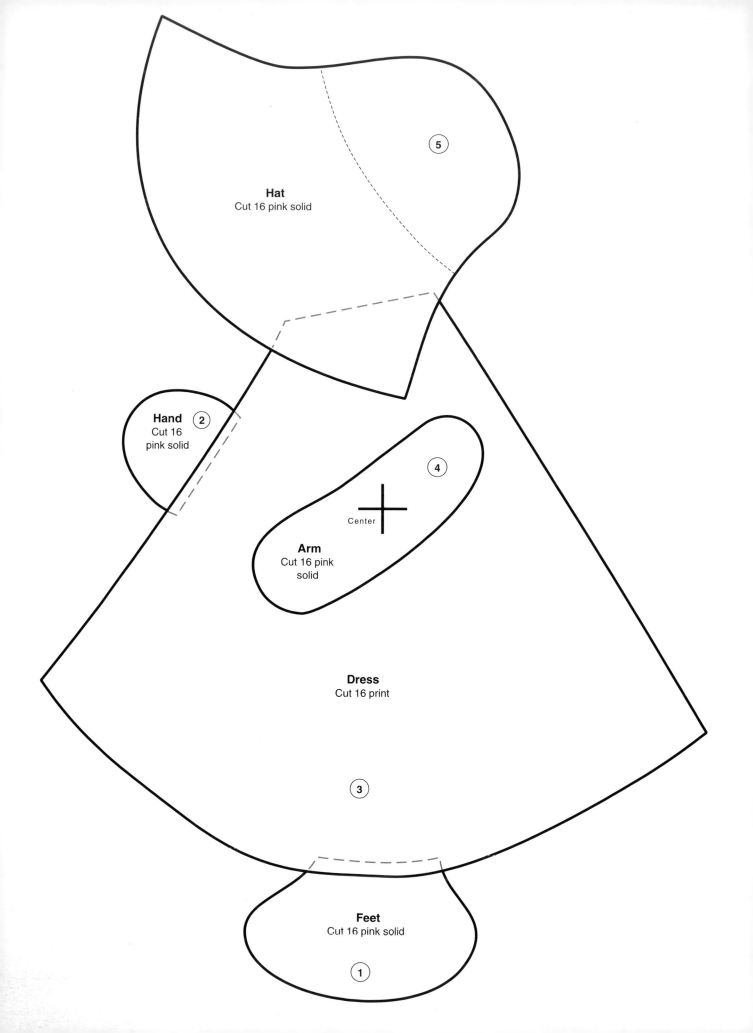

Hat
Cut 16 pink solid

5

Hand
Cut 16
pink solid

2

Arm
Cut 16 pink
solid

4

Center

Dress
Cut 16 print

3

Feet
Cut 16 pink solid

1

FRUIT BASKET

Fabric baskets are favorites among quilters, as evidenced by the variety of basket patterns created in the 1930s. The Fruit Basket design is known by several other names, the most common being the Cake Stand. The amount of quilting on this basket quilt shows that the person who made this treasured heirloom loved to quilt.

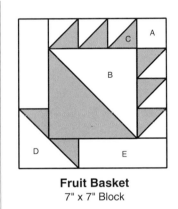

Fruit Basket
7" x 7" Block

FROM THE COLLECTION OF SANDRA L. HATCH

Project Specifications

Skill Level: Intermediate
Quilt Size: Approximately
  73¾" x 83⅝"
Block Size: 7" x 7"
Number of Blocks: 42

Materials

- 5½ yards bleached muslin
- 42 print scraps 10" square for blocks
- Print scraps for border triangles
- Backing 80" x 90"
- Batting 80" x 90"
- 12 yards self-made or purchased binding
- Basic sewing tools and supplies

Project Note

The pieced blocks in this old-time quilt from our grandmothers' era are combined with solid blocks set on point. Each basket uses a different print combined with bleached muslin background pieces to complete the design.

Instructions

Step 1. Cut two muslin strips 6½" x 86" and two strips 6½" x 64" for borders. Set aside.

Step 2. Prepare and cut templates as directed referring to the General Instructions.

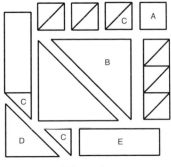

Figure 1

Step 3. Piece one block by sewing a muslin C to a print C; repeat to make six C units. Join three C units; repeat. Arrange with remaining pieces and join referring to Figure 1. Repeat for 42 blocks; press.

Step 4. Cut 30 muslin squares 7½" x 7½".

Step 5. Cut six muslin squares 11⅛" x 11⅛". Cut apart on both diagonals to make side fill-in triangles referring to Figure 2. Cut two muslin squares 5⅞" x 5⅞". Cut once on the diagonal to make corner triangles referring to Figure 2.

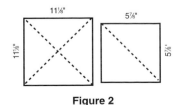

Figure 2

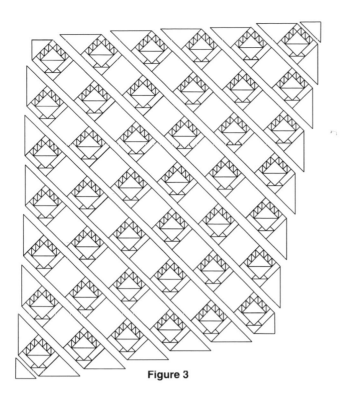

Figure 3

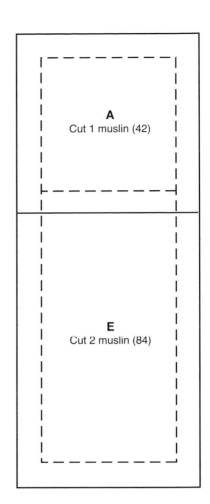

A
Cut 1 muslin (42)

E
Cut 2 muslin (84)

Step 6. Arrange the pieced blocks with the muslin squares and triangles in diagonal rows referring to Figure 3. Join in rows; join the rows to complete the center pieced section; press.

Step 7. Sew 25 print F's to 24 muslin F's as shown in Figure 4; repeat. Sew a strip to the top and bottom of quilt center; press seams toward border strips. **Note:** *Adjust these strips to fit, if necessary.*

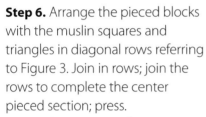

Figure 4

Step 8. Sew 29 print F's to 28 muslin F's to make a long strip;

repeat. Sew a strip to each long side of quilt center; press.

Step 9. Sew the 6½" x 64" muslin border strips to the top and bottom. Press seams toward border strips. Trim excess square at edges. Sew the 6½" x 86" muslin border strips to sides. Press seams toward border strips. Trim excess square at corners.

Step 10. Using the scallop border pattern given and starting in the center of each side border strip, mark the shape on the quilt's edges using a water-erasable marker or pencil. Trim to curved shape. Using a plate of desired size, trace circle shape at corners and trim.

Step 11. Mark the quilting designs given on quilt top referring to the General Instructions.

Step 12. Finish quilt referring to the General Instructions. **Note:** *Use bias binding to finish the curved edges of the quilt, as it will stretch around the border scallops.* ◆

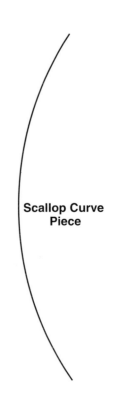

Scallop Curve Piece

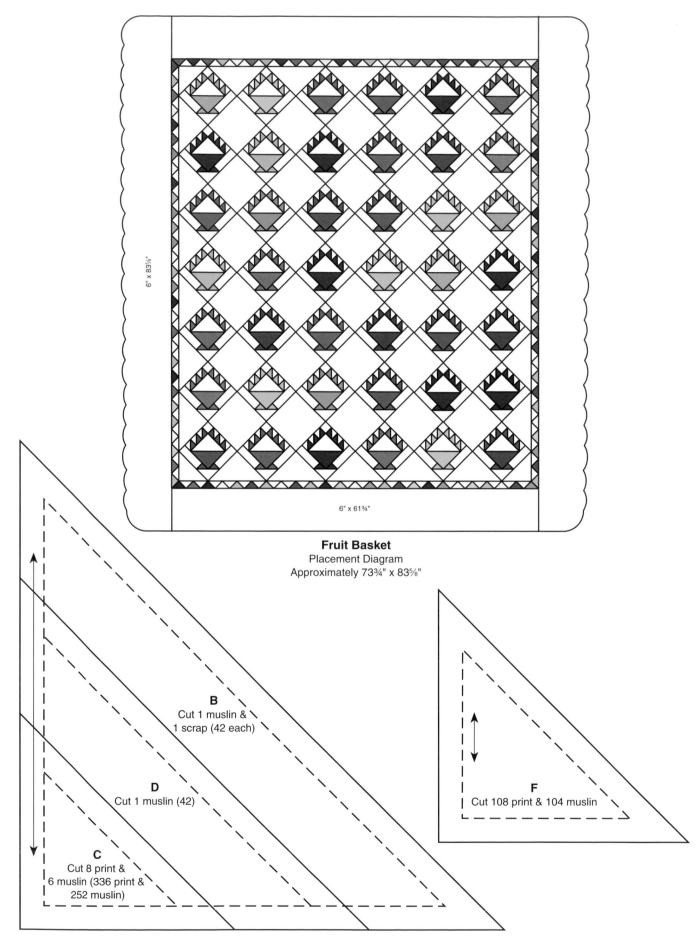

6" x 83⅝"

6" x 61¾"

Fruit Basket
Placement Diagram
Approximately 73¾" x 83⅝"

B
Cut 1 muslin &
1 scrap (42 each)

D
Cut 1 muslin (42)

C
Cut 8 print &
6 muslin (336 print &
252 muslin)

F
Cut 108 print & 104 muslin

Quilting Design for Muslin Blocks

Border Quilting Design

EIGHT-POINTED STAR

The Eight-Pointed Star design is one of the most popular and basic Nine-Patch patterns. There are countless variations from simple to complex. This antique scrap version has an unusual setting. Each block combines only two fabrics, a light and a dark value. The blocks are set together with wide sashing strips on the diagonal without borders. If you like the antique look, antique reproduction fabrics may be found at your local quilt shop.

Eight-Pointed Star
9" x 9" Block

FROM THE COLLECTION OF SANDRA L. HATCH

Project Specifications
Skill Level: Intermediate
Quilt Size: 63¾" x 80¾"
Block Size: 9" x 9"
Number of Blocks: 31

Materials
- 31 pieces each light and dark prints 9" x 12" or 1¼ yards each light and dark prints
- ¾ yard pink-on-pink print
- 2 yards green print
- Backing 70" x 87"

- Batting 70" x 87"
- 8¾ yards self-made or purchased binding
- Coordinating all-purpose thread
- Basic sewing tools and supplies

Instructions
Step 1. Cut one square light print and four squares dark print 3½" x 3½".

Step 2. Cut two squares each light and dark prints 4¼" x 4¼". Cut each of these squares on both diagonals

to make triangles as shown in Figure 1.

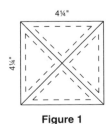

Figure 1

Step 3. Sew a light triangle to a dark triangle on the short sides as shown in Figure 2; repeat for all triangles.

Figure 2

Step 4. Join two triangle units to make a square as shown in Figure 3; repeat for four squares.

Figure 3

Step 5. Arrange the pieced squares with the 3½" x 3½" squares to make a block as shown in Figure 4. Join the pieces in rows; press. Join the rows to complete the block; press. Repeat for 31 blocks.

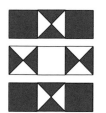

Figure 4

Step 6. Cut 32 sashing squares pink-on-pink print 3½" x 3½".
Step 7. Cut 80 sashing strips from green print 3½" x 9½".
Step 8. Cut five squares 9¾" x 9¾" pink-on-pink print. Cut each

square on both diagonals to make four triangles as shown in Figure 5.

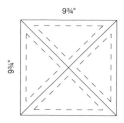

9¾"

9¾"

Figure 5

Step 9. Arrange the pieced blocks, sashing strips and squares and pink triangles in diagonal rows as shown in Figure 6 below. **Note:** *At this time all sashing strips are still rectangles with no angled cuts. The angles will be trimmed later.*
Step 10. Join the units in diagonal rows; press. Trim sashing strips even with edges of outside-edge triangles as shown in Figure 7. Trim corner sashing strips at a 90-

degree angle using any square as a guide for cutting as shown in Figure 8 to complete top.

Figure 7

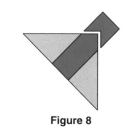

Figure 8

Step 11. Prepare quilt top for quilting and finish referring to the General Instructions. ✦

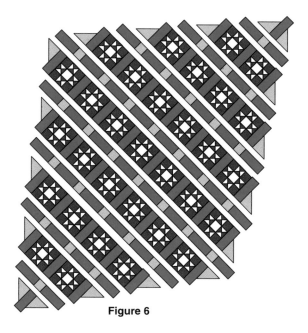

Figure 6

Eight-Pointed Star
Placement Diagram
63¾" x 80¾"

SNOWBALL

No doubt the quilter who stitched this fascinating pattern had a sunny seat by the window where she could watch all the neighborhood children playing in the snow. Notice how the snowball theme is carried into the scalloped border, a clever finishing touch!

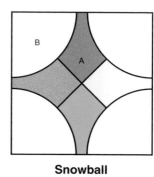

Snowball
6½" x 6½" Block

DESIGN BY CAROL SCHERER

Project Specifications
Skill Level: Intermediate
Quilt Size: 79" x 92"
Block Size: 6½" x 6½"
Number of Blocks: 143

Materials
- Scraps for blocks, including floral prints and coordinating solids
- 8 yards white fabric for blocks and borders
- Backing 85" x 98"
- Batting 85" x 98"
- 12 yards pink bias binding
- Basic sewing tools and supplies

Project Note
Hand-pieced and hand-quilted in the 1930s, this quilt contains a pleasing assortment of floral prints and pastel solids. When the blocks are joined together, perfect round snowball shapes are formed, thus giving the quilt its unusual name.

Instructions
Step 1. Cut the border strips from the white fabric before cutting the pieces for the blocks. First, cut off a little more than 2½ yards, or 94"; trim off the selvage edge. Cut four strips 4" x 94" (the excess will be trimmed later). Set these strips aside. The remaining white fabric is to be used in the blocks.

Step 2. Prepare templates using pattern pieces given. Cut fabric patches as directed on each piece for one block (whole quilt).

Step 3. To piece one block, referring to Figure 1, sew two A pieces together—one print and one solid; repeat. Sew these joined pairs together, matching center seams. Add the curved B pieces to the outside corners to complete one block. Complete 143 blocks to make the quilt as shown. Press blocks.

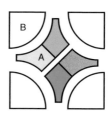

Figure 1

Step 4. Join the blocks in rows; press seams of adjacent rows in opposite directions. Join the rows to complete the pieced center; press seams in one direction.

Step 5. Sew the previously cut border strips to the sides of the quilt center. Mark the strips with the scalloped border pattern given in Figure 2 and cut out. (Straight-sided borders may be substituted if you prefer.) Match the fold line on the border pattern with the center

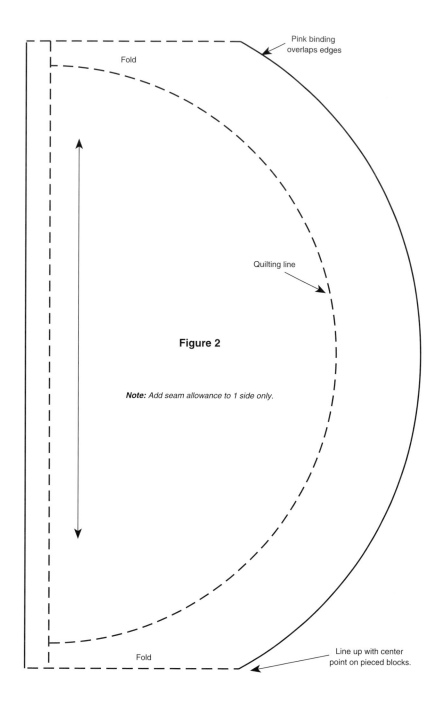

Pink binding overlaps edges

Fold

Quilting line

Figure 2

Note: Add seam allowance to 1 side only.

Fold

Line up with center point on pieced blocks.

of the blocks. Refer to the quilt photograph as needed; press.

Step 6. Sew the remaining borders to the top and bottom in the same manner, mitering corners as shown in the General Instructions. Press and trim off excess at back side of corners.

Step 7. Refer to Figure 3 for quilting design used on the sample quilt. Mark design on finished top with a water-erasable marker or pencil.

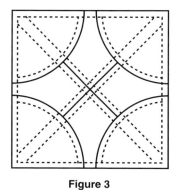

Figure 3

Step 8. Finish quilt referring to the General Instructions. ◆

Snowball
Placement Diagram
79" x 92"

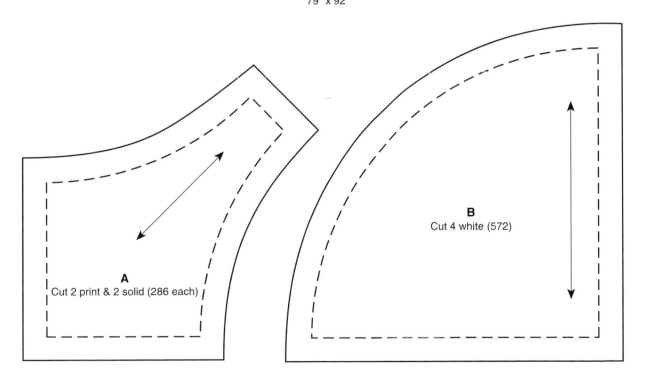

A
Cut 2 print & 2 solid (286 each)

B
Cut 4 white (572)

JOB'S TROUBLES ANTIQUE QUILT

The antique quilt, Job's Troubles, requires set-in seams and precise piecing of points. Although hand piecing is recommended for novice stitchers, more experienced stitchers may successfully use machine-piecing methods.

Job's Troubles
15⅞" x 15" Block

Project Specifications
Skill Level: Intermediate
Quilt Size: 77" x 79½"
Block Size: 15⅞" x 15"
Number of Blocks: 9

Materials
- Scraps navy, burgundy, black, gray and brown prints and plaids for dark A pieces
- Scraps pink and white prints and plaids for light A pieces
- ½ yard each 3 different white shirting prints for borders and C pieces
- ⅔ yard tan stripe for borders and side triangles
- 2 yards dark pink print
- 4 yards muslin (includes binding)
- Backing 83" x 86"
- Batting 83" x 86"
- All-purpose thread to match fabrics
- White hand-quilting thread
- Basic sewing tools and supplies, rotary cutter, mat and ruler, water-erasable marker or pencil, and hole punch or awl

Project Notes
As with most antique quilts, when examined, it seems accuracy in piecing is inconsistent. The quilt shown is no exception. The pink B rectangle pieces on the inside blocks are all the same size, but those used on the outside blocks are almost ¾" narrower. Of course, this means that the C pieces joining these areas are not equilateral triangles as in the blocks. This really doesn't matter because these pieces do not get stitched together with other blocks. Our instructions use the same-size B and C pieces throughout.

The quilt uses a very thick batting, but it is still heavily quilted. We wonder how the quilter did it. The batting has migrated in lumps in areas where the quilting is less than ½" apart. This gives the quilt lots of texture.

This quilt design was shown in Barbara Brackman's *Encyclopedia of Pieced Quilt Patterns* with several variations and different names—Brunswick Star, Rolling Stone and Chained Star are a few examples. Job's Troubles seems like the most appropriate name. It was published in the magazine *Modern Priscilla*, begun in 1897. This magazine was a mail-order source for patterns during the early 1900s until it was bought by *Needlecraft—The Home Arts Magazine* in 1930. The shirting prints along with the navy print clearly date the quilt at the turn of the century.

Instructions

Step 1. Prepare templates for A–E using pattern pieces given; cut as directed on each piece.

Step 2. Using a hole punch or awl, make a hole in the points of the A, C and D templates as shown in Figure 1. Place the templates on the wrong side of the corresponding fabric patches. Using a sharp lead pencil, make a mark through the holes to mark seam joints as shown in Figure 2.

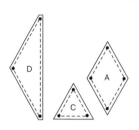

Figure 1

Figure 2

Figure 3   **Figure 4**

Step 3. Sew a dark print A to a light print A, starting and ending seams at the marked dots as shown in Figure 3, securing seams at the beginning and end; set in a muslin A as shown in Figure 4. Repeat for three units. Join the pieced units to create a star unit as shown in Figure 5, again starting and ending seams at the marked

dots; press seams in one direction. Set in a muslin A between dark and light print A pieces, again referring to Figure 5. Press center seam in a swirling pattern as shown in Figure 6. Repeat for 36 star units.

Figure 5   **Figure 6**

Step 4. Sew C to each end of 33 B pieces to make a B-C unit as shown in Figure 7; press seams toward B. Set aside six units.

Figure 7

Step 5. Sew a B-C unit to three straight sides of a star unit as shown in Figure 8; set in B between the B-C units, again referring to Figure 8 and starting and stopping at marked dots to complete a Job's Troubles block. Press seams toward B. Repeat for nine blocks.

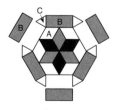

Figure 8

Step 6. Add B and C pieces to nine star units as shown in Figure 9 to create partial blocks. Cut three partial blocks in half as shown in Figure 10.

Figure 9

Figure 10

Step 7. Join three blocks, two partial blocks and two half-partial blocks to make an A row as shown in Figure 11; repeat for three A rows. Press seams toward blocks.

Figure 11

Step 8. Join six star units with five B pieces to make a B row as shown in Figure 12; repeat for three B rows. Press seams toward B pieces.

Figure 12

Step 9. Sew a B-C unit to one edge of each star unit in one B row as shown in Figure 13; set in B pieces on the adjacent edges, again referring to Figure 13. Trim ends even with star units.

Step 10. Join the A and B rows referring to Figure 14 for positioning of rows; press seams toward the A rows.

Step 11. Trim the A rows even with the B rows as shown in Figure 15 to complete the top and bottom of the pieced center.

Trim

Figure 15

Step 12. Set in D triangles between side B pieces and sew E and ER to corners to complete the pieced center as shown in Figure 16.

Step 13. Cut and piece two strips tan stripe 2" x 70½" and two strips white shirting print 2½" x 70½"; sew the tan strips and then the white strips to the top and

Figure 13   **Figure 14**

Job's Troubles Antique Quilt
Placement Diagram
77" x 79½"

bottom of the pieced center. Press seams toward strips.

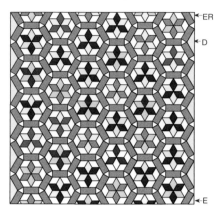

Figure 16

Step 14. Cut and piece two strips of one white shirting print 2" x 80" and two strips of another white shirting print 2½" x 80". Sew the narrower strips to the top and bottom and the wider strips to opposite long sides to complete the pieced top.

Step 15. Sandwich batting between the completed top and prepared backing piece; pin or baste layers together to hold.

Step 16. Quilt as desired by hand or machine. ***Note:*** *The quilt shown was heavily hand-quilted using white quilting thread in a continuous swirling pattern with lines about ½" apart over the entire quilt.*

Step 17. When quilting is complete, trim excess batting and backing edges even with quilted top.

Step 18. Cut eight strips muslin 2¼" by fabric width. Join strips on short ends to make one long strip for binding.

Step 19. Fold binding strip with wrong sides together along length and press. Pin to the quilt top edges with raw edges even. Stitch all around, mitering corners and overlapping ends. Turn binding to the back side; hand-stitch in place to finish. ◆

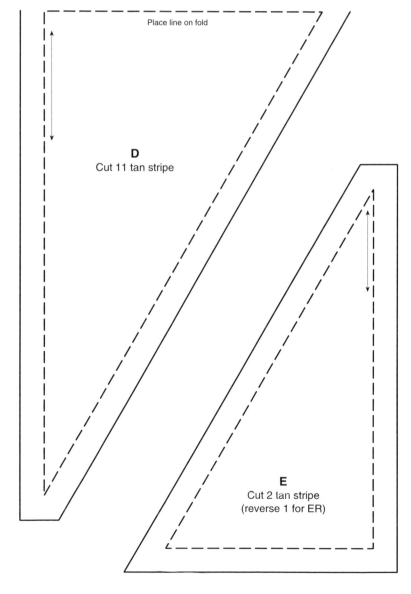

Place line on fold

D
Cut 11 tan stripe

E
Cut 2 tan stripe
(reverse 1 for ER)

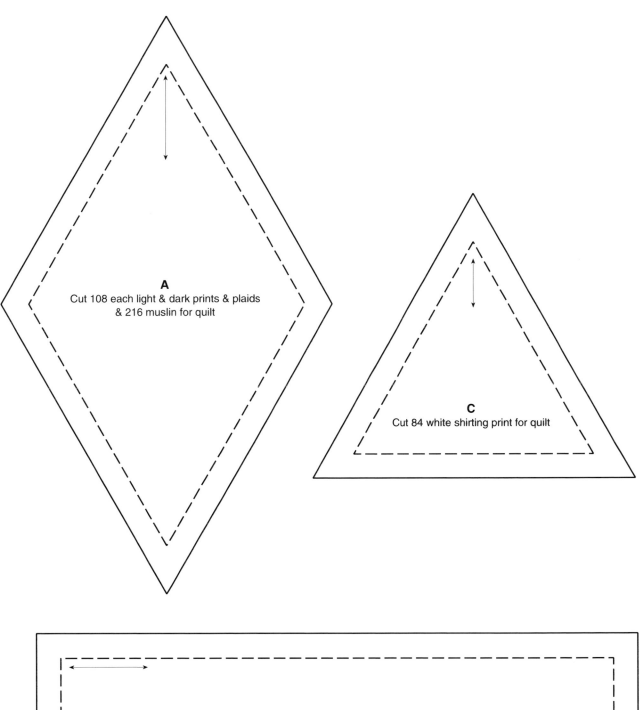

A
Cut 108 each light & dark prints & plaids
& 216 muslin for quilt

C
Cut 84 white shirting print for quilt

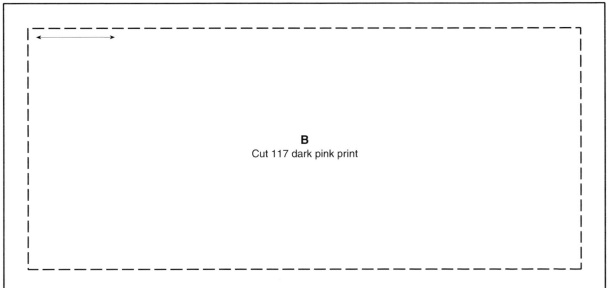

B
Cut 117 dark pink print

ANTIQUE NINE-PATCH

The Nine-Patch block is set on point in this antique scrap quilt. Each block uses only one print with muslin, and some fabrics are used to make several blocks. Here is the perfect opportunity to use up scraps from your collection.

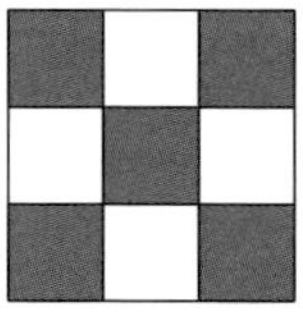

Nine-Patch
6" x 6" Block

FROM THE COLLECTION OF PAULINE LEHMAN

Project Specifications
Skill Level: Beginner
Quilt Size: 75½" x 84"
Block Size: 6" x 6"
Number of Pieced Blocks: 56

Materials
- 5¾ yards bleached muslin
- 1½ yards total medium to dark scraps (a 2½" x 14" strip is needed for each block)
- Backing 81" x 90"
- Batting 81" x 90"
- Off-white all-purpose thread
- 1 spool off-white quilting thread
- 9 yards self-made or purchased binding
- Basic sewing tools and supplies

Project Notes
It is difficult to give quick cutting and piecing instructions because scrap fabrics are used. If you prefer to use these methods, cut muslin strips in 2½" x 14" lengths and combine with scrap strips of the same length referring to the General Instructions or other projects for methods when using strips.

Instructions
Step 1. Cut 14 strips muslin 2½" by fabric width; subcut strips into (224) 2½" segments.

Step 2. Cut five 2½" x 2½" squares medium or dark scraps for each block to total 280 squares for 56 blocks to make the quilt. ***Note:*** *More than one block from each scrap color may be used or each block could be different. The quilt shown has several colors repeated, some more than four times.*

Step 3. To piece one block, sew a scrap square to a muslin square to a scrap square to make one row; repeat. Sew a muslin square to a scrap square to a muslin square to make another row. Press seams toward scraps.

Step 4. Join the rows as shown in Figure 1 to complete one block; press. Repeat for 56 blocks.

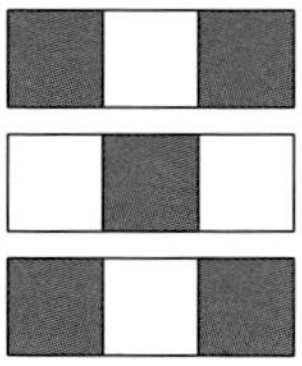

Figure 1

Step 5. Cut 42 squares muslin 6½" x 6½".

Step 6. Cut seven squares muslin 9¾" x 9¾". Cut each square across both diagonals as shown in Figure 2 to make side fill-in triangles.

Step 7. Cut two squares muslin 5⅛" x 5⅛". Cut each square once on the diagonal to make corner triangles.

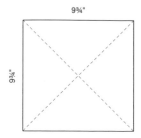

Figure 2

Step 8. Arrange triangles with pieced blocks and solid squares in diagonal rows as shown in Figure 3. Join the units in rows; press. Join the rows; press to complete pieced center.

Step 9. Cut two strips muslin 8½" x 60". Sew to top and bottom of pieced center; press seams toward strips. Cut two more strips 8½" x 84½". Sew to opposite long sides; press seams toward strips.

Step 10. Mark the quilting design given in the muslin squares.

Step 11. Prepare quilt top for quilting and finish referring to the General Instructions. ✦

Figure 3

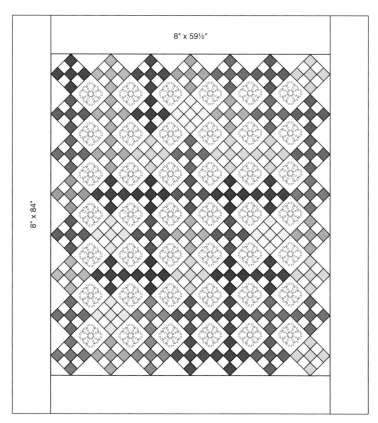

Antique Nine-Patch
Placement Diagram
75½" x 84"

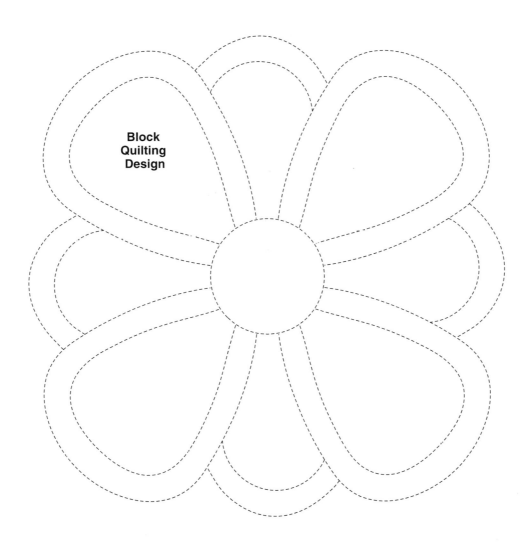

Block
Quilting
Design

CONNECTING STAR

A perfect example of a unit-pieced quilt, the Connecting Star units are joined with orange solid diamonds. You may not prefer the colorful fabric of the antique quilt shown; however, in Grandmother's day, orange was a popular color. Combined with the green solid of the day, you may be surprised how much you like this fascinating color combination.

Connecting Star
4½" x 4½" Unit

Project Specifications
Skill Level: Intermediate
Quilt Size: 67½" x 72"
Unit Size: 4½" x 4½"

Materials
- 4 yards orange solid
- 2 yards green solid
- Assorted dark and light print scraps to total 2½ yards
- Backing 74" x 78"
- Batting 74" x 78"
- 8½ yards self-made or purchased binding
- Basic sewing tools and supplies

Project Note
Regardless of whether you choose the colors Grandmother used or connect your star shapes with a country blue or rose, you will enjoy piecing the star units while using up scraps from your accumulated stash.

Instructions
Step 1. Cut four strips orange solid 2" x 70" and four strips 2" x 74" before cutting templates. Set aside. Cut two strips green solid 2" x 70" and two strips 2" x 74". Set aside. **Note:** *These strips are at least 2" longer than needed to finish the quilt as is to allow for adjustments when sewing. The excess is trimmed after the corners are mitered.*

Step 2. Cut four A pieces per unit—two light prints and 2 dark prints. Join a light print to a dark print twice. Join the two pieced sections to create one Connecting Star unit referring to Figure 1.

Figure 1

Step 3. Complete 182 star units.

Arrange in 14 rows of 13 units each. When you have found a pleasing arrangement, pin units in rows in order. Begin joining rows with B pieces between referring to Figure 2, starting and ending each row with C as shown in Figure 3.

Figure 2

Figure 3

Step 4. Join the rows with B pieces, with C on the edge of the top and bottom rows, referring to Figure 4.

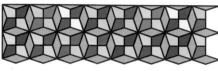

Figure 4

Step 5. Sew a 2" x 70" orange strip to each side of a 2" x 70" green strip; repeat. Press seams to one side.
Step 6. Sew a 2" x 74" orange strip to each side of a 2" x 74" green strip; repeat. Press seams to one side.

Step 7. Sew the longer strips to the long sides of the quilt top and the shorter strips to the short sides, mitering corners as shown in the General Instructions. Press seams toward border strips. Trim off excess from back side of corners. Press completed quilt top.
Step 8. Finish quilt as desired referring to the General Instructions. ◆

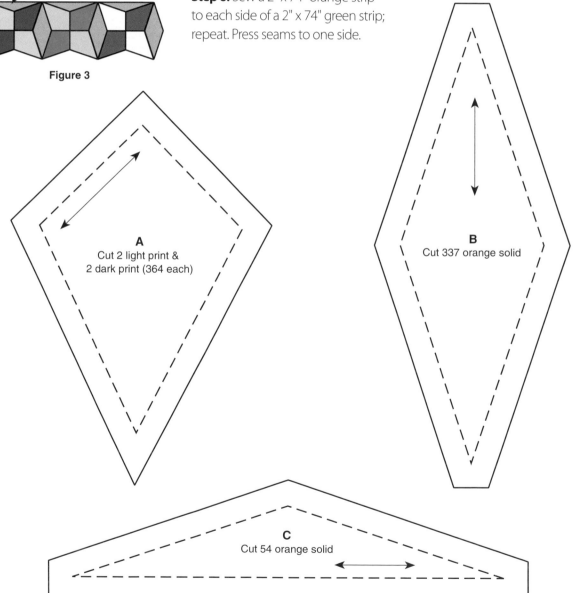

A
Cut 2 light print &
2 dark print (364 each)

B
Cut 337 orange solid

C
Cut 54 orange solid

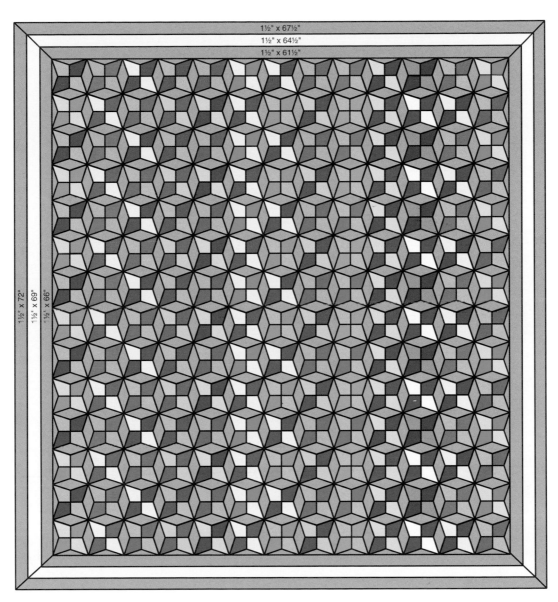

Connecting Star
Placement Diagram
67½" x 72"

GRANDMOTHER'S FLOWER GARDEN

The Grandmother's Flower Garden was one of Grandmother's most popular patterns. The quilt shown is similar to many quilts of this design from those early days. This scrap quilt has worn edges, but it is just as warm as the day it was finished over 75 years ago.

FROM THE COLLECTION OF SANDRA L. HATCH

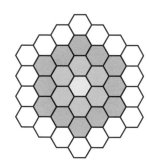

Grandmother's Flower Garden
8¼" x 9¼" Block

Project Specifications
Skill Level: Intermediate
Quilt Size: Approximately
    74¼" x 88½"
Unit Size: 8¼" x 9¼"

Materials
- 4 yards muslin
- 1¾ yards green solid
- 1 yard gold solid
- ⅛–¼ yard each of a variety of solids and prints for flower petals
- Backing 80" x 94"
- Batting 80" x 94"
- 20 yards self-made or purchased binding
- Basic sewing tools and supplies

Project Note
The flowers in this quilt are made with three rounds of hexagons all with the same-color center. The flowers are separated with a row of muslin hexagons and small green triangles. The triangles could have been eliminated and the hexagon shapes stitched to one another, but the green triangles and muslin hexagons create a walkway, or path, in the garden of flowers.

Instructions
Step 1. Cut A fabric patches for one Grandmother's Flower Garden unit referring to Figure 1. Beginning with the first row, sew a solid-color A to each side of the center A, joining as

shown in Figure 2. Add a round of print A's and then a round of muslin A's to complete one flower unit.

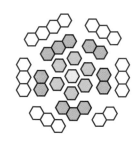

Figure 1

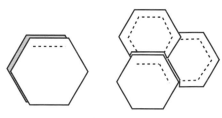

Figure 2

Step 2. Piece 102 flower units.

Step 3. Join nine flower units with solid green B diamonds and C triangles to make a row referring to Figure 3. Repeat for six rows.

Step 4. Complete 10 half-flower shapes as shown in Figure 4. Join two half-units with eight pieced flower units to make five rows, beginning and ending with half-units.

Step 5. Join eight whole flower units to make one row for the top.

Step 6. Join the rows with B diamonds and C triangles referring to the Placement Diagram and Figure 3 again to complete the quilt top.

Step 7. Prepare the pieced top for quilting. **Note:** *The quilt shown was quilted ¼" from seams on all hexagons. This is the most common way to quilt the pattern.*

Step 8. Finish quilt as desired referring to the General Instructions.

Note: *The quilt shown was bound around each hexagon shape on the edge. It was not squared off. This edge finish looks very nice and, although it takes more time than a straight-edge finish, adding pieces to square up the edge would add time to the completion of the quilt top. A double binding would be more durable. The edges on the antique quilt shown are very worn and need to be re-bound.* ✦

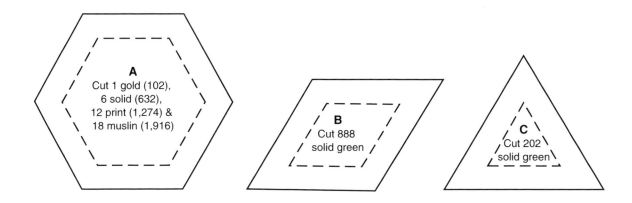

Figure 3

Figure 4

A
Cut 1 gold (102),
6 solid (632),
12 print (1,274) &
18 muslin (1,916)

B
Cut 888
solid green

C
Cut 202
solid green

Grandmother's Flower Garden
Placement Diagram
Approximately 74¼" x 88½"

CHIMNEYS & CORNERSTONES

There is a real challenge in making traditional quilts in new and creative ways. The block unit used for this interesting design is similar to a Log Cabin block in that the block begins in the center and rows are added around it.

DESIGN BY NORMA COMPAGNA

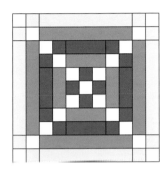

Block A
11" x 11" Block

Block B
11" x 11" Block

Project Specifications
Skill Level: Intermediate
Quilt Size: 45" x 59"
Block Size: 11" x 11"
Number of Blocks: 12

Materials
- 1¼ yards fabric 1 (lightest color)
- 1¼ yards fabric 2 (medium/light)
- 1¼ yards fabric 3 (medium/dark)
- 2½ yards fabric 4 (dark)
- Backing 51" x 65"
- Batting 51" x 65"
- All-purpose thread to match fabrics
- 6 yards self-made or purchased binding
- Basic sewing tools and supplies

Project Notes
The center of the block unit used in the Chimneys & Cornerstones quilt shown is a Nine-Patch. The subsequent rounds are added in log cabin fashion.

As the rounds are added, a diagonal design takes form as the corner squares create the cornerstones and the strips form the chimneys as mentioned in the quilt's name.

More blocks may be added to create a larger quilt; remember to adjust the materials list accordingly.

Instructions
Step 1. Cut fabrics into 1½" by fabric width strips as follows: fabric 1—cut 20 strips; fabric 2—cut 13 strips; fabric 3—cut 26 strips; and fabric 4—cut 38 strips.

Step 2. Sort strips into colors.

Step 3. Sew one strip set of each color set using fabrics 1 and 4 for Nine-Patch A units as shown in Figure 1. Repeat for two strip sets of the 1-4-1 combination. Cut strips into 1½" segments.

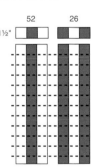

Figure 1

Step 4. Join the cut segments to create Nine-Patch A units as shown in Figure 2. Complete 26 of these units for blocks and sashing.

Figure 2

Step 5. Repeat with one strip set of each color set using fabrics 1 and 3 for Nine-Patch B units as shown in Figure 3. Complete six Nine-Patch B units for blocks.

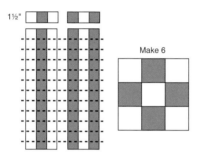

Make 6

Figure 3

Step 6. Sew four strips each fabrics 3 and 4 together and cut into 3½" segments as shown in Figure 4. You will need 48 segments to complete the quilt as shown.

Step 7. Sew four strips each fabrics 2 and 4 together and cut into 7½" segments as shown in Figure 5. You will need 24 segments for Block B.

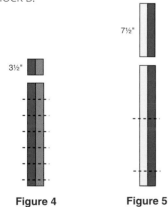

3½"

7½"

Figure 4   **Figure 5**

Step 8. Sew four strips each fabrics 2 and 3 together and cut into 7½" segments as shown in Figure 6. You will need 24 segments for Block A.

7½"

Figure 6

Step 9. Sew two fabric 4 strips to one fabric 3 strip as shown in Figure 7. Cut into 11½" segments. Repeat for 11 strip units. You will need 31 segments for sashing.

11½"

Figure 7

Step 10. Sew four strip sets fabrics 4 and 1 for Four-Patch A units as shown in Figure 8. Cut into 1½" segments. You will need 48 segments. Re-stitch to make 24 Four-Patch A units. Repeat with

fabrics 3 and 1 for 48 segments to make 24 Four-Patch B units and with fabrics 2 and 1 for 96 segments for 48 Four-Patch C units.

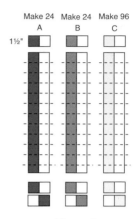

Make 24   Make 24   Make 96
A   B   C

1½"

Figure 8

Step 11. Arrange Four-Patch units with Nine-Patch centers and sew together to make six A blocks as shown in Figure 9.

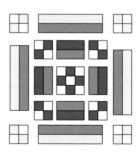

Figure 9

Step 12. Arrange Four-Patch units with Nine-Patch centers and sew together to make six B blocks as shown in Figure 10.

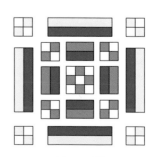

Figure 10

Step 13. Sew sashing Nine-Patch units with sashing strips as shown in Figure 11; repeat for five strip units.

Step 14. Referring to Figure 12, join four sashing strips with two A blocks and one B block to make a row; press seams toward sashing strips. Repeat to make two rows. Repeat with two B blocks and one A block to make two rows.

Step 15. Arrange sashing-strip rows with block rows referring to the Placement Diagram; join in rows and press.

Step 16. Finish quilt in chosen method referring to the General Instructions. ◆

Figure 11

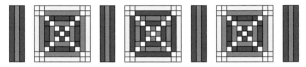

Figure 12

Color Key
☐ Fabric 1—light
☐ Fabric 2—medium/light
▨ Fabric 3—medium/dark
■ Fabric 4—dark

Chimneys & Cornerstones
Placement Diagram
45" x 59"

RAINBOW OF RINGS

Making the Nine-Patch blocks for this quilt is the easy part! Putting them together is a bit more complicated. The original maker found that out when she put her quilt together, as you can see from the interruption of the rings on the quilt.

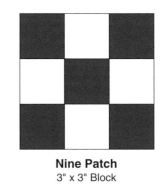

Nine Patch
3" x 3" Block

Project Specifications
Skill Level: Experienced
Quilt Size: Approximately 70" x 90"
Block Size: 3" x 3"
Number of Blocks: 318

Materials
- 2½ yards total various light and dark prints
- 5¾ yards muslin
- Backing 76" x 96"
- Batting 76" x 96"
- Off-white all-purpose thread
- 1 spool off-white quilting thread
- Basic sewing tools and supplies

Project Notes
The quilt shown was made in the 1930s using pastel prints from that era. Our instructions do not recommend putting the blocks together in the exact same manner as the quilt shown. Although many of the rows are consistent as to the placement of the A hexagon, some are not. When the placement of A is changed, the pattern does not make the allover concentric circles. Notice that the circles are not always the same size on the quilt.

If you look at the drawings given in Figure 7, where lines have been removed, the pattern does make the same-size circles throughout. You may prefer the mixed-up look, but if you want the pattern to really show, be very careful when sewing the blocks together to get all A pieces with points going up and down.

Instructions
Step 1. Prepare templates using pattern pieces given. Cut as directed on each piece. ***Note:*** *Strips of muslin and prints may be cut 1½" wide, stitched together and cut in 1½" segments as shown in Figure 1. If a planned color arrangement is used, this is recommended.*

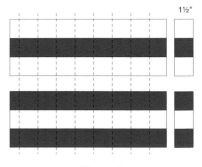

Figure 1

Step 2. Sew a muslin B to a scrap B to a muslin B to make a row; repeat. Sew a scrap B to a muslin B to a scrap B to make a row.

Step 3. Join the pieced B rows as shown in Figure 2 to complete one Nine-Patch block; repeat for 318 blocks.

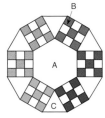

Figure 2

Step 4. Sew a Nine-Patch block to each side of A; set in C pieces to complete one block as shown in Figure 3; press. Repeat for 53 blocks.

Figure 3

Step 5. Join eight blocks in a row with C pieces as shown in Figure 4; repeat for four rows. **Note:** *When piecing, be careful to place piece A with points going from top to bottom rather than side to side. Piece D may*

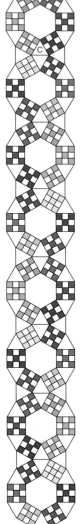

Figure 4

Figure 5

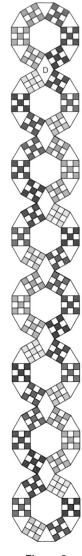

Figure 6

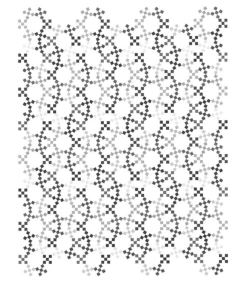

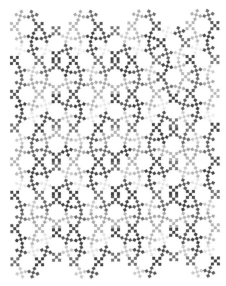

Figure 7

be substituted for piece C to eliminate some seams. Doing this complicates row construction and makes piecing units necessary. It is really easier to use piece C with more seams than to substitute D. We have given piece D for those who prefer this method, but we give no drawings or instructions for using this piece except for the drawing given in Figure 6.

Step 6. Join seven blocks in a row with C pieces as in Step 5; repeat for three rows.

Step 7. Join the rows, setting in C as necessary as shown in Figure 5.

Step 8. Mark the quilting design given in piece A.

Step 9. Prepare quilt top for quilting and finish referring to the General Instructions. ✦

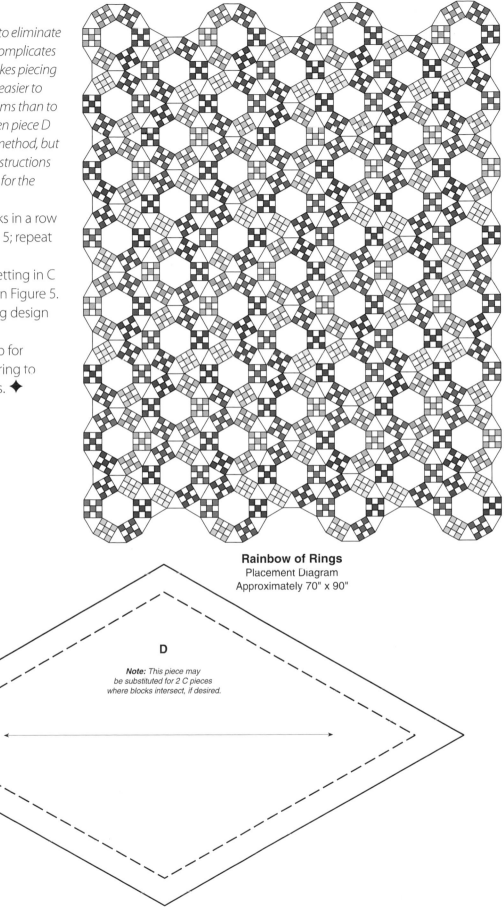

Rainbow of Rings
Placement Diagram
Approximately 70" x 90"

D

Note: *This piece may be substituted for 2 C pieces where blocks intersect, if desired.*

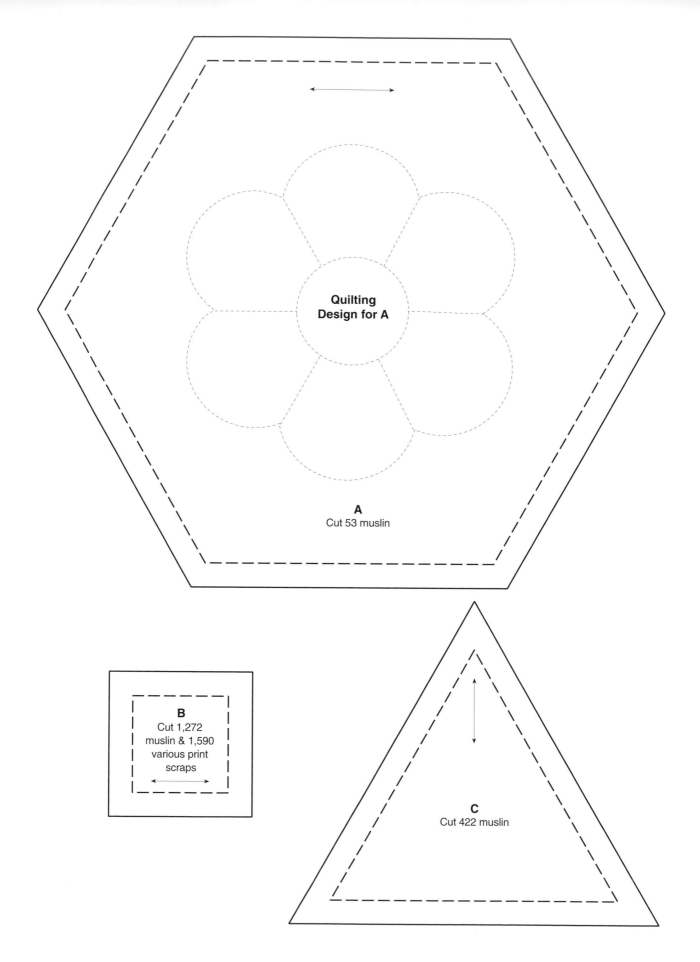

**Quilting
Design for A**

A
Cut 53 muslin

B
Cut 1,272
muslin & 1,590
various print
scraps

C
Cut 422 muslin

BROKEN WHEEL

A variety of white shirting fabrics combine with black, indigo and pink fabrics in this pretty one-block-design quilt.

FROM THE COLLECTION OF SANDRA L. HATCH

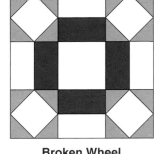

Broken Wheel
9" x 9" Block

Bed Quilt

Project Specifications
Skill Level: Intermediate
Quilt Size: 67¾" x 75⅛"
Block Size: 9" x 9"
Number of Blocks: 20 whole,
   14 half and 2 quarter

Materials
- ⅝ yard muslin
- ¾ yard total dark prints
- 1⅜ yards total medium prints
- 2¼ yards total light prints
- 3 yards pink tonal
- Backing 74" x 81"
- Batting 74" x 81"
- Neutral color all-purpose thread
- Quilting thread
- Basic sewing tools and supplies

Cutting
Step 1. Cut seven 9½" by fabric width strips pink tonal; subcut strips into (25) 9½" A squares.
Step 2. Cut two 14" x 14" squares pink tonal; cut each square on both diagonals to make eight AA triangles. Set aside three triangles for another project.

Step 3. Cut (10) 2" by fabric width strips each light (B) and dark (C) prints.
Step 4. Cut (10) 3½" by fabric width strips light prints; subcut strips into (114) 3½" D squares.
Step 5. Cut (18) 2" by fabric width strips medium prints; subcut strips into (376) 2" E squares.
Step 6. Cut four 5½" x 5½" squares light prints; cut each square in half on both diagonals to make 16 F triangles. Set aside two triangles for another project.
Step 7. Cut two 2⅝" by fabric width strips light prints. Prepare template for H; place H on strips and cut 32 H pieces.
Step 8. Prepare template for G; cut as directed.
Step 9. Cut one 2⅜" by fabric width strip medium print; subcut strip into (16) 2⅜" squares. Cut each square on one diagonal to make 32 I triangles.
Step 10. Cut one 3" x 3" square light print; cut in half on one diagonal to make two J triangles.
Step 11. Cut four 3" by fabric width strips pink tonal. Join strips

on short ends to make one long strip; press seams open. Subcut strip into two 64¼" K strips.
Step 12. Cut four 2½" by fabric width strips pink tonal. Join strips on short ends to make one long strip; press seams open. Subcut strip into two 75⅝" L strips.
Step 13. Cut eight 2¼" by fabric width strips muslin for binding.

Piecing Broken Wheel Blocks
Step 1. Sew a B strip to a C strip with right sides together along length; press seams toward C. Repeat for 10 strip sets.
Step 2. Subcut strip sets into (110) 3½" B-C units as shown in Figure 1; set aside 30 units for half- and quarter-blocks.

Figure 1

Step 3. Mark a diagonal line from corner to corner on the wrong side of each E square.
Step 4. Referring to Figure 2, place an E square on one corner of D; stitch on the marked line. Trim

seam to ¼"; press E to the right side. Repeat on each corner of D to complete a D-E unit, again referring to Figure 2; repeat for 94 D-E units; set aside 14 units for half-blocks.

Figure 2

Step 5. To complete one Broken Wheel block, sew a B-C unit to opposite sides of D as shown in Figure 3; press seams toward the B-C units.

| **Figure 3** | **Figure 4** |

Step 6. Sew a D-E unit to opposite sides of a B-C unit as shown in Figure 4; press seams toward the B-C unit. Repeat for two units.

Step 7. Join the pieced units as shown in Figure 5 to complete one block; repeat for 20 blocks. Press seams toward the center.

Figure 5

Piecing Half-Blocks

Step 1. To complete one half-block, sew G to each short end of H and add I as shown in Figure 6; press seams toward G and I. Repeat for 32 G-H-I units; set aside four units for quarter-blocks.

| **Figure 6** | **Figure 7** |

Step 2. Sew a G-H-I unit to one end of a B-C unit as shown in Figure 7; repeat for a reversed unit, again referring to Figure 7. Press seams toward B-C units. Repeat for 16 units and 16 reversed units.

Step 3. Sew a pieced unit to one side of F as shown in Figure 8; press seam away from F.

| **Figure 8** | **Figure 9** |

Step 4. Sew a D-E unit to the B-C end of a reversed unit as shown in Figure 9; press seams away from the D-E unit.

Step 5. Join the pieced units to complete a half-block as shown in Figure 10; repeat for 14 half-blocks.

Figure 10

Piecing Quarter-Blocks

Step 1. Sew a G-H-I unit to opposite sides of a B-C unit and add J as shown in Figure 11; press seams toward B-C and J to complete one quarter-block. Repeat for two quarter-blocks.

Figure 11

Broken Wheel
Placement Diagram
67¾" x 75½"

Completing the Quilt Top

Step 1. Arrange the whole blocks with the half- and quarter-blocks and the A squares and AA triangles in diagonal rows referring to Figure 12; join in rows. Press seams toward A. Join the rows to complete the pieced center; press seams in one direction.

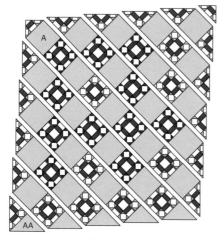

Figure 12

Step 2. Sew a K strip to the top and bottom and L strips to opposite sides of the pieced center; press seams toward strips.

Step 3. Finish quilt referring to the General Instructions.

Wall Quilt

Project Specifications
Skill Level: Beginner
Quilt Size: 35" x 35"
Block Size: 9" x 9"
Number of Blocks: 4

Materials
- ½ yard black print
- ¾ yard red tonal
- 1¼ yards white print
- Backing 41" x 41"
- Batting 41" x 41"
- Neutral color all-purpose thread
- Quilting thread
- Basic sewing tools and supplies

Cutting

Step 1. Cut two 2" by fabric width strips each white (B) and black (C) prints.

Step 2. Cut three 3½" by fabric width strips white print; subcut strips into (33) 3½" D squares.

Step 3. Cut six 2" by fabric width strips red tonal; subcut strips into (116) 2" E squares.

Step 4. Cut three 1½" by fabric width F strips black print.

Step 5. Cut six 1½" by fabric width G strips white print.

Step 6. Cut four 1½" x 27½" I strips black print.

Step 7. Cut four 1½" x 1½" H squares red tonal.

Step 8. Cut four 3½" x 29½" J strips white print.

Step 9. Cut four 2¼" by fabric width strips red tonal for binding.

Piecing the Blocks

Step 1. Complete 16 B-C units referring to Steps 1 and 2 for Piecing Broken Wheel Blocks.

Step 2. Complete 29 D-E units referring to Steps 3 and 4 for Piecing Broken Wheel Blocks; set aside 13 units for sashing and borders.

Step 3. Complete four Broken Wheel blocks referring to Steps 5–7 for Piecing Broken Wheel Blocks.

Completing the Wall Quilt

Step 1. Sew a G strip to opposite sides of an F strip with right sides together along length; press seams toward F. Repeat for three strip sets.

Step 2. Subcut the strip sets into (12) 9½" F-G units as shown in Figure 13.

Step 3. Join three F-G units with two blocks to complete a block row as shown in Figure 14; press seams toward F-G units. Repeat for two block rows.

Figure 13

Figure 14

Step 4. Join two F-G units with three D-E units to complete a sashing row referring to Figure 15; press seams toward F-G units. Repeat for three sashing rows.

Figure 15

Step 5. Join the block rows with the sashing rows to complete the pieced center; press seams toward sashing rows.

Step 6. Sew an I strip to opposite sides of the pieced center; press seams toward I.

Step 7. Sew an H square to each end of the remaining I strips; press seams toward I.

Step 8. Sew an H-I strip to the remaining sides of the pieced center; press seams toward H-I.

Step 9. Sew a J strip to opposite sides of the pieced center; press seams toward J.

Step 10. Sew a D-E unit to each end of the remaining J strips; press seams toward J.

Step 11. Sew a D-E-J strip to the remaining sides of the pieced center; press seams toward D-E-J to complete the top.

Step 12. Finish quilt referring to the General Instructions. ◆

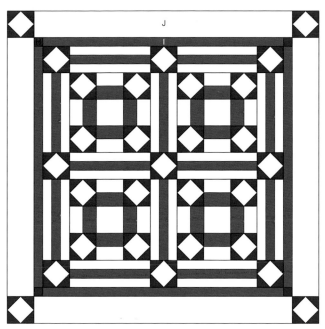

Broken Wheel Wall Quilt
Placement Diagram
35" x 35"

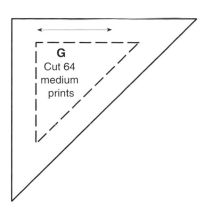

G
Cut 64
medium
prints

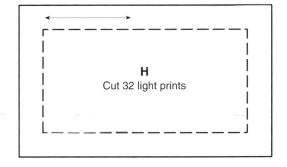

H
Cut 32 light prints

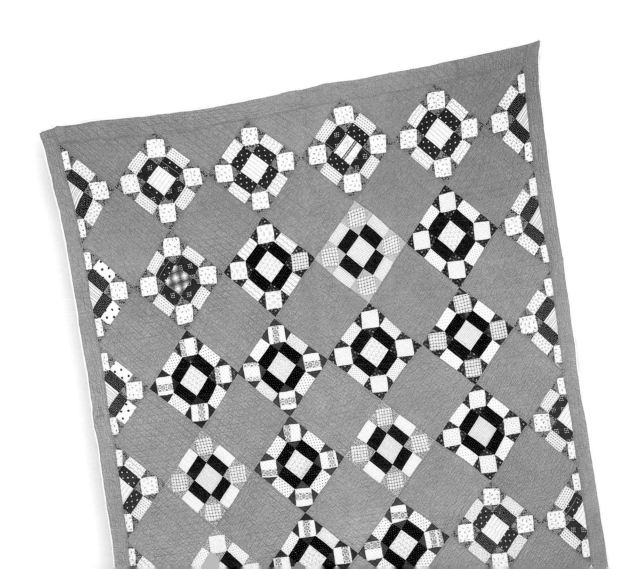

SCRAPPY STARS

Most quilters have enough scraps on hand to make many quilts. Scrap quilts work best if they are combined with a background fabric that is used throughout the quilt to tie everything together. In this quilt, muslin is that fabric—scraps make up the star designs.

Scrappy Stars
6" x 6" Block

DESIGN BY RUTH SWASEY

Project Specifications
Skill Level: Intermediate
Quilt Size: 60" x 60"
Block Size: 6" x 6"
Number of Blocks: 64

Materials
- ¾ yard each pink and green prints for border
- 2 yards total medium to dark scraps
- 4 yards muslin
- Backing 66" x 66"
- Batting 66" x 66"
- 7 yards self-made or purchased binding
- Neutral color all-purpose thread
- Basic sewing tools and supplies

Instructions
Step 1. Prepare templates for blocks and borders using pattern pieces given. Cut as directed on D and E for one block; repeat for 64 blocks. Cut as directed on pieces A, B and C for borders; set aside.

Step 2. To piece one block, join four E pieces, sewing only to the end of the marked seam allowance. Set in D pieces as shown in Figure 1 to complete one block; repeat for 64 blocks. Press and square up to 6½" x 6½".

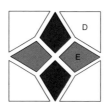

Figure 1

Step 3. Arrange blocks in eight rows of eight blocks each. Join blocks in rows; join rows to complete pieced center. Press seams in one direction.

Step 4. To piece border sections, sew a pink print C to a green print CR, sewing only to the end of the marked seam allowance; set in muslin B pieces as shown in Figure 2. Press; repeat for 32 units.

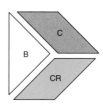

Figure 2

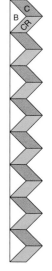

Step 5. Join eight C-CR-B units to make a strip as shown in Figure 3; repeat for four strips.

Step 6. Sew a pieced strip to each side

Figure 3

of the pieced center; press.

Step 7. To make corner units, sew C to CR; set in two B pieces and A as shown in Figure 4. Sew one of these units to each corner of the pieced quilt to complete quilt top.

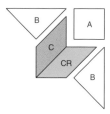

Figure 4

Step 8. Prepare quilt top for quilting and finish referring to the General Instructions. ✦

Scrappy Stars
Placement Diagram
60" x 60"

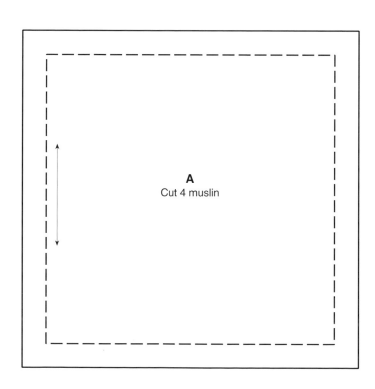

A
Cut 4 muslin

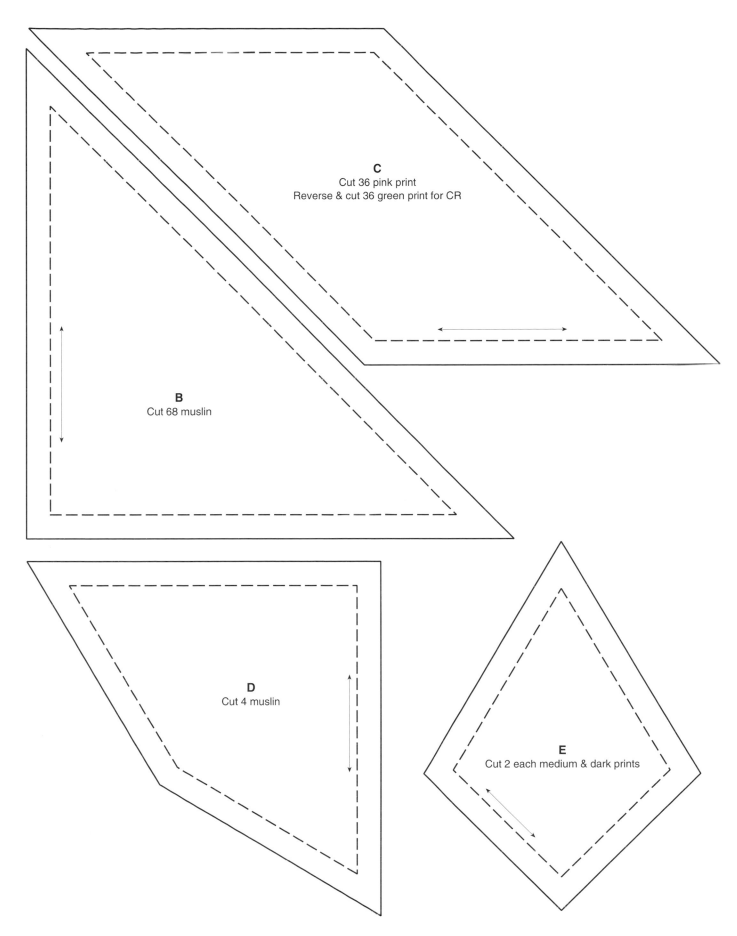

C
Cut 36 pink print
Reverse & cut 36 green print for CR

B
Cut 68 muslin

D
Cut 4 muslin

E
Cut 2 each medium & dark prints

TIPSY TRAIL

Whether you prefer the green-and-pink combination of the antique quilt or a newer version made with pink and white, this pattern will make you a little tipsy during construction.

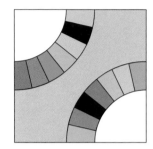

Tipsy Trail
7" x 7" Block

FROM THE COLLECTION OF EUNICE BROWER

Project Specifications
Quilt Size: 92" x 106"
Block Size: 7" x 7"
Number of Blocks: 168

Materials
- Assorted scraps
- 1 yard burgundy solid
- ¾ yard cream-with-pink print for binding
- 3 yards muslin
- 4½ yards pink solid
- Backing 98" x 112"
- Batting 98" x 112"
- Neutral color all-purpose thread
- Cream hand-quilting thread
- Basic sewing supplies and tools

Project Notes
My grandmother made the green-and-pink quilt shown over 70 years ago. She called it Drunkard's Path, but it is not like any of the Drunkard's Path quilts I have ever seen. I tried to find the pattern, but had no success, so I asked my computer-savvy son-in-law to draft one for me.

I have now made my own version of my grandmother's quilt, and I call it Tipsy Trail. It is made with assorted scraps and creates an unusual pattern when the blocks are all stitched together. I substituted a burgundy solid piece for the red solid piece Grandmother used in the pieced sections.

Instructions
Step 1. Prepare templates using pattern pieces given. Cut as directed on each piece for one block; repeat for 168 blocks.
Step 2. To piece one block, join seven C pieces, including one burgundy solid C, to create a C unit as shown in Figure 1; repeat for two units. Press seams in one direction.

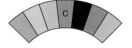

Figure 1

Step 3. Match the center of B to the center of a C unit; pin corners and ease the remaining fabric as shown in Figure 2. Stitch; clip seams if necessary. Repeat for two B-C units.

Figure 2

Step 4. Match the center of A with the center of one B-C unit; pin corners. Ease the remaining fabric along curve; stitch. Clip curves; press seam toward A. Repeat with a second B-C unit to complete one block as shown in Figure 3; repeat for 168 blocks.

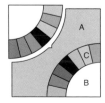

Figure 3

Step 5. Join 12 blocks to make a row referring to the Placement Diagram for positioning; press seams in one direction. Repeat for 14 rows.

Step 6. Join the rows to complete the pieced center; press seams in one direction.

Step 7. Cut and piece two strips each 4½" x 94½" and 4½" x 108½" pink solid. Center and sew the shorter strips to the top and bottom and longer strips to opposite sides of the pieced center, mitering corners; press seams toward strip. Trim excess at mitered corner seam; press seams open.

Step 8. Mark a chosen quilting design in the large open areas, if desired.

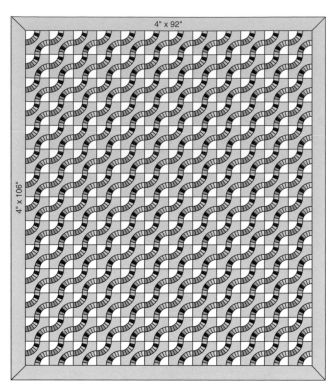

Tipsy Trail
Placement Diagram
92" x 106"

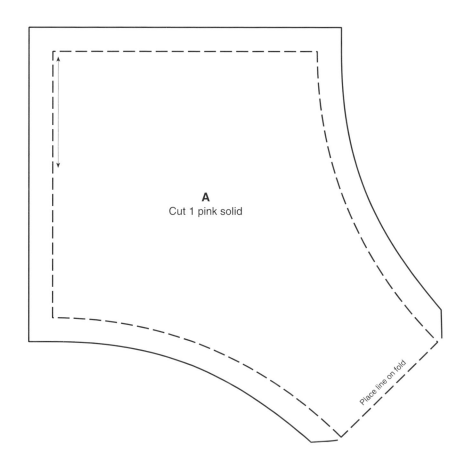

A
Cut 1 pink solid

Place line on fold

Step 9. Sandwich batting between completed top and prepared backing; pin or baste to hold.

Step 10. Quilt as desired by hand or machine. ***Note:*** *The quilt shown was hand-quilted in a diagonal 1" grid using cream hand-quilting thread.*

Step 11. When quilting is complete, remove pins or basting; trim backing and batting even with quilt top.

Step 12. Cut 10 strips cream-with-pink print 2¼" by fabric width; join on short ends to make one long strip for binding. Fold the strip in half along length with wrong sides together; press. Sew binding to quilt edges, mitering corners and overlapping ends. Turn binding to the backside; hand- or machine-stitch in place to finish. ✦

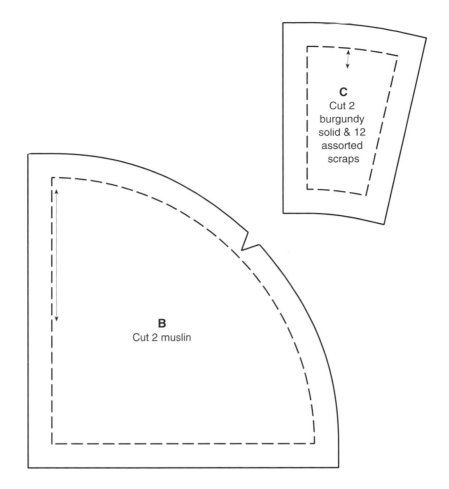

C
Cut 2 burgundy solid & 12 assorted scraps

B
Cut 2 muslin

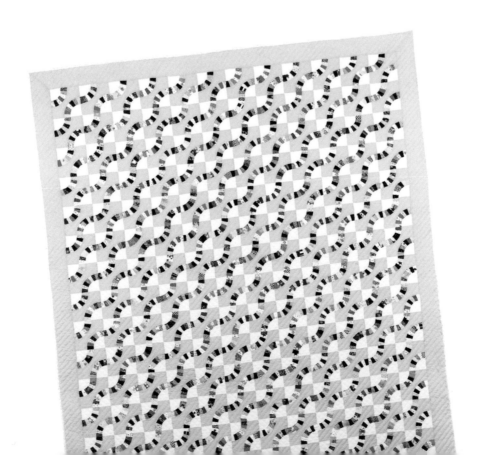

DELECTABLE MOUNTAINS VARIATIONS

Whether you choose the quick method or the traditional method, you will enjoy the charm of this antique quilt.

FROM THE COLLECTION OF BARB SPRUNGER

Delectable Mountains Variation
7½" x 7½" Block

Project Specifications
Skill Level: Intermediate
Quilt Size: 77" x 84½"
Block Size: 7½" x 7½"
Number of Blocks: 72

Materials
- 72 rectangles assorted prints 8" x 10" or 2¾ yards total print scraps
- ½ yard peach solid
- 4½ yards white solid
- Backing 83" x 91"
- Batting 83" x 91"
- 9½ yards self-made or purchased binding
- All-purpose thread to match fabrics
- White quilting thread
- Basic sewing supplies and tools and rotary-cutting tools

Traditional Method
Step 1. Prepare templates using full-size patterns given; cut as directed on each piece for one block. Repeat for 72 blocks. **Note:** *If using 8" x 10" rectangles for prints, cut border triangles from portions left after cutting blocks.*

Step 2. To piece one block, sew a print A to a white solid A; repeat for seven A-A units.

Step 3. Join three A-A units to make a strip; repeat with four A-A units to make another strip referring to Figure 1.

Figure 1

Step 4. Sew a peach solid A triangle to one end of each strip as shown in Figure 2.

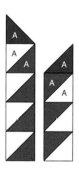

Figure 2

Step 5. Sew the three-unit strip to one short side of B and add the four-unit strip to the other short side of B as shown in Figure 3.

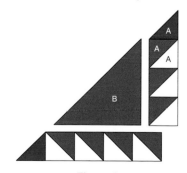

Figure 3

Step 6. Add C to the pieced unit to complete one block as shown in Figure 4; press. Repeat for 72 blocks.

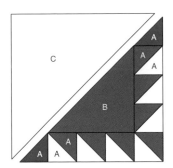

Figure 4

Step 7. Join eight blocks to make a row as shown in Figure 5; repeat for nine rows. Press seams in one direction. Join pieced rows referring to the Placement Diagram to complete pieced center.

Figure 5

Step 8. Cut and piece two strips white solid 2" x 60½". Sew a strip to the top and bottom of the pieced center; press seams toward strips.

Step 9. Cut A pieces as directed on template for borders. Sew a print A to a white solid A along the diagonal to make an A-A unit; press seams toward the print A. Repeat to make 178 A-A units.

Step 10. Join 40 A-A units to make a strip referring to the Placement Diagram; press. Repeat for two strips.

Step 11. Sew a pieced strip to the top and bottom of the pieced center; press seams toward white solid strips.

Step 12. Cut and piece two strips white solid 2" x 74". Sew a strip to opposite long sides of the pieced center; press seams toward strips.

Step 13. Join 49 A-A units to make a strip referring to the Placement Diagram; press. Repeat for two strips.

Step 14. Sew a pieced strip to opposite long sides of the pieced center; press seams toward white solid strips.

Step 15. Cut and piece two strips each white solid 6" x 66½" and 6" x 85". Sew the shorter strips to the top and bottom and longer strips to opposite sides of the pieced center; press seams toward white solid strips.

Step 16. Mark the quilting designs given in C and on borders referring to General Instructions.

Step 17. Prepare top for quilting and finish as desired referring to the General Instructions.

Quick Method

Step 1. Cut 8" x 10" print rectangles into one 5⅜" x 5⅜" square and six 2⅜" x 2⅜" squares as shown in Figure 6.

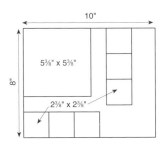

Figure 6

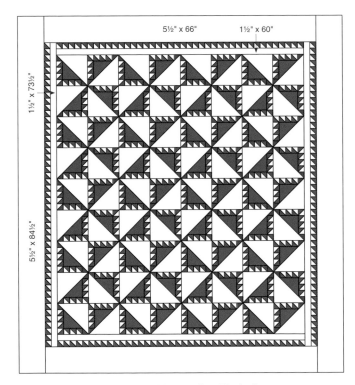

Delectable Mountains Variation
Placement Diagram
77" x 84½"

Step 2. Cut each 2⅜" x 2⅜" square in half on one diagonal to make A triangles. Select seven triangles of each print for blocks; set aside remainder for borders.

Step 3. Cut the 5⅜" x 5⅜" square in half on one diagonal to make B triangles. Set aside one triangle for another project.

Step 4. Cut peach solid into five strips 2⅜" by fabric width. Subcut strip into 2⅜" segments; you will need 72 segments. Cut each segment in half on one diagonal to make A triangles. You will need two peach solid A triangles for each block or 144 for the whole quilt.

Step 5. Cut eight strips white solid 7⅞" by fabric width. Subcut each strip into 7⅞" segments. You will need 36 segments. Cut each segment in half on one

diagonal to make 72 C triangles.

Step 6. Cut 21 strips white solid 2⅜" by fabric width. Subcut each strip into 2⅜" segments. Cut each segment in half on one diagonal to make A triangles. You will need seven white solid A triangles for each block and 178 for borders (total needed is 682).

Step 7. Join pieces to make blocks and complete quilt referring to Steps 2–16 of Traditional Method to finish. ✦

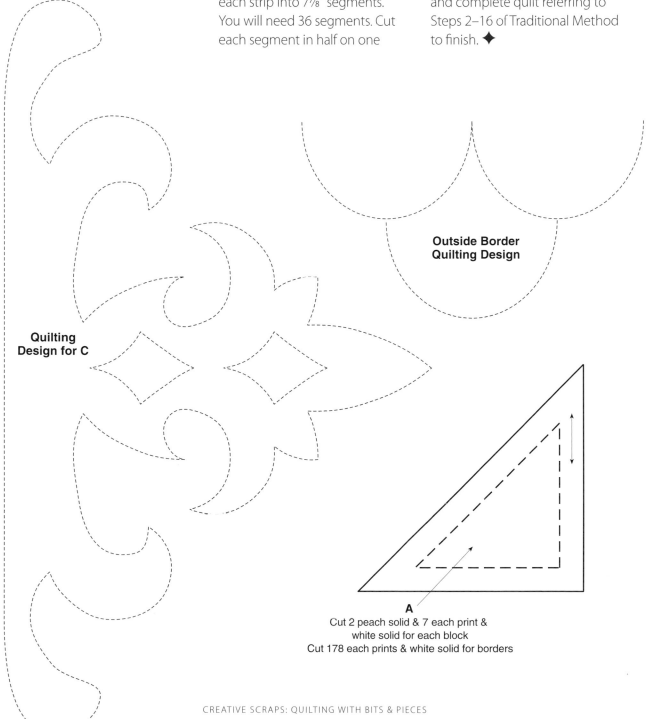

Outside Border Quilting Design

Quilting Design for C

A
Cut 2 peach solid & 7 each print &
white solid for each block
Cut 178 each prints & white solid for borders

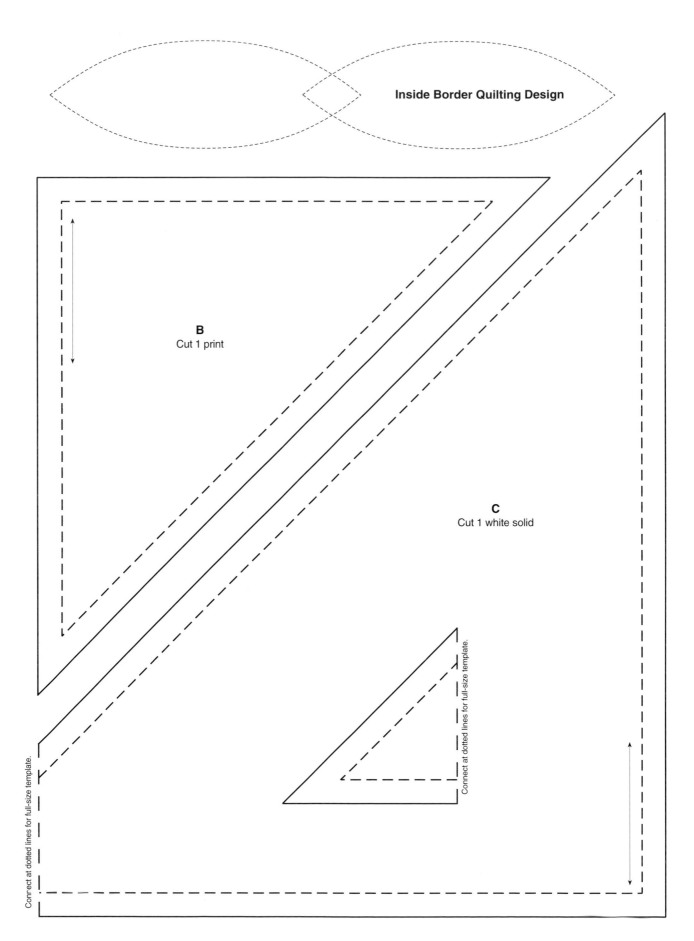

Inside Border Quilting Design

B
Cut 1 print

C
Cut 1 white solid

Connect at dotted lines for full-size template.

Connect at dotted lines for full-size template.

SUNFLOWER STAR

A wide variety of pastels, shades of brown and shirting fabrics date this quilt as early as the 20th century.

FROM THE COLLECTION OF MARY JO KURTEN

Sunflower Star
9" x 9" Block

Project Specifications

Skill Level: Advanced
Quilt Size: 63¾" x 76½"
Block Size: 9" x 9"
Number of Blocks: 20 plain
   and 30 pieced

Materials

- 3½ yards white solid
- Wide variety of light, medium and dark brown and pastel scraps totaling 2½ yards
- Backing 70" x 83"
- Batting 70" x 83"
- 8¼ yards self-made or purchased binding
- White all-purpose thread
- 2 spools white quilting thread
- Basic sewing tools and supplies

Project Note

There is really no quick way to piece the blocks in this lovely old quilt. The circular design surrounding the center star is best hand-pieced for accuracy. Adding the A and B pieces around the outside is also a difficult task and not for the beginner.

Instructions

Step 1. Prepare templates using full-size patterns given; cut as directed on each piece for one block. Repeat for 30 blocks.

Step 2. To piece one block, sew a dark print D to a medium print D, starting at the center dot and stopping at the ¼" seam allowance as shown in Figure 1; repeat for four units. Join two units; repeat. Join these two units to complete pieced star as shown in Figure 2.

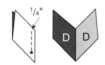

Figure 1

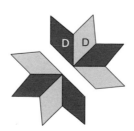

Figure 2

Step 3. Set C pieces into pieced star unit as shown in Figure 3.

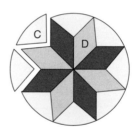

Figure 3

Step 4. Sew F to E; repeat for all F and E pieces. Join pieced units to make a circle; stitch to the C-D center star unit.

Step 5. Set in A and B pieces around the edges of the pieced unit referring to Figure 4 to finish one block; repeat for 30 blocks.

Step 6. Cut 20 squares white solid 9½" x 9½". Cut five squares white solid 14" x 14". Cut in half on both diagonals to make side fill-in triangles; discard two. Cut two squares white solid 7¼" x 7¼"; cut in half on one diagonal to make corner triangles.

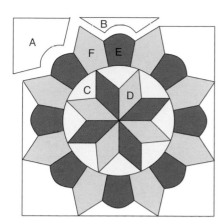

Figure 4

Step 7. Lay out pieced blocks, plain blocks and side and corner triangles in diagonal rows as shown in Figure 5. Join blocks and triangles in rows; join rows to complete pieced center. Press seams in one direction.

9½" x 9½"

Figure 5

Step 8. Mark the quilting design given on plain blocks referring to the General Instructions.

Step 9. Prepare top for quilting and finish as desired referring to the General Instructions. ✦

Sunflower Star
Placement Diagram
63¾" x 76½"

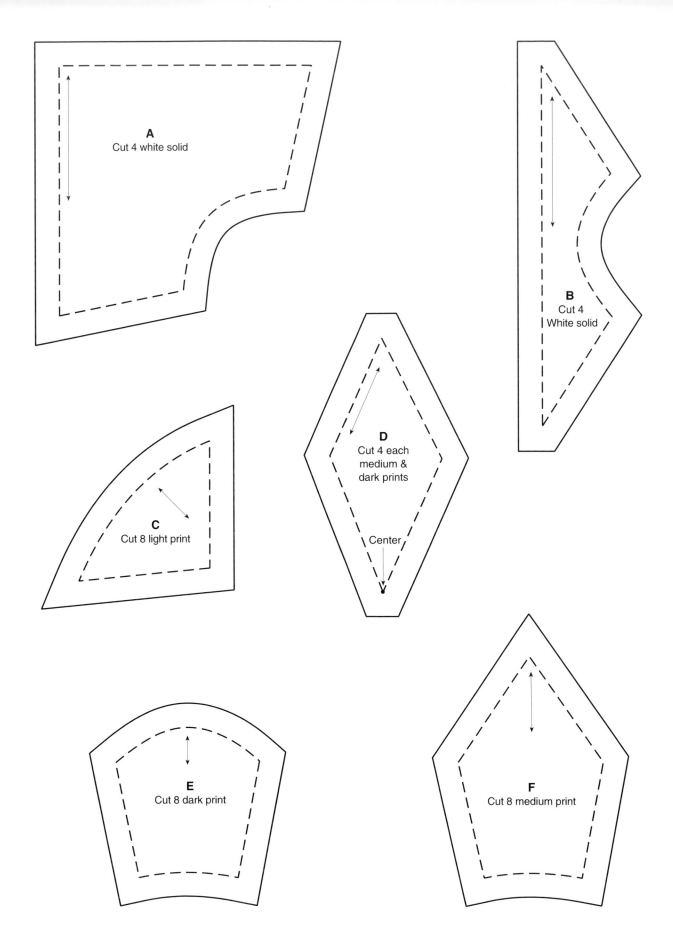

A
Cut 4 white solid

B
Cut 4
White solid

C
Cut 8 light print

D
Cut 4 each
medium &
dark prints

Center

E
Cut 8 dark print

F
Cut 8 medium print

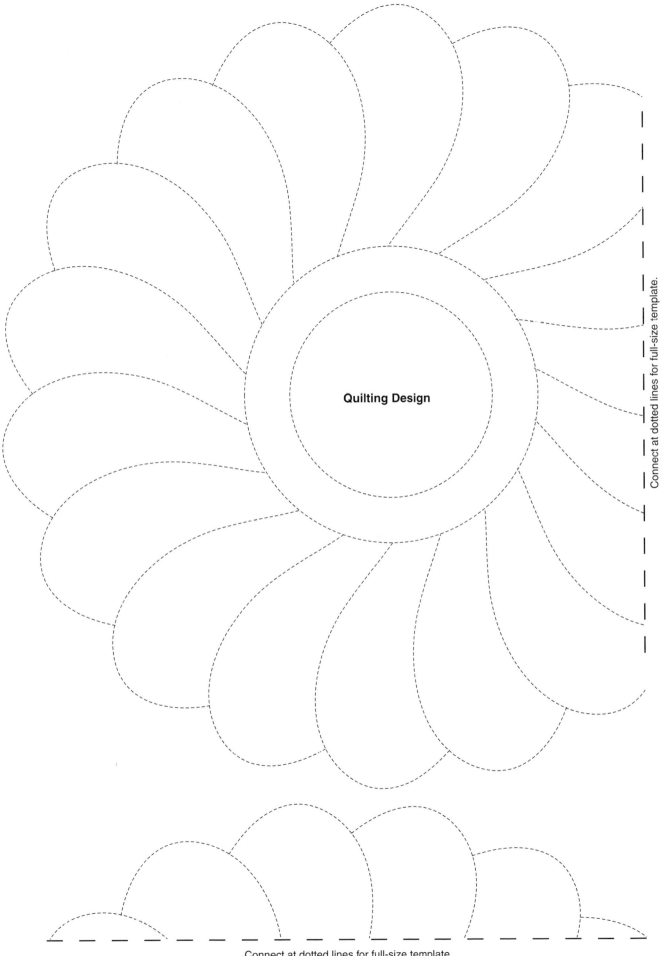

Quilting Design

Connect at dotted lines for full-size template.

Connect at dotted lines for full-size template.

LAZY LOG CABIN

Scrap strips combine to make this quick and easy Log Cabin bed-size quilt.

DESIGN BY ANN BOYCE

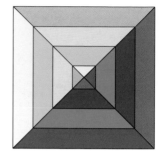

Lazy Log Cabin
10⅞" x 10⅞" Block

Project Specifications

Skill Level: Beginner
Quilt Size: 87" x 87"
Block Size: 10⅞" x 10⅞"
Number of Blocks: 64

Materials

- 5 yards total light prints
- 5 yards total dark prints
- Backing 93" x 93"
- Batting 93" x 93"
- 10 yards self-made or purchased binding
- All-purpose thread to match fabrics
- Basic sewing tools and supplies, rotary cutter, self-healing mat and acrylic ruler

Instructions

Step 1. Cut all fabrics into 2" by fabric width strips; you will need 88 strips each light and dark prints.

Step 2. Choose four strips dark prints. Sew strips together along length to make a strip set as shown in Figure 1; press seams in one direction. Repeat for 22 strip sets each light and dark prints.

Step 3. Prepare template for A triangle using pattern given. Place the A template on a strip set as shown in Figure 2. Cut 128 each light and dark A triangles.

Step 4. Sew two dark print A triangles together as shown in Figure 3. Repeat with all dark and light print triangles, sewing dark to dark and light to light.

Figure 3

Step 5. Join a dark print triangle pair to a light print triangle pair to complete one block as shown in Figure 4; repeat for 64 blocks.

Figure 4

Step 6. Arrange blocks in eight rows of eight blocks each, making a Barn-Raising design referring to the Placement Diagram for positioning of blocks. Join blocks in rows; join rows to complete quilt top. Press seams in one direction.

Step 7. Prepare quilt top for quilting and finish referring to the General Instructions. ◆

Figure 1

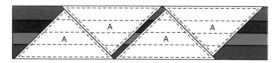

Figure 2

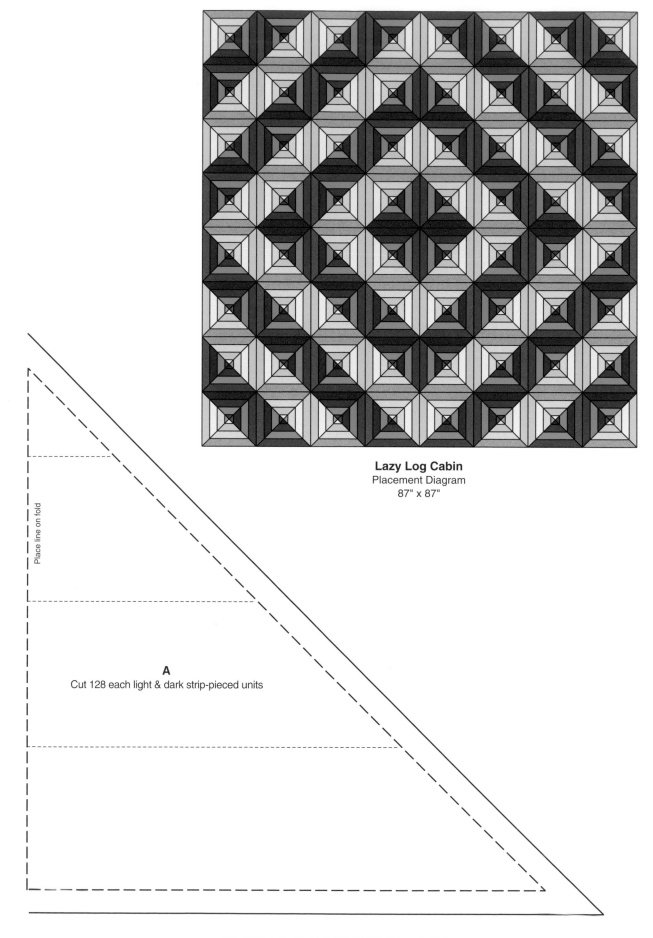

Lazy Log Cabin
Placement Diagram
87" x 87"

Place line on fold

A
Cut 128 each light & dark strip-pieced units

HARVEST FOUR-PATCH QUILT

Select warm autumn colors to carry out the harvest theme of this small quilt.

DESIGN BY JANET J. WORLEY

Harvest Four-Patch
14" x 14" Block

Project Specifications
Skill Level: Beginner
Quilt Size: 44" x 44"
Block Size: 14" x 14"
Number of Blocks: 4

Materials
- ⅝ yard beige print for background
- ⅛ yard chicken print for segment centers
- 1 yard novelty print for wide border
- Wide variety of medium- and dark-value scraps that coordinate with wide border fabric
- ⅜ yard plaid for narrow border
- Backing 50" x 50"
- Batting 50" x 50"
- All-purpose thread to blend with patchwork fabrics
- 1 spool natural quilting thread
- 5 yards purchased or self-made binding
- Rotary-cutting tools
- Basic sewing tools and supplies

Instructions
Step 1. From beige print background fabric, cut 64 rectangles 1½" x 2½". From a wide variety of medium- and dark-value scraps, cut 64 rectangles 1½" x 2½". Sew one beige and one medium or dark rectangle together to make 64 squares 2½" x 2½".

Step 2. From medium- and dark-value scraps, cut 64 squares 2½" x 2½". From chicken print fabric, cut 16 squares 2½" x 2½".

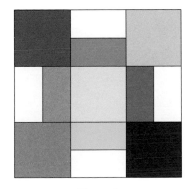

Figure 1

Step 3. Referring to Figure 1, join 2½" squares from Steps 1 and 2 to make 16 block segments as shown.

Step 4. Cut 16 beige rectangles 2½" x 6½" and four strips 2½" x 14½". From plaid narrow border fabric, cut five squares 2½" x 2½". Using four block segments, four beige strips 2½" x 6½" and one plaid square, assemble a block as shown in the block diagram. Repeat for four blocks

Step 5. Stitch a 2½" x 14½" beige strip between two blocks as shown in Figure 2. Repeat for two strips. Sew one plaid 2½" square

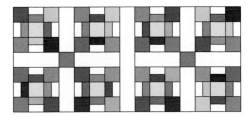

Figure 2

between two 2½" x 14½" strips. Assemble as shown in Figure 3.

Step 6. From plaid narrow border fabric, cut two strips each 2½" x 34½" and 2½" x 30½". Sew shorter strips to the sides of the quilt and longer strips to the top and bottom.

Step 7. From novelty print, cut five 5½" strips across width of fabric.

Piece as necessary to make two strips each 5½" x 44½" and 5½" x 34½". Sew shorter strips to the sides of the quilt and longer strips to the top and bottom.

Step 8. Prepare for quilting as shown in the General Instructions. Quilt as desired by hand or machine. Bind to finish. ✦

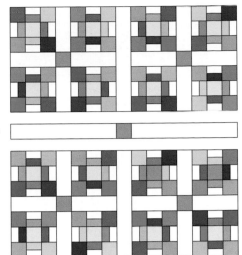

Figure 3

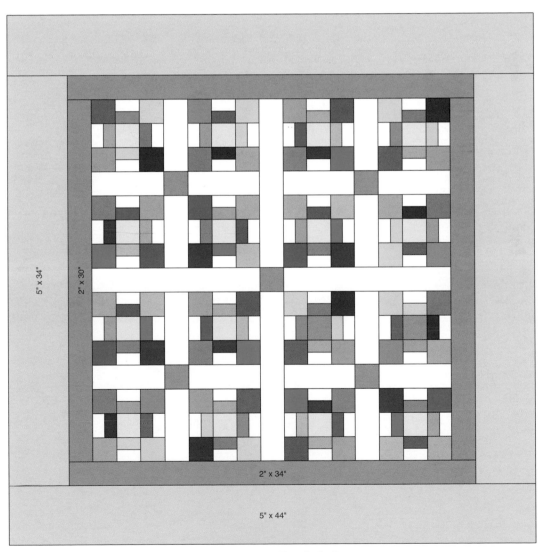

5" x 34"

2" x 30"

2" x 34"

5" x 44"

Harvest Four-Patch Quilt
Placement Diagram
44" x 44"

KANSAS DUGOUT

Search your scrap basket for dark and light fabrics to create a pattern that can easily expand to make a quilt of any size.

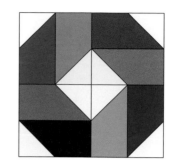

Kansas Dugout
8" x 8" Block

DESIGN BY NANCY BRENAN DANIEL

Project Specifications

Skill Level: Beginner
Quilt Size: 36" x 44"
Block Size: 8" x 8"
Number of Blocks: 12

Materials

- ¼ yard red print
- ¾ yard assorted light background scraps
- 1 yard teal print
- 1 yard assorted medium/dark scraps
- Backing 42" x 50"
- Batting 42" x 50"
- All-purpose thread to match fabrics
- Basic sewing tools and supplies, rotary cutter, mat and ruler

Project Note

The color palette of scraps chosen for the sample quilt was limited to red-rust, blues, blacks and browns. The design has the cohesion of a planned color scheme rather than a palette of scraps of all colors.

Instructions

Step 1. Cut 156 squares light background scraps 2½" x 2½" for A. Set aside 60 A squares for borders. Mark a diagonal line from corner to corner on the wrong side of the remaining 96 A squares.

Step 2. Cut 96 rectangles medium/dark scraps 2½" x 4½" for B.

Step 3. To piece one block, join two B pieces as shown in Figure 1; repeat for four B units.

Figure 1

Step 4. Place an A square on two corners of one B unit and stitch on marked lines as shown in Figure 2.

Figure 2

Step 5. Trim ¼" beyond seam line and press to create an A-B unit as shown in Figure 3; repeat for four A-B units.

Figure 3

Step 6. Join the four A-B units to complete one Kansas Dugout block as shown in Figure 4; repeat for 12 blocks.

Figure 4

Step 7. Join three blocks to make a row; repeat for four rows. Press seams in one direction.

Step 8. Join rows to complete the pieced center; press seams in one direction.

Step 9. Join 16 A squares to make a side strip; repeat for two strips. Sew a strip to opposite sides of the pieced center; press seams toward the A strips.

Step 10. Join 14 A squares to make another strip; repeat for two strips. Sew a strip to the top and bottom of the pieced center; press seams toward the A strips.

Step 11. Cut two strips each 1½" x 38½" and 1½" x 28½" red print. Sew the shorter strips to the top

and bottom, and longer strips to opposite sides; press seams toward strips.

Step 12. Cut (and piece) two strips each 3½" x 44½" and 3½" x 30½" teal print. Sew the shorter strips to the top and bottom and longer strips to opposite long sides of the pieced center; press seams toward strips.

Step 13. Sandwich batting between prepared backing and pieced top; pin or baste to hold.

Step 14. Hand- or machine-quilt as desired. ***Note:*** *The sample shown was machine-quilted ¼" away from some seams.*

Step 15. Trim backing and batting even with top; remove pins or basting.

Step 16. Cut five 2½" by fabric width strips teal print. Join the strips on the short ends to make one long strip for binding; press strips in half with wrong sides together along length. Bind edges with binding to finish. ✦

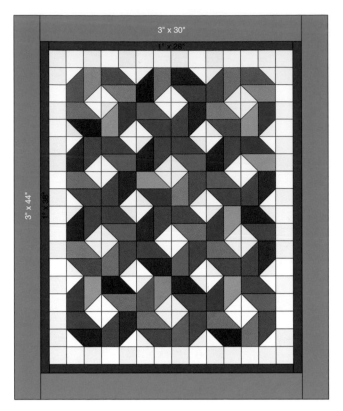

Kansas Dugout
Placement Diagram
36" x 44"

NINE-PATCH & FOUR-PATCH STARS

Red, tan and blue fabrics create a homespun look in simple Four-Patch and Nine-Patch blocks with appliquéd stars.

DESIGN BY KATE LAUCOMER

Four-Patch Stars A
18" x 18" Block

Four-Patch Stars B
18" x 18" Block

Project Specifications
Skill Level: Beginner
Quilt Size: 68" x 82"
Block Size: 18" x 18"
Number of Blocks: 4 Four-Patch
  Stars and 5 Nine-Patch

Materials
- ¾ yard total gold prints and plaids
- 2 yards total red prints and plaids
- 2½ yards total background prints and plaids in tan, white or cream
- 3 yards total blue prints and plaids
- Backing 74" x 88"
- Batting 74" x 88"
- 8¾ yards self-made or purchased blue binding
- All-purpose thread to match fabrics
- Black machine topstitching thread
- 2 yards fusible web
- 2 yards fabric stabilizer

- Basic sewing tools and supplies, rotary cutter, mat and ruler

Project Note
Collect a variety of plaids and prints in darker red, tan, gold and blue colors to make a scrappy yet coordinated-looking quilt. If you prefer a more planned look, purchase the total yardage listed of one fabric in each color and cut half the number of fabric strips listed across the width of the fabric to create Four-Patch and Nine-Patch units and all background pieces.

Instructions
Step 1. Cut four 5" x 22" strips each from four different red and background prints and plaids.
Step 2. Sew a red strip right sides together with a background strip along length; press seam toward red fabric. Repeat for four strip sets.
Step 3. Subcut each strip set into 5" segments; you will need 16

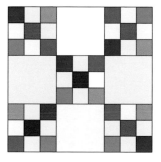

Nine-Patch
18" x 18" Block

segments. Join two segments as shown in Figure 1 to make a Four-Patch unit; repeat for eight units. Press seams in one direction.

Figure 1

Step 4. Cut eight 9½" x 9½" squares from background prints and plaids.

Step 5. Prepare template for large star shape using pattern given. Reverse and trace eight large star shapes onto the paper side of the fusible web. Cut out, leaving a margin around each shape.

Step 6. Fuse the large star shapes onto the wrong side of the gold prints and plaids. Cut out shapes on traced lines; remove paper backing.

Step 7. Position a star shape on the center of each 9" x 9" background square referring to the block drawing for positioning of star; fuse in place.

Step 8. Cut fabric stabilizer to fit behind star shapes; pin in place on the wrong side of each fused square.

Step 9. Using black machine topstitching thread in the top of the machine and all-purpose thread in the bobbin, buttonhole-stitch around each star shape. When stitching is complete, remove fabric stabilizer.

Step 10. Join two star squares with two Four-Patch units to complete one Four-Patch Stars A block as shown in Figure 2; repeat for two A blocks and two B blocks. Press seams toward Four-Patch units.

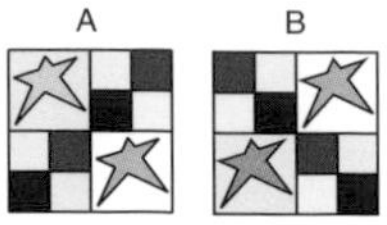

Figure 2

Step 11. Cut 15 strips background prints and plaids, 14 strips blue prints and plaids and four strips red prints and plaids 2½" x 22".

Step 12. Join two background strips with one red strip with right sides together along length as shown in Figure 3; press seams toward red fabrics. Repeat for four strip sets. Subcut each strip set into 2½" segments, again referring to Figure 3; you will need 25 segments.

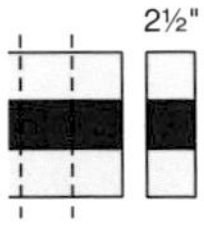

Figure 3 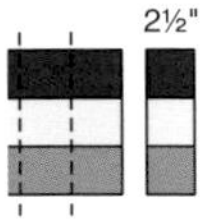   **Figure 4**

Step 13. Join two blue strips with one background strip with right sides together along length as shown in Figure 4; press seams toward blue fabrics. Repeat for seven strip sets. Subcut each strip set into 2½" segments, again referring to Figure 4; you will need 50 segments.

Step 14. Join segments referring to Figure 5 to make a Nine-Patch unit; repeat for 25 units. Press seams in one direction.

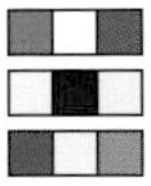

Figure 5

Step 15. Cut 20 squares background prints and plaids 6½" x 6½".

Step 16. Join four background squares with five Nine-Patch units to complete one Nine-

Patch block referring to Figure 6; press seams toward background squares.

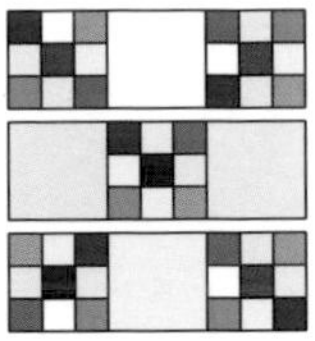

Figure 6

Step 17. Join two Nine-Patch blocks with one Four-Patch Stars A block to make a row; repeat for two rows. Press seams away from Nine-Patch blocks. Join one Nine-Patch block with two Four-Patch Stars B blocks to make a row; press seams away from Nine-Patch block.

Step 18. Join the rows to complete the pieced center; press seams in one direction.

Step 19. Cut a variety of red print and plaid strips 3½" wide and join to create two 3½" x 54½" strips for side borders. Sew a pieced strip to opposite sides of the pieced center; press seams toward pieced strips.

Step 20. Cut a variety of red print and plaid strips 6½" wide and join to create two 6½" x 60½" strips for the top and bottom. Sew a pieced strip to the top and bottom of the pieced center; press seams toward pieced strips.

Step 21. Cut a variety of blue print and plaid strips 4½" wide and join to create two 4½" x 66½" strips for side borders. Sew a pieced strip to opposite sides of the pieced center; press seams toward pieced strips.

Step 22. Cut a variety of blue print and plaid strips 8½" wide and join to create two 8½" x 68½" strips for top and bottom borders.

Step 23. Prepare template for small star shape using pattern given and prepare star shapes for appliqué as in Steps 5 and 6.

Step 24. Arrange seven small stars along one 8½" x 68½" border strip for quilt top strip referring to the Placement Diagram for positioning; fuse in place. Repeat with six small stars on remaining border strip for bottom.

Step 25. Cut fabric stabilizer and machine-appliqué in place as in Steps 8 and 9 for large stars.

Step 26. Sew the seven-star strip to the top and the six-star strip to the bottom of the pieced center; press seams toward pieced strips.

Step 27. Sandwich batting between completed top and prepared backing piece; pin or baste layers together to hold flat.

Step 28. Quilt as desired by hand or machine. **_Note:_** _The quilt shown was machine-quilted in a meandering pattern using threads to match fabrics._

Step 29. When quilting is complete, trim excess batting and backing even with quilted top.

Step 30. Bind edges with self-made or purchased blue binding to finish. ✦

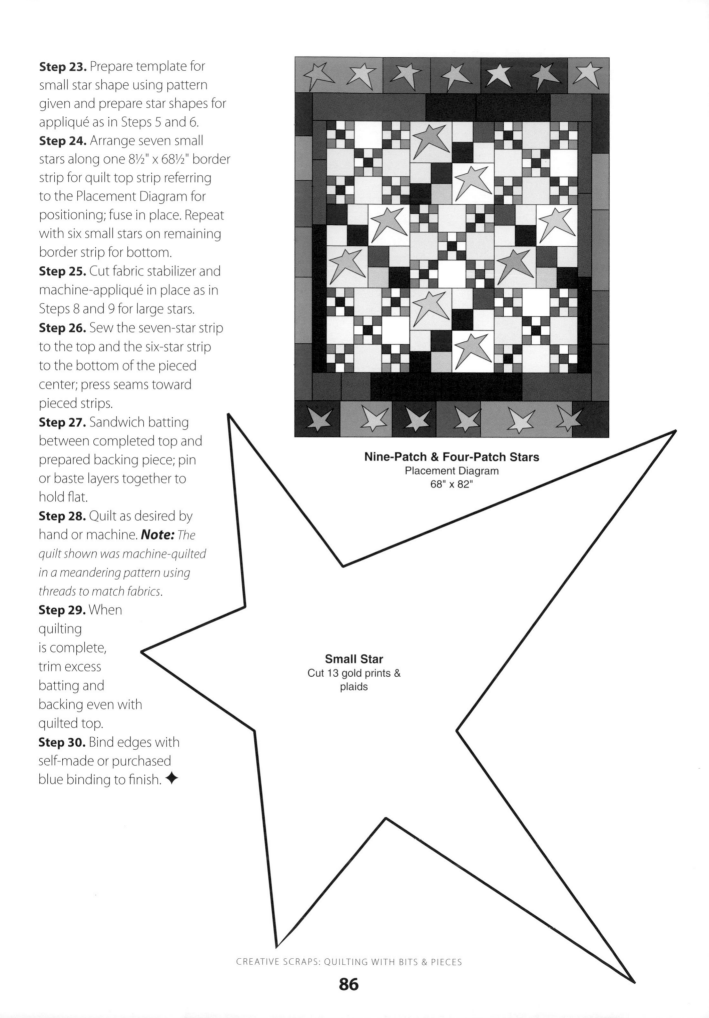

Nine-Patch & Four-Patch Stars
Placement Diagram
68" x 82"

Small Star
Cut 13 gold prints & plaids

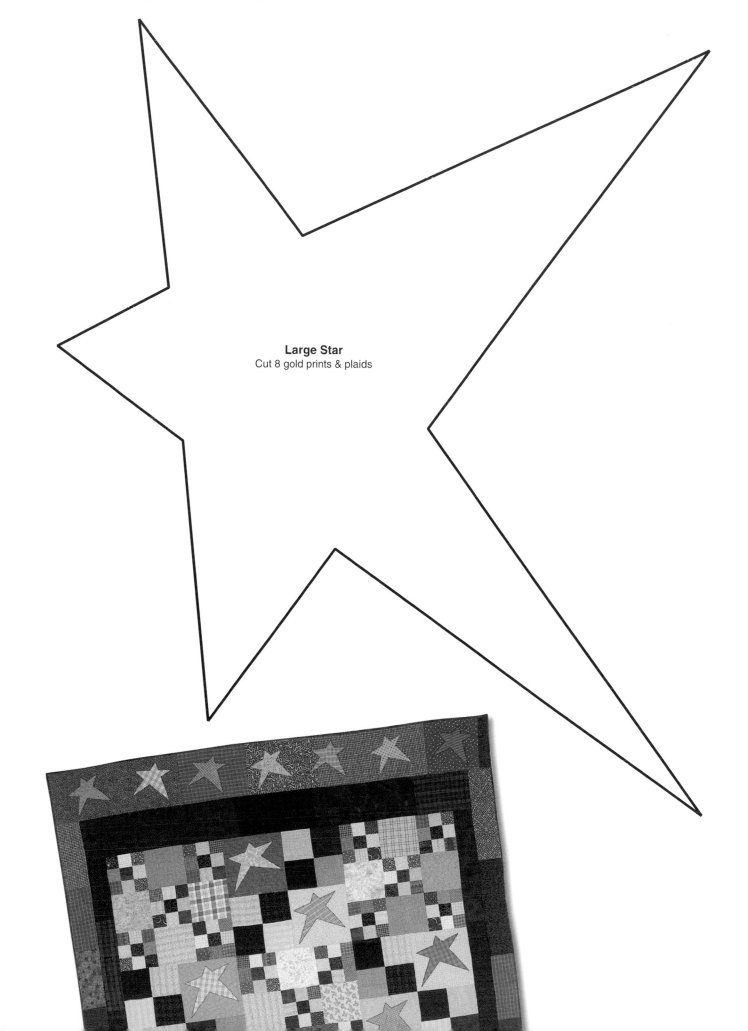

Large Star
Cut 8 gold prints & plaids

SQUARES & TRIANGLES

Dig out those blue, green and cream scraps to make this simple-to-stitch bed-size quilt.

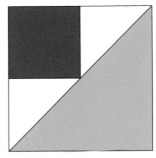

Squares & Triangles
8" x 8" Block

DESIGN BY RUTH SWASEY

Project Specifications

Skill Level: Beginner
Quilt Size: 94" x 94"
Block Size: 8" x 8"
Number of Blocks: 121

Materials

- 61 different 8⅞" x 8⅞" squares medium and dark green and blue prints or tonals for A
- 121 different 4½" x 4½" squares medium and dark green and blue prints or tonals for B
- 121 different 4⅞" x 4⅞" light prints or tonals for C
- 10 different 2¼" by fabric width strips blue prints or tonals for binding
- 1 yard white print for border
- Backing 100" x 100"
- Batting 100" x 100"
- Neutral color all-purpose thread
- Quilting thread
- Basic sewing tools and supplies

Piecing Blocks

Step 1. Cut each A and C square in half on one diagonal to make A and C triangles. Set aside one A triangle for another use.

Step 2. To piece one block, select one A and two C triangles and one B square.

Step 3. Sew C to two adjacent sides of B as shown in Figure 1; press seams toward B.

Figure 1

Step 4. Sew the B-C unit to A as shown in Figure 2 to complete one block; press seam toward A. Repeat for 121 blocks.

Figure 2

Step 5. Select 11 blocks; arrange and join the blocks to make a row as shown in Figure 3; repeat for 11 rows. Press seams in one direction.

Step 6. Join the rows to complete the pieced center; press seams in one direction.

Step 7. Cut nine 3½" by fabric width strips white print; join strips on short ends to make one long strip. Press seams to one side.

Step 8. Cut strip into two 88½" D strips and two 94½" E strips.

Step 9. Sew a D strip to opposite sides and an E strip to the top and bottom of the pieced center to complete the quilt top. Press seams toward D and E strips.

Finishing the Quilt

Step 1. Sandwich the batting between the completed top and prepared backing piece; pin or baste to hold.

Step 2. Hand- or machine-quilt as desired.

Step 3. Trim batting and backing even with the quilted top.

Figure 3

Step 4. Join the binding strips on short ends with a diagonal seam to make a long strip; press seams toward one side.

Step 5. Press the strip in half along length with wrong sides together to complete the binding strip. Bind edges of quilt to finish. ✦

Squares & Triangles
Placement Diagram
94" x 94" Block

LOG CABIN STARS AT MIDNIGHT

A black solid background makes the jewel-tone fabrics stand out in this beautiful star-design quilt.

DESIGN BY MARY EDWARDS

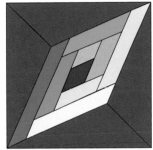

Black Star
10" x 10" Block

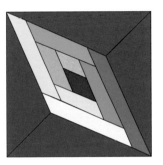

Black Star Reversed
10" x 10" Block

Log Cabin
5" x 5" Block

Project Specifications
Skill Level: Advanced
Quilt Size: 82" x 102"
Block Size: 10" x 10" and 5" x 5"
Number of Blocks: 56 and 48

Materials
- ⅜ yard red mottled
- ½ yard gray mottled
- ⅝ yard light blue mottled
- ⅔ yard aqua mottled
- ⅔ yard green mottled
- 1 yard light green mottled
- 1 yard light teal mottled
- 1⅛ yards dark green mottled
- 1⅓ yards lavender mottled
- 9 yards black solid
- Backing 88" x 108"
- Dark batting 88" x 108"
- All-purpose thread to match fabrics
- Quilting thread
- Spray starch
- 6" and 12½" acrylic squares with 45-degree-angle lines
- Basic sewing tools and supplies

Project Notes
It is helpful to wash, apply spray starch and iron all fabrics before cutting. The starch helps to prevent distortion when cutting.

When sewing, guide the fabric—don't handle the strips or pieces by hand. Press using a dry iron; do not move the iron around, just follow the seam. Use the guideline on the square to maintain the 45-degree angle on each piece when cutting.

Cutting
Step 1. Cut four 1¾" by fabric width A strips and two 1½" by fabric width X strips red mottled. Open fold; press strips flat.

Step 2. Place the 45-degree line of the 6" acrylic square along the top of one A strip as shown in Figure 1; cut end of strip at an angle.

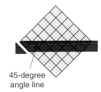

45-degree
angle line

Figure 1

Step 3. Cut (28) A pieces from two A strips, aligning the 45-degree line

on the square ruler with the edge of the strip and matching the 1¾" line on the ruler with previously cut edge to cut one A piece as shown in Figure 2. Repeat to cut 28 AR pieces, again referring to Figure 2.

Step 4. Cut the following 1½" by fabric width strips: eight gray (B); 12 each lavender (C) and light blue (D); 14 each aqua (E) and green (F); 20 each light green (G) and light teal (H); and 22 dark green mottled (I).

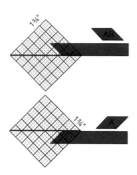

Figure 2

Step 5. Cut eight 3⅝" J strips along the length of the black solid. Prepare template for J using pattern given. Layer two J strips with wrong sides together; place the J template on top and cut to make one J and one JR piece. Repeat for 112 J and 112 JR pieces.

Step 6. Cut one 5½" strip along the length of the black solid; subcut strip into two 70½" K strips and two 50½" L strips.

Step 7. Cut two 1½" strips along the length of the black solid; subcut strips into two 100½" M and two 82½" N strips.

Step 8. Cut (10) 2½" by fabric width strips lavender mottled for binding.

Piecing Black Star Blocks

Step 1. Place one B strip right side up on your sewing machine table; place an A piece right sides together with strip starting 3" from end of B as shown in Figure 3. Stitch A to B. Continue adding A pieces to the B strips, butting each A piece against the previous one until 28 A pieces are sewn to B strips. Repeat with 28 AR pieces on B strips, again referring to Figure 3.

Figure 3

Step 2. When stitching is complete, press seams toward B strip.

Step 3. Align edge of ruler with edge of A and cut along B to continue the 45-degree angle as shown in Figure 4; repeat for all A and AR pieces to complete 28 each A-B and AR-B units.

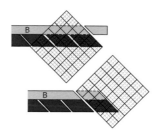

Figure 4

Step 4. Stack the like units wrong side up with color B facing away from you as shown in Figure 5. Place one C strip right side up and place an A-B unit on the C strip as shown in Figure 6; stitch. Continue until all A-B and AR-BR units are stitched to the C strips.

Figure 5   **Figure 6**

Step 5. Press seams toward C and cut units as in Step 3 and as shown in Figure 7.

Figure 7

Step 6. Continue adding strips in alphabetical order around the center to complete 28 each A and AR units as shown in Figure 8.

Step 7. Sew J and JR to the sides of the A and AR units, stitching

mitered seam between J and JR last, to complete the Black Star and Black Star Reversed blocks as shown in Figure 9; press mitered seams open and long seams toward J and JR.

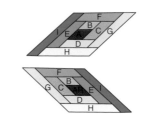

Figure 8

Figure 9

Piecing Log Cabin Blocks

Step 1. Sew an X strip to a B strip with right sides together along length; press seam toward B. Repeat for two X-B strips.

Step 2. Subcut strip sets into (48) 1½" X-B units as shown in Figure 10.

Figure 10

Step 3. Stack X-B units wrong side up with B facing you.

Step 4. Place a C strip right side up on your sewing machine table; place an X-B unit on C and stitch as shown in Figure 11; repeat for all X-B units on C.

Figure 11

Step 5. Press seams toward C strips; cut C strip even with X-B unit to complete an X-B-C unit as shown in Figure 12. Repeat for 48 units.

Figure 12

Step 6. Repeat Steps 4 and 5, adding units to strips in alphabetical order to complete 48 Log Cabin blocks as shown in Figure 13.

Figure 13

Completing the Top

Step 1. Arrange 12 Black Star and 12 Black Star Reversed blocks in six rows of four blocks each referring to Figure 14 for positioning of blocks. Join blocks in rows; press seams of adjacent rows in opposite directions.

Figure 14

Step 2. Join rows to complete the pieced center; press seams in one direction.

Step 3. Join 12 Log Cabin blocks to make a side strip as shown in Figure 15; repeat for two side strips. Repeat with 10 blocks to make top and bottom strips, again referring to Figure 15; press seams in one direction.

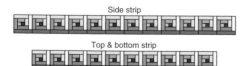

Side strip

Top & bottom strip

Figure 15

Step 4. Sew a side strip to opposite sides and the remaining strips to the top and bottom of the pieced center; press seams toward Log Cabin strips.

Step 5. Sew a K strip to opposite long sides of the pieced center; press seams toward K. Sew a Log Cabin block to each end of each L strip, referring to the Placement Diagram for positioning of blocks; press seams toward L. Sew the L strips to the top and bottom of the pieced center; press seams toward L strips.

Step 6. Join four Black Star and four Black Star Reversed blocks to make a strip referring to Figure 16

for positioning; press seams in one direction. Repeat for two strips.

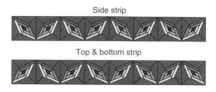

Side strip

Top & bottom strip

Figure 16

Step 7. Sew a strip to opposite long sides of the pieced center; press seams toward K.

Step 8. Join four Black Star and four Black Star Reversed blocks to make a strip, again referring to Figure 16; press seams in one direction. Repeat for two strips.

Log Cabin Stars at Midnight
Placement Diagram
82" x 102"

Step 9. Sew a strip to the top and bottom of the pieced center; press seams toward L.

Step 10. Sew an M strip to opposite long sides and an N strip to the top and bottom of the pieced center; press seams toward M and N to complete the top.

Finishing the Quilt

Step 1. Sandwich the batting between the completed top and prepared backing; pin or baste layers together to hold.

Step 2. Hand- or machine-quilt as desired. When quilting is complete, trim batting and backing even with top; remove pins or basting.

Step 3. Join binding strips on short ends to make one long strip. Fold the strip in half along length with wrong sides together; press.

Step 4. Sew binding to quilt edges, mitering corners and overlapping ends. Fold binding to the back side and stitch in place to finish. ◆

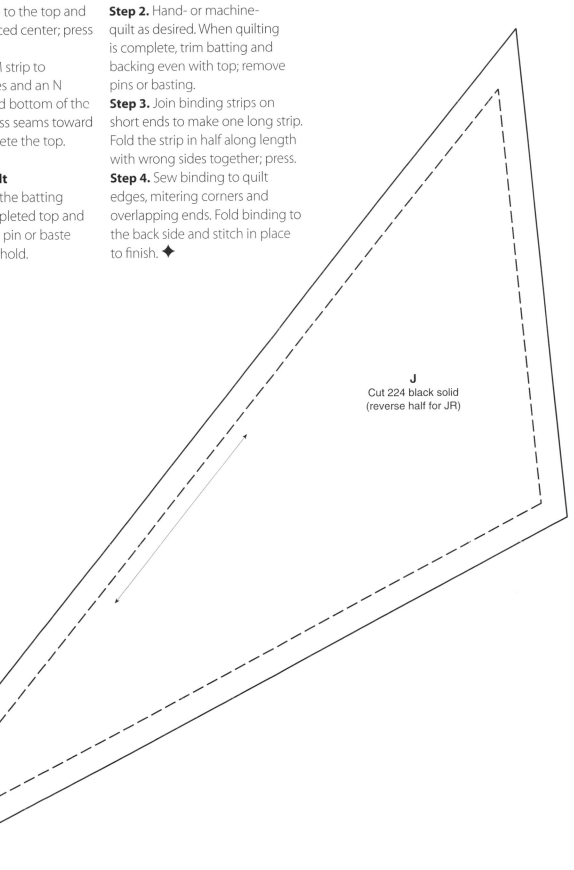

J
Cut 224 black solid
(reverse half for JR)

T IS FOR TULIPS

The Crossed T's blocks combine with appliquéd tulip blocks to make a pretty quilt with an antique look.

Small Tulip
4½" x 4½"

Project Specifications
Skill Level: Intermediate
Quilt Size: 47¼" x 47¼"
Block Size: 9" x 9" and 4½" x 4½"
Number of Blocks: 13 and 4

Materials
- ¼ yard each 9 different dark prints for Crossed T's blocks
- ¼ yard pink print for tulip appliqué
- ¼ yard pink print for inner border
- ½ yard binding fabric
- ⅝ yard white shirting print for A and B background squares
- ⅝ yard blue print for outer border
- ¾ yard total 1 or more white shirting prints for Crossed T's blocks
- ¾ yard total 1 or more dark brown prints for H and I triangles and tulip appliqué
- Backing 53" x 53"
- Batting 53" x 53"
- Neutral color all-purpose thread
- Machine-appliqué thread to match pink and brown prints
- Quilting thread
- 1 yard lightweight fusible web
- ⅝ yard fabric stabilizer
- Basic sewing tools and supplies

Making Large & Small Tulip Blocks
Step 1. Prepare templates for appliqué shapes using patterns given.
Step 2. Trace shapes onto the paper side of the lightweight fusible web referring to patterns for number to cut. Cut out shapes, leaving a margin around each one.
Step 3. Fuse paper shapes to the wrong side of fabrics as directed on pieces for color; cut out shapes on traced lines. Remove paper backing.
Step 4. Cut four 9½" x 9½" A squares and four 5" x 5" B squares white shirting fabric. Fold and crease to mark the diagonal center.
Step 5. Center one large stem shape on the diagonal of each A square as shown in Figure 1; fuse in place. Repeat with small stems and B squares.

Figure 1

Step 6. Arrange two large leaves and one large tulip shape with

Large Tulip
9" x 9" Block

Crossed T's
9" x 9" Block

the fused stem shape on each A square; fuse in place. Repeat with small leaves and small tulip shapes on B.
Step 7. Cut four 9½" x 9½" and four 5" x 5" squares fabric stabilizer; pin squares behind same-size fused squares.
Step 8. Using machine-appliqué thread to match fabrics, satin-stitch shapes in place. When

stitching is complete, remove fabric stabilizer to complete the blocks.

Making Crossed T's Blocks

Step 1. To make one Crossed T's block, cut (16) 2" x 2" C squares, one 3½" x 3½" D square and two 3⅞" x 3⅞" E squares from one of the nine dark prints. Cut each E square in half on one diagonal to make E triangles.

Step 2. Cut eight 2" x 3½" F rectangles and two 3⅞" x 3⅞" G squares from white shirting print. Cut each G square in half on one diagonal to make G triangles.

Step 3. Mark a diagonal line on the wrong side of each C square. Referring to Figure 2, pin C to F and stitch on the marked line; trim seam to ¼" and press C to the right side. Repeat on opposite end of F to complete one C-F unit, again referring to Figure 2; repeat for eight units.

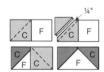

Figure 2

Step 4. Sew E to G to make an E-G unit as shown in Figure 3; press seam toward E. Repeat for four units.

Figure 3   **Figure 4**

Step 5. To complete one block, join two C-F units as shown in Figure 4; repeat for four joined units.

Step 6. Join two E-G units with a joined C-F unit to make a row as shown in Figure 5; repeat for two rows. Press seams toward E-G units.

Figure 5

Step 7. Join D with two joined C-F units to make a row as shown in Figure 6; press seams toward D.

Figure 6

Step 8. Join the rows to complete one Crossed T's block referring to Figure 7; press. Repeat for nine blocks.

Figure 7

Completing the Top

Step 1. Cut two 14" x 14" squares dark brown print; cut each square in half on both diagonals to make H triangles.

Step 2. Cut two 7¼" x 7¼" squares dark brown print; cut each square in half on one diagonal to make I triangles.

Step 3. Arrange the blocks in diagonal rows with H and I triangles as shown in Figure 8. Join in rows; join rows to complete the quilt center. Press seams in one direction.

Figure 8

Step 4. Cut four 1½" x 36¾" J strips pink print and four 4" x 36¾" K strips blue print. Cut eight 1½" x 5" L strips pink print.

Step 5. Sew a J strip to a K strip with right sides together along length; press seams toward K. Sew L to each end as shown in Figure 9; press seams toward L. Repeat for four J-K-L strips.

Figure 9

Step 6. Sew a J-K-L strip to opposite sides of the pieced center; press seams toward strips.

Step 7. Sew a Small Tulip block to each end of the remaining J-K-L strips, keeping blocks upright on each end; press seams away from blocks. Sew these strips to the top and bottom of the quilt center; press seams toward strips.

Finishing the Quilt

Step 1. Sandwich the batting between the completed top and prepared backing; pin or baste layers together to hold.

Step 2. Hand- or machine-quilt as desired. When quilting is complete, trim batting and backing even with top; remove pins or basting.

Step 3. Cut five 2¼" by fabric width strips binding fabric. Join the strips on short ends to make one long strip. Fold the strip in half along length with wrong sides together; press.

Step 4. Sew binding to quilt edges, mitering corners and overlapping ends. Fold binding to the back side and stitch in place. ✦

T Is for Tulips
Placement Diagram
47¼" x 47¼"

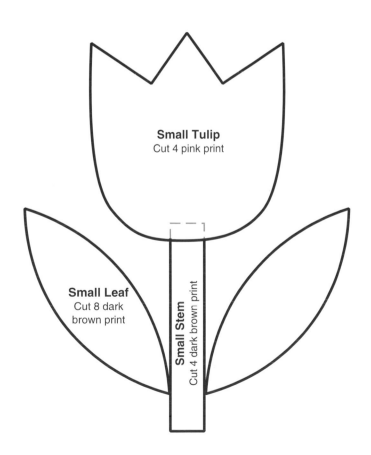

Small Tulip
Cut 4 pink print

Small Leaf
Cut 8 dark
brown print

Small Stem
Cut 4 dark brown print

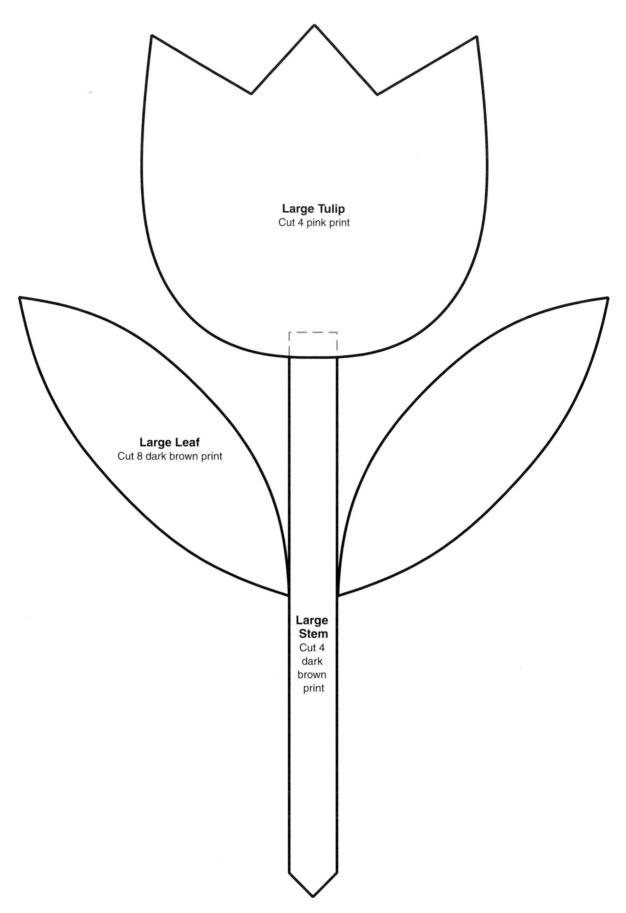

Large Tulip
Cut 4 pink print

Large Leaf
Cut 8 dark brown print

Large Stem
Cut 4 dark brown print

ZOI'S VIOLETS

The violet print combines with coordinating fabrics in this summertime quilt.

DESIGN BY CATE TALLMAN-EVANS

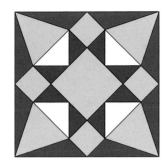

Zoi's Violet A
12" x 12" Block

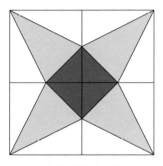

Zoi's Violet B
12" x 12" Block

Project Specifications

Skill Level: Intermediate
Quilt Size: 85" x 102"
Block Size: 12" x 12"
Number of Blocks: 32

Materials

- ¾ yard light green print
- 1⅛ yards dark green print
- 1½ yards tan tonal
- 1⅝ yards dark purple tonal
- 1¾ yards cream print
- 2¼ yards purple floral
- 2⅝ yards lavender print
- Backing 91" x 108"
- Batting 91" x 108"
- All-purpose thread to match fabrics
- Basic sewing tools and supplies

Cutting

Step 1. Prepare templates using pattern pieces given. Use templates to cut pieces from strips as directed in the steps that follow.

Step 2. Cut nine 4¾" by fabric width strips lavender print; subcut three strips into (20) 4¾" A squares and six strips into 80 E triangles using the E template as shown in Figure 1.

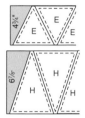

Figure 1

Step 3. Cut five 2⅝" by fabric width strips lavender print; subcut strips into (80) 2⅝" D squares.

Step 4. Cut four 6⅞" by fabric width strips lavender print; subcut strips into 48 H triangles using the H template, again referring to Figure 1.

Step 5. Cut five 4¾" by fabric width strips cream print; subcut strips into (80) 2⅝" B rectangles.

Step 6. Cut (10) 3½" by fabric width strips cream print; subcut strips into 48 each I and IR triangles using the I template as shown in Figure 2.

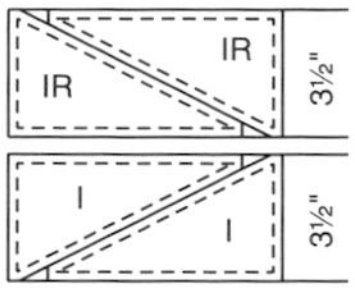

Figure 2

Step 7. Cut (10) 2⅝" by fabric width strips dark purple tonal; subcut strips into (160) 2⅝" C squares.

Step 8. Cut (18) 2" by fabric width strips dark green print; subcut strips into 80 each F and FR triangles using the F template as shown in Figure 3.

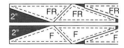

Figure 3

Step 9. Cut three 3⅞" by fabric width strips purple floral; subcut strips into (24) 3⅞" squares. Cut each square in half on one diagonal to make 48 G triangles.

Step 10. Cut four 18¼" x 18¼" squares tan tonal; cut each square in half on both diagonals to make 14 J triangles. Set aside two triangles for another project.

Step 11. Cut two 9⅜" x 9⅜" squares tan tonal. Cut each square in half on one diagonal to make four K triangles.

Step 12. Cut eight 2½" by fabric width strips light green print. Join strips on short ends to make one long strip; subcut strip into two 85½" L strips and two 72½" M strips.

Step 13. Cut nine 7" by fabric width strips purple floral. Join strips on short ends to make one long strip; subcut strip into two 89½" N strips and two 85½" O strips.

Step 14. Cut (10) 2¼" by fabric width strips dark purple tonal for binding.

Piecing A Blocks

Step 1. Draw a line from corner to corner on the wrong side of each C square.

Step 2. Referring to Figure 4, place C right sides together with B; stitch on the marked line. Trim seam to ¼"; press C to the right side. Repeat on the other end of B, again referring to Figure 4, to complete one B-C unit; repeat for 80 units.

Figure 4

Step 3. Sew a B-C unit to two opposite sides of A as shown in Figure 5; press seams toward A. Repeat for 20 A-B-C units.

Step 4. Sew D to each end of the remaining B-C units, again referring to Figure 5; press seams toward D. Repeat for 40 B-C-D units.

Figure 5

Step 5. Sew a B-C-D unit to opposites sides of an A-B-C unit to complete a block center unit, again referring to Figure 5; press seams toward B-C-D units. Repeat for 20 block centers.

Step 6. Sew F and FR to each long side of E as shown in Figure 6; press seams toward F and FR. Repeat for 80 E-F units.

Figure 6

Step 7. Sew an E-F unit to each side of the center unit to complete one A block as shown in Figure 7; press seams toward the E-F units. Repeat for 20 A blocks.

Figure 7

Piecing B Blocks

Step 1. Sew I and IR to opposite long sides of H as shown in Figure 8; press seams toward I and IR. Repeat for 48 H-I units.

Figure 8

Step 2. Sew G to an H-I unit as shown in Figure 9; press seams toward G. Repeat for 48 G-H-I units.

Figure 9

Step 3. Join four G-H-I units to complete one B block as shown in Figure 10; press seams in one direction. Repeat for 12 B blocks.

Figure 10

Completing the Top

Step 1. Arrange and join the A and B blocks with J and K in diagonal rows referring to Figure 11. Press seams toward B blocks and J and K triangles. Join rows to complete the pieced center; press seams in one direction.

Figure 11

Step 2. Sew L strips to opposite long sides and M strips to the top and bottom of the pieced center; press seams toward L and M strips.

Step 3. Sew N strips to opposite long sides and O strips to the top and bottom of the pieced center to complete the pieced top; press seams toward N and O strips.

Step 4. Finish quilt referring to the General Instructions. ◆

E
Cut 80 lavender print
from 4¾"-wide strips

F
Cut 160 dark green print
from 2"-wide strips
(reverse 80 for FR)

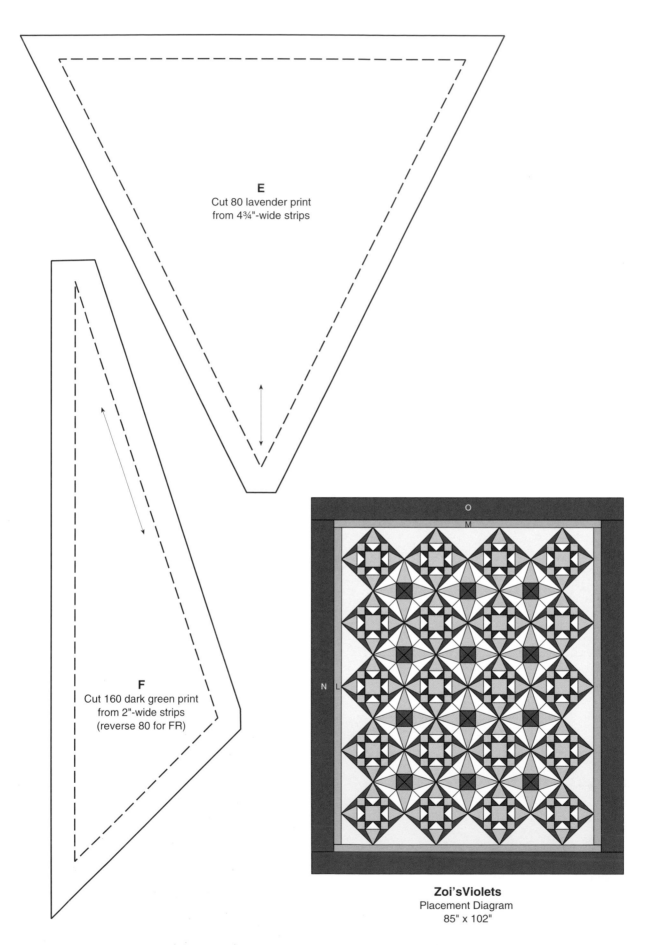

Zoi's Violets
Placement Diagram
85" x 102"

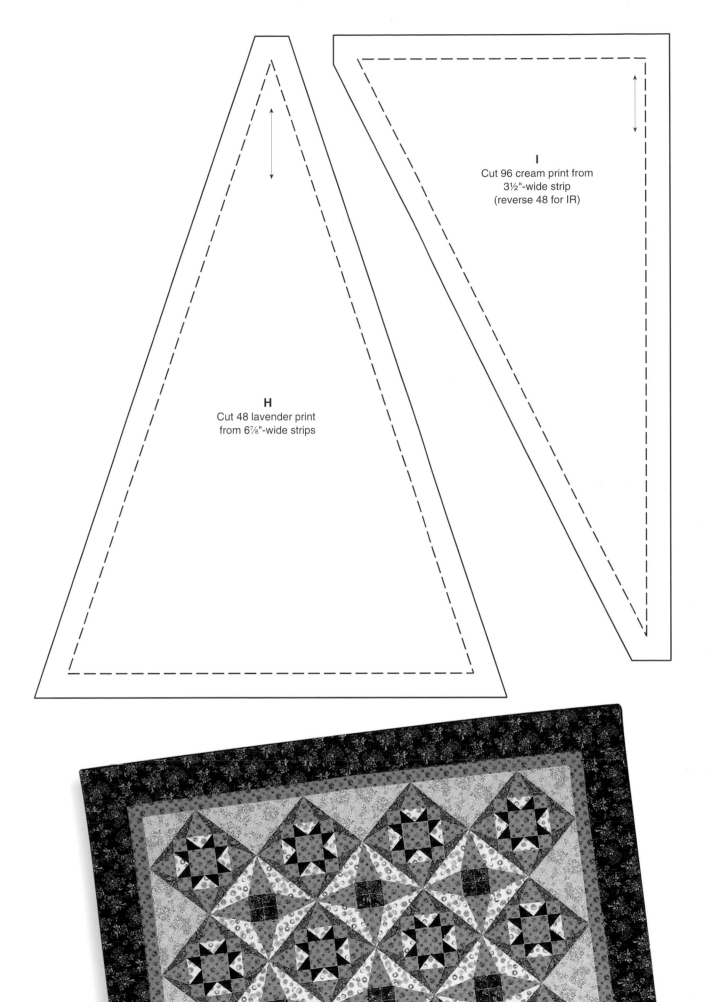

I
Cut 96 cream print from
3½"-wide strip
(reverse 48 for IR)

H
Cut 48 lavender print
from 6⅞"-wide strips

LOVE OF PATCHWORK FRIENDSHIP QUILT

Friendship quilts are wonderful reminders of special people and can be made for someone of any age. The quilt shown has children's signatures and will be a reminder of friends for many years in the future.

DESIGN BY JUDITH SANDSTROM

Stripe
3" x 3" Block

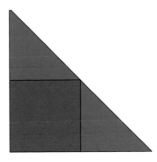

Half Four-Patch
3" x 4¼" Block

Four-Patch
3" x 3" Block

Project Specifications
Skill Level: Beginner
Quilt Size: 39" x 47½"
Block Size: 3" x 3" and 3" x 4¼"
Number of Blocks: 31 Four-Patch,
40 Stripe and 18 Half Four-Patch

Materials
- ¼ yard each dark green, dark blue, light green, yellow and light blue prints
- ⅜ yard floral print for border
- ½ yard white-on-white print
- ⅝ yard rose print
- Backing 45" x 54"
- Batting 45" x 54"
- Neutral color all-purpose thread
- 3 or 4 colored extra-fine-point fabric marking pens
- Quilt basting spray
- Basic sewing tools and supplies, rotary cutter, self-healing mat and acrylic ruler

Instructions
Step 1. Cut three strips white-on-white print 3½" by fabric width; subcut into 3½" square segments. Set aside 32 squares for signatures. Cut seven squares white-on-white print 3⅞" x 3⅞"; cut each square in half on one diagonal to make 14 A triangles for edges. Cut one square white-on-white print 4¼" x 4¼"; cut in half on both diagonals to make four small B triangles for corners.

Step 2. Cut three strips each dark green and dark blue prints and four strips each light green, yellow, light blue and rose prints 2" by fabric width.

Step 3. Stitch strips with right sides together along length as follows: dark green/dark blue; light green/yellow; and light blue/rose. Repeat for three strip sets dark green/dark blue and four strip sets of the remaining combinations.

Step 4. Cut dark green/dark blue strip sets in 2" segments; repeat for 62 segments.

Step 5. Join two dark green/dark blue segments to make a Four-Patch block as shown in Figure 1; press. Repeat for 31 blocks.

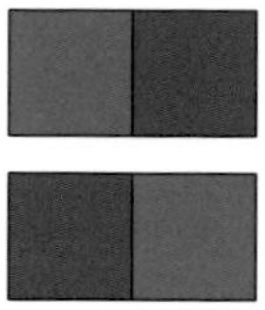

Figure 1

Step 6. Cut the light green/yellow and the light blue/rose strip sets into 3½" segments; repeat for 40 segments of each combination referring to Figure 2.

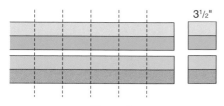

Figure 2

Step 7. Cut one strip dark blue print 2" by fabric width. Subcut into 18 squares 2" x 2". Cut nine 2⅜" x 2⅜" squares dark green print; cut each square in half on one diagonal. Join two dark green print triangles with one dark blue print square as shown in Figure 3; repeat to make 18 Half Four-Patch blocks.

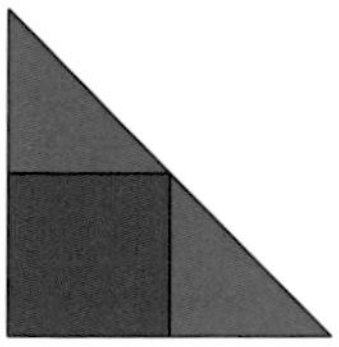

Figure 3

Step 8. Using colored extra-fine-point fabric marking pens, collect signatures on the 32 white-on-white print squares, placing signatures on point as shown in Figure 4. ***Note:*** *If you find it difficult to write on the fabric squares, press freezer paper to the wrong side of the square for a stabilizer; remove paper after signature has been added.* Press all squares to permanently set the ink.

Figure 4

Step 9. Join seven white-on-white print signature squares with eight light green/yellow segments and one A triangle in a diagonal row, reversing the yellow and green sequence as shown in Figure 5.

Step 10. Join seven light blue/rose segments with six dark green/dark blue Four-Patch blocks and two Half Four-Patch blocks in a diagonal row, reversing color sequence as shown in Figure 6.

Step 11. Stitch remaining rows referring to Figure 7 for color sequence and number of units in a row.

Figure 7

Step 12. Lay out rows in the proper sequence, again referring to Figure 7; sew A triangles to ends of rows. Join rows; sew a B triangle to each corner to complete pieced center.

Step 13. Cut two strips each floral print 3" x 39½" and 3" x 43". Sew the longer strips to opposite long sides and shorter strips to the top and bottom; press seams toward strips.

Step 14. Prepare 5½ yards self-made binding from rose print, prepare quilt for quilting and finish referring to the General Instructions. ◆

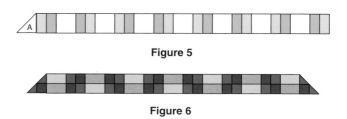

Figure 5

Figure 6

2½" x 39"

2½" x 42½"

Love of Patchwork Friendship Quilt
Placement Diagram
39" x 47½"

STARS & DIAMONDS

Any color of fabric can be used to make this quilt; the only requirement is that there be true value changes from light to medium to dark. Before you start, divide your scraps into three stacks and estimate the amount of fabric in each pile. The Materials list gives the approximate amount of light, medium and dark fabric needed. If you need more fabric of a certain value, treat yourself to a few fat quarters. The scrappier this quilt is the better.

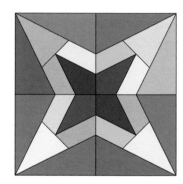

Stars & Diamonds
12" x 12" Block

DESIGN BY JANICE MCKEE

Project Specifications
Skill Level: Intermediate
Quilt Size: 59" x 59"
Block Size: 12" x 12"
Number of Blocks: 16

Materials
- ⅔ yard dark scraps
- 1¼ yards medium scraps
- 1¾ yards navy print for borders
- 2 yards light scraps
- Backing 65" x 65"
- Batting 65" x 65"
- 7 yards self-made or purchased binding
- Neutral color all-purpose thread
- Basic sewing tools and supplies and water-erasable marker

Instructions
Step 1. Prepare templates using pattern pieces given. Cut as directed on each piece for one block; repeat for 12 blocks.
Step 2. To piece one block, sew B and BR to A; add C, D and DR referring to Figure 1; repeat for four units. Join four units to complete one block as shown in Figure 2; repeat for 16 blocks. Press and square up blocks to 12½" x 12½", if necessary.

Figure 1

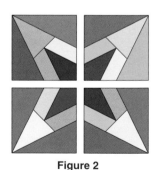

Figure 2

Step 3. Arrange blocks in four rows of four blocks each. Join blocks in rows; join rows to complete pieced center. Press seams in one direction.
Step 4. Cut four strips navy print 6" x 59½" from fabric length. Sew a strip to each side of the

pieced center, mitering corners; press seams toward strips.

Step 5. Mark desired quilting design in border strips using water-erasable marker. Refer to Figure 3 for suggested quilting design for blocks.

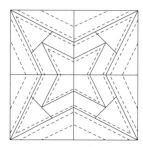

Figure 3

Step 6. Prepare quilt top for quilting and finish referring to the General Instructions. ✦

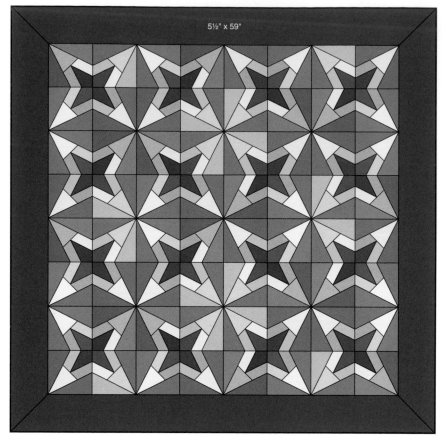

5½" x 59"

Stars & Diamonds
Placement Diagram
59" x 59"

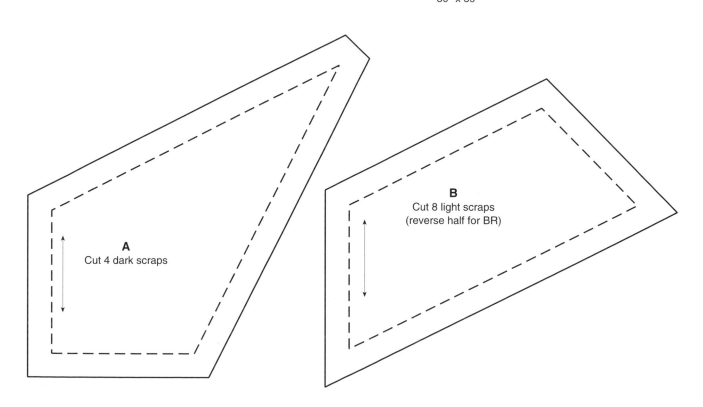

A
Cut 4 dark scraps

B
Cut 8 light scraps
(reverse half for BR)

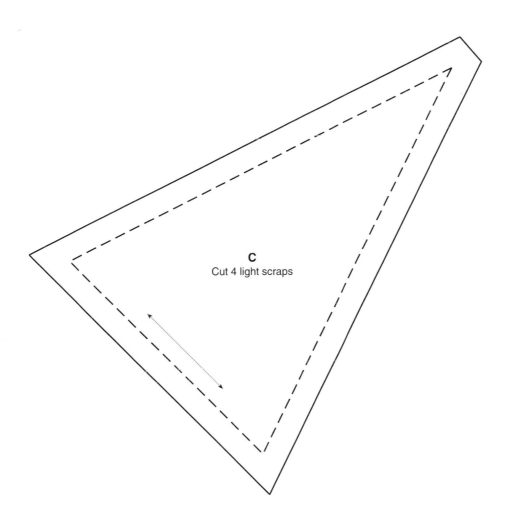

C
Cut 4 light scraps

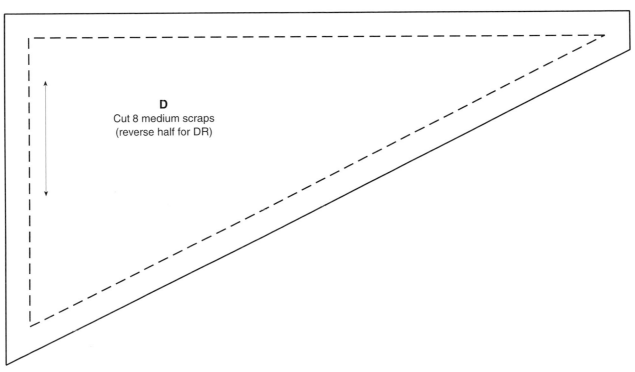

D
Cut 8 medium scraps
(reverse half for DR)

SCRAPPY PRAIRIE QUEEN

Select a variety of light and dark scraps to make this quick bed-size quilt.

DESIGN BY SANDRA L. HATCH

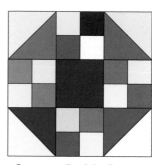

Scrappy Prairie Queen
15" x 15"

Project Specifications
Skill Level: Beginner
Quilt Size: 85" x 100"
Block Size: 15" x 15"
Number of Blocks: 20

Materials
- ¾ yard cream tonal
- 2¾ yards total light scraps
- 2¾ yards dark floral print
- 3½ yards total dark scraps
- Backing 91" x 106"
- Batting 91" x 106"
- Neutral color all-purpose thread
- Quilting thread
- Basic sewing tools and supplies

Cutting
Step 1. Cut 40 squares each light and dark scraps 5⅞" x 5⅞" for A.
Note: *Six 5⅞" by fabric width strips to equal 1 yard each light and dark are needed if cutting strips from scrap fabric.*
Step 2. Cut and piece 3"-wide strips from light and dark scraps to equal (18) 3" x 42" strips each for B units. ***Note:*** *If using unpieced scrap strips, only 16 strips (or 1½ yards total) are needed.*

Step 3. Cut 24 squares dark scraps 5½" x 5½" for C.
Step 4. Cut seven 3" by fabric width strips cream tonal for D and E.
Step 5. Cut nine 8" by fabric width strips dark floral print for F.
Step 6. Cut (10) 2¼" by fabric width strips dark floral print for binding.

Piecing the Blocks
Step 1. Draw a diagonal line from corner to corner on the wrong side of each light A square.
Step 2. Place a marked A square right sides together with a dark A square; stitch ¼" on each side of the marked line as shown in Figure 1. Repeat for all A squares.

Figure 1

Step 3. Cut a stitched A unit on the marked line; press seams toward the dark A pieces to complete two A units as shown in Figure 2. Repeat for all A units.

Figure 2

Step 4. Sew a light B strip to a dark B strip with right sides together along length; press seams toward dark B. Repeat for 18 strip sets.
Step 5. Subcut strip sets into (214) 3" B segments as shown in Figure 3; set aside 54 segments for borders. Join two B segments to complete a B unit; repeat to make 80 B units.

Figure 3

Step 6. To piece one block, join two A units with a B unit as shown in Figure 4; press seams open. Repeat for two A-B rows.

Figure 4

Step 7. Join two B units with C referring to Figure 5; press seams toward C.

Figure 5

Step 8. Join the A-B rows with the B-C row to complete one block as shown in Figure 6; press seams open. Repeat for 20 blocks.

Figure 6

Completing the Top

Step 1. Arrange the blocks in five rows of four blocks each. When satisfied with the arrangement, join blocks in rows; press seams open. Join the rows to complete the pieced center; press seams open.

Step 2. Join 15 B units on short ends to make a border strip as shown in Figure 7; repeat for two strips. Repeat with 12 B units to complete two strips.

Make 2

B

Make 2

Figure 7

Step 3. Join the D and E strips on the short ends to complete one long strip; press seams open. Cut two 75½" D strips and two 60½" E strips from the strip.

Step 4. Sew a D strip to each 15-unit B strip and an E strip to each 12-unit B strip; press seams toward D and E. Sew a D strip to opposite sides of the pieced center, with B units on the outside edge, referring to the Placement Diagram.

Step 5. Sew a C square to each end of each B-E strip; press seams away from C. Sew a strip to the top and bottom of the pieced center, with B units on the outside edge, referring to the Placement Diagram.

Step 6. Join the F strips on the short ends to make one long strip; press seams open. Cut four 85½" F strips from the strip.

Step 7. Sew an F strip to opposite long sides and to the top and bottom of the pieced center to complete the top; press seams toward F.

Finishing the Quilt

Step 1. Sandwich the batting between the completed top and prepared backing; pin or baste layers together to hold.

Step 2. Hand- or machine-quilt as desired. When quilting is complete, trim batting and backing even with top; remove pins or basting.

Step 3. Join the previously cut binding strips on short ends to make one long strip. Fold the strip in half along length with wrong sides together; press.

Step 4. Sew binding to quilt edges, mitering corners and overlapping ends. Fold binding to the back side and stitch in place to finish. ◆

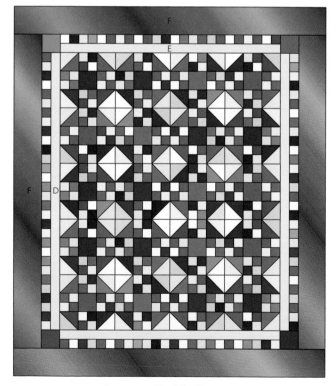

Scrappy Prairie Queen
Placement Diagram
85" x 100"

STAINED GLASS DIAMONDS

Black solid strips create the stained glass look in this simple quilt made with easy pieced blocks in jewel-tone colors.

Stained Glass Diamonds
12" x 12" Block

DESIGN BY HOLLY DANIELS

Project Specifications
Skill Level: Beginner
Quilt Size: 72" x 84"
Block Size: 12" x 12"
Number of Blocks: 42

Materials
- 5 yards total 12–20 jewel-tone solids, tone-on-tones or mottleds
- 5¼ yards black solid
- Backing 78" x 90"
- Batting 78" x 90"
- Neutral color all-purpose thread
- Quilting thread
- Basic sewing tools and supplies

Making Blocks
Step 1. Cut four 3½" by fabric width strips black solid; cut strips into 3½" segments for X. You will need 42 X squares.
Step 2. Cut 75 strips black solid 2" by fabric width; subcut strips to make 168 segments each in the following sizes: 3½" for D, 10½" for E and 4½" for G.

Step 3. Cut 2" by fabric width strips from jewel-tone fabrics and cut to make 84 segments each in the following sizes: 3½" for A and 6½" for B. Cut remaining strips as follows to make 168 segments each in the following sizes: 6½" for C and 6½" for F.
Step 4. To piece one Stained Glass Diamond block, stitch any color A piece to opposite sides of X as shown in Figure 1; press seams away from X.

Figure 1

Step 5. Sew any color B piece to opposite sides of the A-X unit; press seams toward B.
Step 6. Add any color C piece to opposite sides of the A-X-B unit; press seams toward C.
Step 7. Add D to opposite sides of the pieced unit by centering D on C and sewing as shown in Figure 2. Trim block to measure 10½" x 10½" as shown in Figure 3.

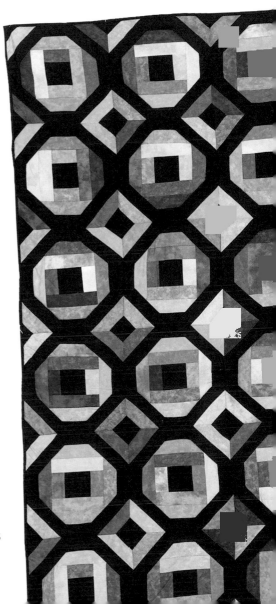

Figure 2

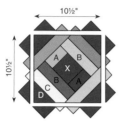

Figure 3

Step 8. Sew pieces E, F and G together, matching centers of pieces as shown in Figure 4; repeat for four units. Press seams toward G.

Figure 4

Step 9. Sew one E-F-G unit to each side of the pieced unit as shown in Figure 5; press seams away from pieced center.

Figure 5

Step 10. Trim pieced block to 12½" x 12½" as shown in Figure 6; repeat for 42 blocks.

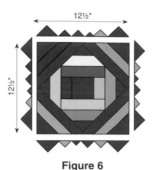

Figure 6

Completing the Top
Step 1. Arrange blocks in seven rows of six blocks each; join blocks in rows. Press seams in one direction.

Step 2. Join the rows, alternating directions of seam allowances, to complete the pieced top.

Finishing the Quilt
Step 1. Prepare quilt top for quilting and quilt.
Step 2. When quilting is complete, trim batting and backing edges even with the quilted top.
Step 3. Prepare 9 yards black solid binding and bind edges of quilt to finish. ✦

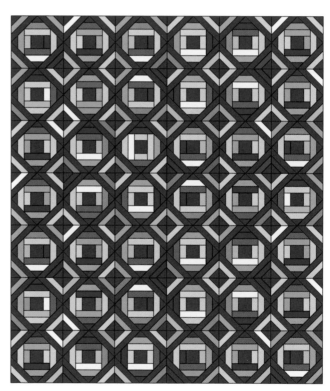

Stained Glass Diamonds
Placement Diagram
72" x 84"

PEEKABOO YO-YO QUILT

Twinkling stars and peekaboo yo-yos make this quilt a sparkling addition to any collection. Try this new technique that makes yo-yos appear to have holes on both sides.

Star Block
4" x 4"

DESIGN BY BETTY ALDERMAN

Project Specifications
Skill Level: Intermediate
Wall Quilt Size: 26" x 31"
Block Size: 4" x 4"
Number of Blocks: 20

Materials
- ⅛ yard each of 20 different medium and dark prints for stars
- 1½ yards light fabric for star backgrounds, sashing and yo-yos
- ½ yard border and binding fabric
- Backing 32" x 37"
- Batting 32" x 37"
- 2 skeins embroidery floss to match border fabric
- All-purpose thread to match fabric
- Basic sewing tools and supplies

Instructions
Step 1. Cut for each star block:

four rectangles 1½" x 2½" and four squares 1½" x 1½" from light fabric; cut eight squares 1½" x 1½" and one square 2½" x 2½" from the same dark or medium print.

Step 2. Place, right sides together, one 1½" print square with one 1½" x 2½" light rectangle and stitch as in Figure 1. Trim corner as in Figure 2 and fold back square (Figure 3). Repeat on opposite edge (Figure 4) to complete two star points. Repeat three more times for each star.

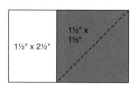

Figure 1

1½" x 2½" 1½" x 1½"

Figure 2

Figure 3

Figure 4

Step 3. Assemble with center and four corner squares as shown in the Star block. Make a total of 20 Star blocks.

Step 4. Make (20) 1½" yo-yos from light fabric following instructions for making yo-yos on page 122.

Step 5. Cut a ¾" circle from each of the star prints. Slip a matching circle inside each yo-yo, right side up, and tack in place as shown in Figure 5 to create a peekaboo yo-yo.

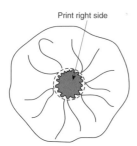

Print right side

Figure 5

Step 6. Appliqué a peekaboo yo-yo to the center of each matching star. Use a blind stitch and thread to match the yo-yo.

Step 7. Cut 16 rectangles 4½" x 1½" from light fabric. Sew five star blocks together with sashing as shown in Figure 6. Repeat to make four strips.

1½" x 4½"

Figure 6

Step 8. Cut five strips 1½" x 24½" from light fabric. Referring to Placement Diagram, sew strips to sashed blocks, beginning and ending with strips.

Step 9. Cut two strips 1½" x 21½" from light fabric. Stitch to top and bottom of quilt.

Peekaboo Yo-Yo Quilt
Placement Diagram
26" x 31"

Step 10. Cut two strips 2¾" x 21½" and two strips 2¾" x 31" border fabric. Sew shorter strips to top and bottom and longer strips to sides.

Step 11. Make 30 more yo-yos from light fabric and appliqué at each intersection of the sashing. Refer to the photo for placement.

Step 12. Layer top, batting and backing and baste.

Step 13. Using 6 strands of embroidery floss, make a tie through all layers, in the center of each yo-yo and at sashing intersections. Make more ties in the border to secure all layers. If you prefer, quilt the layers together.

Step 14. Square the quilt and bind with 3½ yards of self-made binding referring to the General Instructions. ◆

Instructions for a 1½" Yo-yo
The size of the finished yo-yo will be approximately one-half the size of the circle cut.

Step 1. Cut a 3" circle from fabric.

Step 2. Thread a needle with about 18" of thread. Knot one end.

Step 3. Turn under the edge of the circle ¼", wrong sides together.

Step 4. Sew a running stitch around the edge of the circle, through both thicknesses of the turned-under edge. Long running stitches will make a small opening in the center of the yo-yo; tiny stitches will make a larger opening.

Step 5. Gather the circle, right side out and tack stitch in place.

WINTER SNOWFLAKE

Here's a quilt of apparent intricacies—but so much easier than you'd think!

DESIGN BY BARBARA CLAYTON

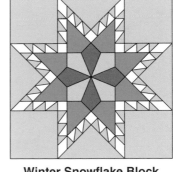

Winter Snowflake Block
15½" x 15½"

Project Specifications
Skill Level: Intermediate
Wall Quilt Size: Approximately
    44½" x 44½"
Block Size: 15½" x 15½"
Number of Blocks: 4

Materials
- ½ yard white solid fabric
- 1 yard light blue print (#1)
- ¾ yard medium blue print (#2)
- ½ yard dark teal print (#3)
- ½ yard medium blue/navy floral print (#4)
- ½ yard navy print (#5)
- Backing 50" x 50"
- Thin batting 50" x 50"
- Rotary-cutting tools
- All-purpose threads to blend with fabrics
- Clear nylon monofilament
- 1 spool each white and medium blue quilting thread
- Stylus
- Basic sewing tools and supplies

Blocks
Step 1. Prepare templates using patterns given.
Step 2. For each block with light blue

(#1) background, cut four A pieces each from #1 and #5. Cut eight B pieces from #4. Cut eight white C squares and eight white D diamonds. From light blue (#1), cut 16 E triangles, four corner squares 4⅞" x 4⅞" and one square 7½" x 7½". Cut the 7½" square in half on both diagonals to make four middle triangles.

Step 3. For each block with light blue (#1) background, cut two 1½" by fabric width strips each of white solid and light blue print (#1). Sew a white and a #1 fabric strip together on one long side. Press toward #1. Repeat with remaining two strips.

Step 4. Rotary-cut 16 G rectangles by aligning the diagonal line on the template with the seam line on one pair of strips. Reverse the template and cut 16 rectangles from the second pair of strips.

Step 5. Piece star centers by joining A pieces, alternating #1 and #5 colors as shown in Figure 1. Sew from dots to the center points. Press seams open.

Step 6. Add color #4 B star pieces as shown in Figure 2. Start and end stitching at dots; press.

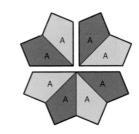

Figure 1

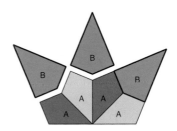

Figure 2

Step 7. Sew one pair of G units and one pair of G units reversed as shown in Figure 3. Add E triangles, C square and D diamonds as shown in Figure 4. Sew strips to corner square as shown in Figure 5. Repeat for four corners. Set corners into star as shown in Figure 6.

Step 8. Sew one pair of G units and one pair of G units reversed, again referring to Figure 3. Add E triangles and C square as shown in Figure 7. Repeat for four strips each.

Figure 3

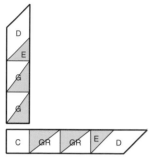

Figure 4

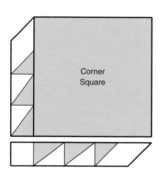

Figure 5

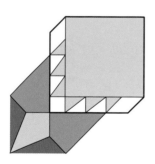

Figure 6

Step 9. Join pieces, again referring to Figure 7. Set the longer strip into the star unit first and then the shorter. Then set in the middle triangle; press. The middle triangles tend to shrink toward the center. For that reason they were cut slightly larger than necessary. When construction is complete,

trim block to 15½" x 15½" square. Repeat for two blocks.

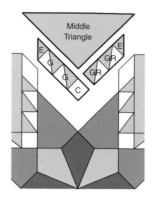

Figure 7

Step 10. For each block with medium blue (#2) background, cut four A pieces each from #2 and #5. Cut eight B pieces from #3. Cut eight white C squares and eight white D diamonds. From medium blue (#2), cut 16 E triangles, four corner squares 4⅞" x 4⅞" and one square 7½" x 7½". Cut the 7½" square in half on both diagonals to make four middle triangles.

Step 11. Repeat Steps 2 and 3 with #2 and white fabrics.

Step 12. Repeat Step 4, alternating #2 and #5 colors. Add color #3 star pieces as in Step 5. Repeat Steps 6–8 to complete two blocks with medium blue (#2) background.

Step 13. Referring to Placement Diagram for color placement, join four blocks to make two rows; join rows to complete the pieced center. Press row seams in opposite directions and the pieced center seam in one direction.

Borders

Step 1. Prepare templates using patterns given.

Step 2. Cut two white strips each 2" x 30½" and 2" x 33½" . Sew shorter strips to top and bottom and longer strips to sides of the pieced center; press seams away from white border strips.

Step 3. Cut two light blue (#1) strips each 3½" x 33½" and 3½" x 39½". Sew to quilt as in Step 1; press seam allowance away from white border strips.

Step 4. For Dresden Plate borders, cut 23 F pieces each from fabrics #2, #3, #4 and #5. Sew a strip sequence of 23 pieces, alternating colors as shown in Figure 8. Repeat for four strips.

Figure 9

Step 5. For border corners, cut eight F pieces fabric #2 and four each of fabrics #3, #4 and #5 for border corners. Complete four corner sections as shown in Figure 9.

Step 6. Join the four sides of border by sewing corner sections between adjacent sides. This will make a large, square border frame. Carefully mark the centers of all sides of border and quilt. Match centers and pin border in place. Turn the inside edges of the border under ¼" all the way around the quilt, carefully folding

Figure 8

the points to make them sharp. This border piece should be placed on the light blue border and machine-stitched in place as an appliqué with clear nylon monofilament and a narrow blind-hemstitch. Trim away excess light blue border fabric under Dresden Plate border to ¼".

Finishing

Step 1. Mark quilting lines ¼" from outer edges of corner squares and middle triangles. Referring to Placement Diagram, mark diagonal lines ¾" apart on corner squares of each block. Mark lines ¾" apart perpendicular to border on middle triangles. Transfer the Diamond Quilting Pattern to the white border.

Step 2. Place quilt top and backing right sides together. Pin corners and several places in the center. Place pinned layers on batting square and pin in many places to secure. Sew around perimeter ¼" from edges of Dresden Plate border, leaving an area open on one side for turning.

Step 3. Trim excess batting and backing, trim points and clip curves. Turn right side out and carefully poke out each point using the stylus; press with a warm iron. Turn edges of opening under ¼" and close with hand stitches. Baste layers for quilting.

Step 4. If machine quilting, use a walking foot and clear nylon monofilament. Quilt in the ditch

along all seam lines. If hand quilting, stitch in the ditch with white thread. With medium blue thread, hand-quilt diamond pattern on white border, ¼" from edge of white border and inner edges of Dresden Plate border.

Step 5. With white thread, quilt ¼" from seam lines of center stars and corner squares and middle triangles of blocks that have #2 background. With medium blue thread, quilt ¼" from seam lines of center stars and corner squares and middle triangles of blocks that have #1 background.

Step 6. Make sleeve for hanging as shown in the General Instructions. ◆

Winter Snowflake
Placement Diagram
Approximately 44½" x 44½"

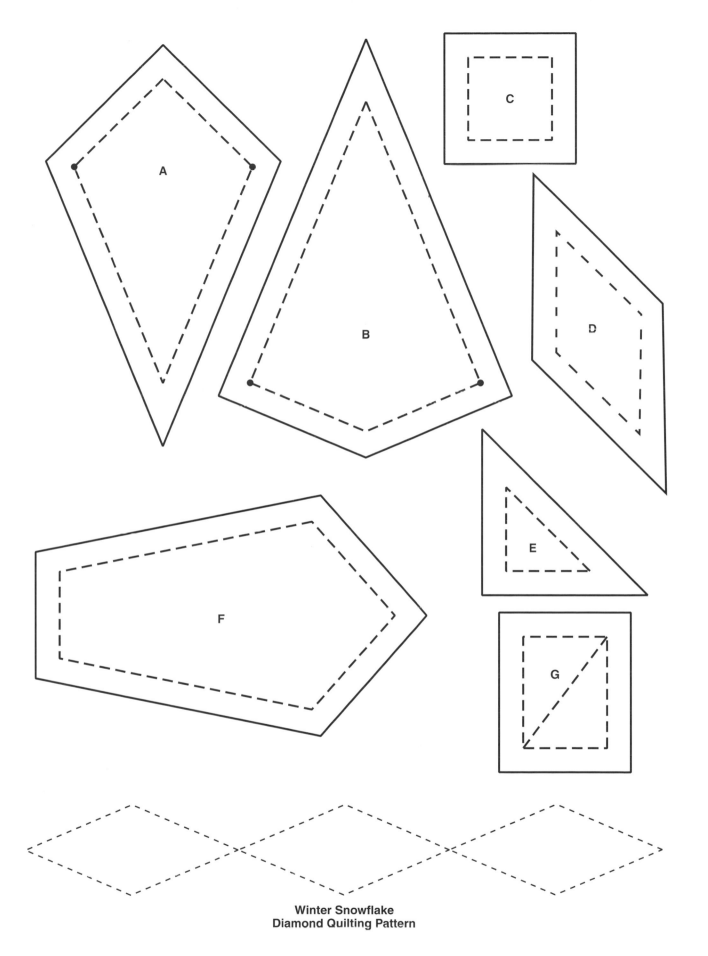

**Winter Snowflake
Diamond Quilting Pattern**

WINDING WAYS

Wind your way around the world in this pretty spring quilt.

DESIGN BY MARTI MICHELL

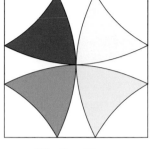

Winding Ways
8½" x 8½" Block

Project Specifications
Skill Level: Intermediate
Quilt Size: 55" x 72"
Block Size: 8½" x 8½"
Number of Blocks: 35

Materials
- ⅓ yard dark blue tonal
- 1⅓ yards total yellow tonals or prints
- 1½ yards yellow/blue print
- 2 yards total blue tonals or prints
- 3 yards white tonal
- Backing 61" x 78"
- Batting 61" x 78"
- Neutral color all-purpose thread
- Quilting thread
- Basic sewing tools and supplies

Project Note
To create the design formed by the blocks in this quilt, color placement in each block is important. Be very careful to keep colors in the right places when joining units for each block.

Cutting
Step 1. Prepare templates for pieces A, B and C using patterns given; cut as directed on each piece.

Step 2. Cut six strips dark blue tonal 1¾" by fabric width; join strips on short ends to make one long strip. Subcut strip into two 43" D strips, two 60" E strips and eight 5½" F strips.

Step 3. Cut four 1¾" x 1¾" G squares white tonal.

Step 4. Cut six 5½" by fabric width strips yellow/blue print; join strips on short ends to make one long strip. Subcut strip into two 43" H strips, two 60" I strips and four 5½" x 5½" J squares.

Step 5. Cut seven 2¼" by fabric width strips yellow/blue print for binding.

Piecing the Blocks
Step 1. Refer to Figure 1 for color placement when piecing all blocks.

Step 2. Lay out the A, B and C pieces for one block as they would appear in the finished block.

Step 3. Referring to Figure 2, and with A on top of B, match center marks and pin; pin at ends of corner seams.

Step 4. Stitch, matching raw edges as you sew; press seams toward A. Repeat for four A-B units.

Make 15	Make 3	Make 4	Make 3	Make 2	Make 8

Figure 1

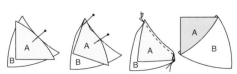

Figure 2

Step 5. Join two A-B units with C, matching raw edges as you sew as shown in Figure 3; repeat for two A-B-C units. Press seams toward B.

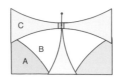 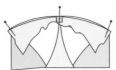 

Figure 5

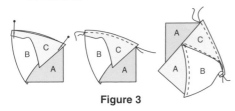

Figure 3

Step 6. Join the remaining two C pieces at the small end seam as shown in Figure 4; press seam open.

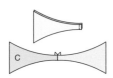

Figure 4

Step 7. Pin C between two A-B-C units, matching center seams as shown in Figure 5; pin at end of seams. Match raw edges as you sew; press seams toward B.

Step 8. Repeat to complete 35 blocks in color combinations shown in Figure 1.

Completing the Top

Step 1. Arrange the pieced blocks in five rows of seven blocks each referring to the Placement Diagram for positioning to create the overlapping circle designs.

Join blocks in rows; press seams in adjacent rows in opposite directions. Join rows to complete the pieced center; press seams in one direction.

Step 2. Sew D strips to the top and bottom; press seams toward D.

Step 3. Sew a G square to each end of each E strip; press seams toward G. Sew an E-G strip to opposite sides of the pieced center; press seams toward E-G strips.

Step 4. Sew an F strip to each end of each H strip; press seams toward F. Sew an H-F strip to the top and bottom of the pieced center; press seams toward H-F.

Step 5. Sew an F strip and a J square to each end of each I strip; press seams toward F. Sew an F-J-I strip to opposite long sides of the pieced center to complete the pieced top. Press seams toward F-J-I strips.

Step 6. Finish the quilt referring to the General Instructions. ✦

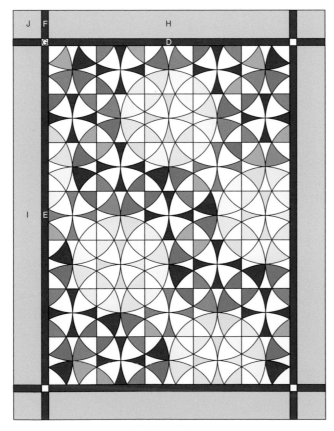

Winding Ways
Placement Diagram
55" x 72"

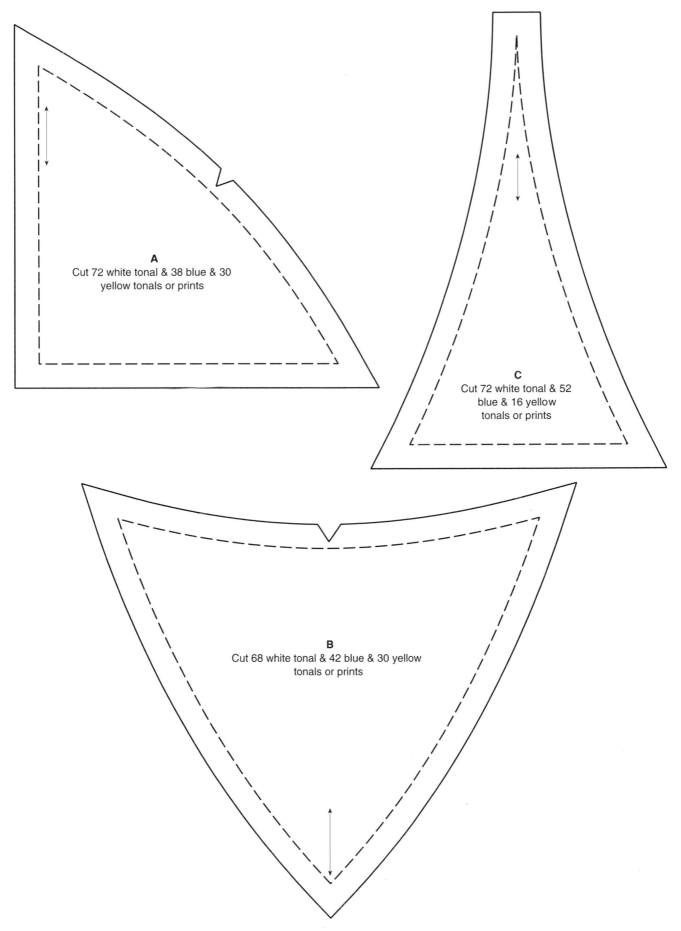

A
Cut 72 white tonal & 38 blue & 30 yellow tonals or prints

C
Cut 72 white tonal & 52 blue & 16 yellow tonals or prints

B
Cut 68 white tonal & 42 blue & 30 yellow tonals or prints

TULIPS AROUND THE CABIN

Gather up your light and dark scraps to make this combination pieced-and-appliquéd quilt.

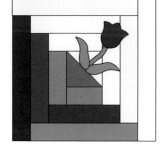

Tulips Around the Cabin
12" x 12" Block

DESIGN BY SHIRLEY PALMER

Project Specifications
Skill Level: Beginner
Quilt Size: 88½" x 88½"
Block Size: 12" x 12"
Number of Blocks: 36

Materials
- ⅛ yard each yellow, red, blue and purple mottleds for flowers
- ¼ yard dark green print for stems and leaves
- 1 yard white print for block centers and sashing
- 1 yard burgundy print for outside border
- 2 yards black print for block centers, sashing, border and binding
- 3 yards total each light and dark scraps for block piecing
- Backing 95" x 95"
- Batting 95" x 95"
- Neutral color and black all-purpose thread
- Quilting thread
- 1¼ yards fusible web
- 1⅔ yards fabric stabilizer
- Basic sewing tools and supplies

Making Log Cabin Blocks
Step 1. Cut 18 squares each white and black prints 3⅞" x 3⅞" for A. Draw a line from corner to corner on the wrong side of the white print A squares.

Figure 1

Step 2. Place a white print A on a black print A with right sides together; stitch ¼" on each side of the marked line as shown in Figure 1. Cut apart on the marked line and press open to make two A units as shown in Figure 2; repeat for 36 A units.

Figure 2

Step 3. Cut the light and dark scraps into 2"-wide strips; cut into 36 pieces of each of the following lengths: light strips—5" , 6½" , 8" , 9½" , 11" and 12½" ; dark strips—3½" , 5" , 6½" , 8" , 9½" and 11" .

Step 4. Sew the shortest dark strip to the dark print side of an A unit; press seam toward strip. Continue to add strips to the sides of the center as shown in Figure 3. Press all seams toward the most recently added strip. Complete 36 blocks.

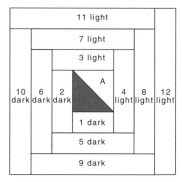

Figure 3

Step 5. Trace appliqué shapes onto the paper side of the fusible web as directed on the pieces for number to cut. Cut out shapes leaving a margin around each one.

Step 6. Fuse shapes to the wrong side of the fabrics as directed on pieces for color; cut out shapes on the traced lines. Remove paper backing.

Step 7. Arrange one tulip, one stem, and one each leaf and reversed leaf on the light side of a completed Log Cabin block referring to the block drawing for positioning; fuse shapes in place. Repeat for all blocks.

Step 8. Cut (36) 5" x 6"rectangles fabric stabilizer; pin behind each fused shape.

Step 9. Using black all-purpose thread, buttonhole-stitch around each shape. When stitching is complete, remove fabric stabilizer.

Completing the Top

Step 1. Cut and piece two 2" x 80" J strips and two 2" x 83" K strips black print; set aside for borders. Cut nine 2¼" by fabric width strips black print; set aside for binding.

Step 2. Cut the remaining white and black prints into 2" by fabric width strips for sashing strips. Subcut the white print strips into (22) 12½" B, two 14" C and two 26" D sashing strips. Subcut the black print strips into (16) 12½" E, six 14" F, four 15½" G, one 26" H and two 29" I sashing strips.

Step 3. Join six blocks with B and E sashing strips to make a block row as shown in Figure 4; press seams toward sashing strips. Repeat for six block rows.

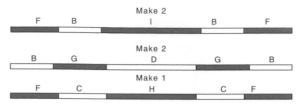

Figure 5

Step 4. Join remaining sashing strips to make sashing rows as shown in Figure 5; press seams toward white print strips.

Step 5. Join the block rows and sashing rows to complete the pieced center as shown in Figure 6; press seams toward sashing rows.

Step 6. Sew J strips to opposite sides and K strips to the top and bottom of the pieced center; press seams toward J and K.

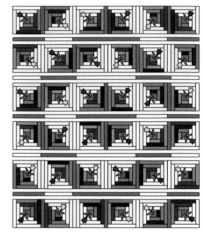

Figure 6

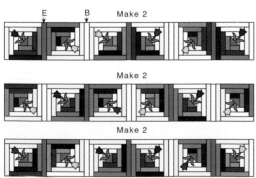

Figure 4

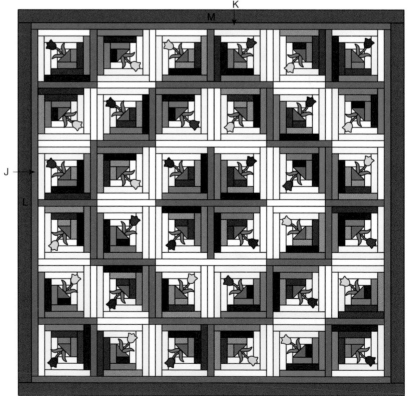

Tulips Around the Cabin
Placement Diagram
88½" x 88½"

Step 7. Cut and piece two 3½" x 83" L strips and two 3½" x 89" M strips burgundy print. Sew L strips to opposite sides and M strips to the top and bottom of the pieced center; press seams toward L and M.

Finishing the Quilt

Step 1. Prepare quilt top for quilting and quilt.

Step 2. When quilting is complete, trim batting and backing edges even with the quilted top.

Step 3. Prepare 10⅜ yards black print binding using previously cut strips and bind edges of quilt to finish. ◆

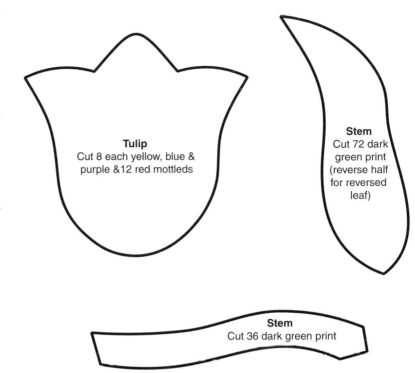

Tulip
Cut 8 each yellow, blue & purple &12 red mottleds

Stem
Cut 72 dark green print (reverse half for reversed leaf)

Stem
Cut 36 dark green print

PLAID LAP ROBE

Use paper foundations to piece accurate triangle-shaped Log Cabin blocks with woven plaids in a variety of colors.

Plaid Lap Robe Block
6" x 7" Block

DESIGN BY CONNIE KAUFFMAN

Project Specifications
Skill Level: Intermediate
Quilt Size: 42" x 48"
Block Size: 6" x 7"
Number of Blocks: 88 full blocks and 16 half-blocks

Materials
- ⅛ yard tan solid
- ¼ yard each 12 light plaids
- ¼ yard each 12 dark plaids
- ½ yard black solid
- Backing 48" x 56"
- Fusible batting 48" x 56"
- Neutral color all-purpose thread
- Quilting thread
- Basic sewing tools and supplies

Making Pieced Units
Step 1. Cut all plaid fabrics into 1½" by fabric width strips.
Step 2. Cut two 1½" by fabric width strips tan solid; subcut into (51) 1½" squares for piece 1. Repeat with black solid to make 40 squares for piece 1.
Step 3. Make 88 copies of the A unit pattern and eight copies each of the B and B unit-reversed patterns.

Step 4. Pin a piece 1 tan solid square to the unmarked side of the A unit paper pattern to cover the piece 1 area on the marked side; pin a light plaid piece 2 to piece 1.
Step 5. Stitch strips in numerical order to the paper pattern to complete 48 light plaid A units referring to Figure 1. Repeat with black solid No. 1 pieces to complete 40 dark plaid A units as shown in Figure 2. **Note:** *Vary the fabric strips used in piece 4, as these pieces will be touching each other in the finished top.*

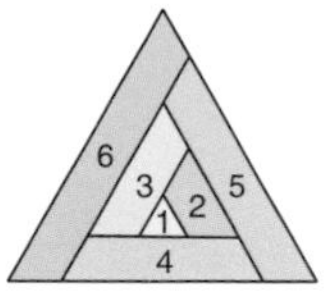

Figure 1

Figure 2

Step 6. Repeat to complete eight each dark plaid B and BR units referring to Figure 3.

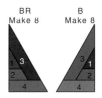

BR
Make 8

B
Make 8

Figure 3

Completing the Top
Step 1. Join five dark and six light plaid A units to make a row as shown in Figure 4; repeat for eight rows; press seams toward darker units.
Step 2. Sew B and BR to the end of each row, again referring to Figure 4; press seams toward B and BR.

B   A   BR

Figure 4

Step 3. Join the rows referring to the Placement Diagram for positioning; press seams in one direction.

Finishing the Quilt
Step 1. Prepare quilt top for quilting using fusible batting

referring to manufacturer's instructions and quilt.

Step 2. When quilting is complete, trim batting and backing edges even with quilted top.

Step 3. Prepare 5½ yards black solid binding and bind edges of quilt. ✦

Plaid Lap Robe
Placement Diagram
42" x 48"

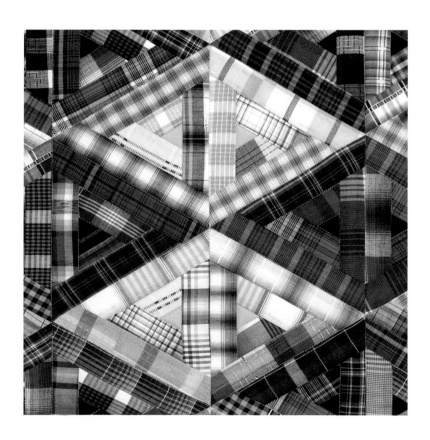

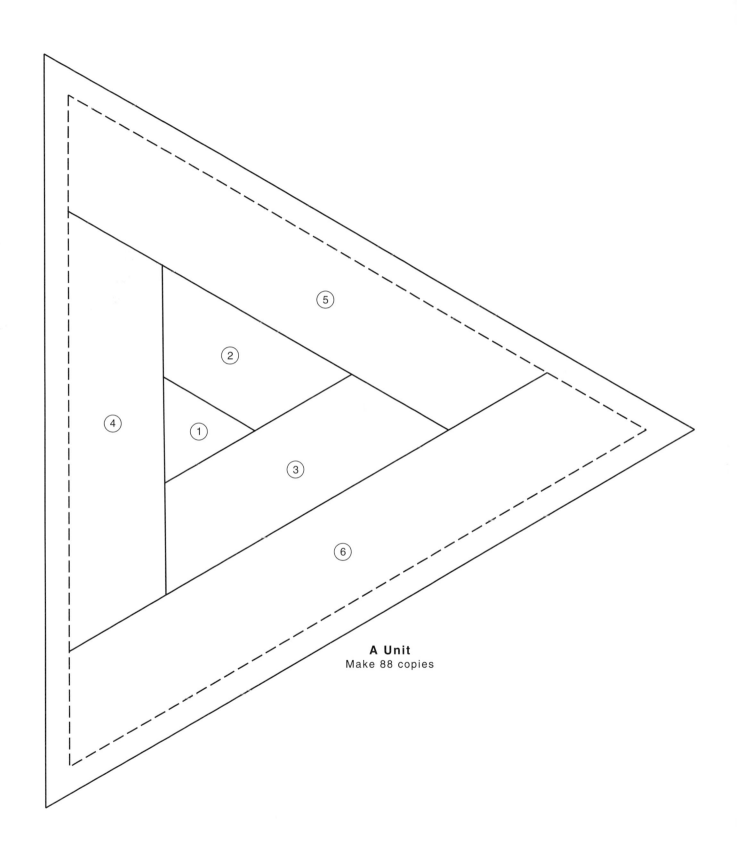

A Unit
Make 88 copies

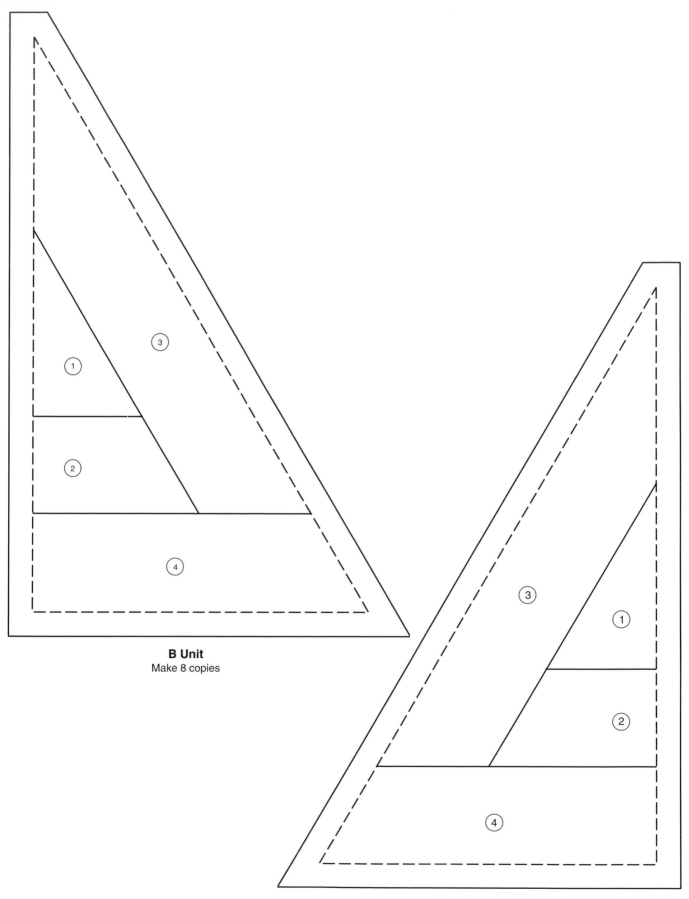

B Unit
Make 8 copies

B Unit Reversed
Make 8 copies

TURNING LEAVES

Select a variety of autumn-colored hand-dyed fabrics to make this beautiful quilt.

Turning Leaf
12" x 12" Block

DESIGN BY JULIE WEAVER

Project Specifications
Skill Level: Intermediate
Quilt Size: 85" x 105½"
Block Size: 12" x 12"
Number of Blocks: 18

Materials
- 18 fat quarters assorted hand-dyed mottleds
- 3⅝ yards multicolor batik
- 4¾ yards tan mottled
- Backing 91" x 112"
- Batting 91" x 112"
- All-purpose thread to match fabric
- Quilting thread
- 2 yards 12"-wide fusible web
- Basic sewing tools and supplies

Cutting
Note: *Steps 1–4 refer to the cutting diagram in Figure 1.*
Step 1. Cut a 94" length tan mottled; cut a 21¾" strip along the 94" length. Set aside remainder of length for Step 3.
Step 2. Cut the 21¾"-wide strip into two 12⅞" x 12⅞" H squares and three 21¾" x 21¾" G squares.

Cut each H square in half on one diagonal to make four H triangles. Cut each G square in half on both diagonals to make 12 G triangles. Set aside two G triangles for another project.
Step 3. Cut nine 8½" strips from the remainder of the 94" tan mottled strip; subcut strips into (18) 8½" A squares.
Step 4. Cut six 2½" strips from remainder of tan mottled strip; subcut strips into (36) 2½" D squares.

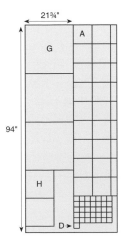

Figure 1

Step 5. From the remaining tan mottled yardage, cut (12) 2⅞" by fabric width strips; subcut strips into (162) 2⅞" B squares.
Step 6. Cut nine 2⅞" x 2⅞" C squares from each of the 18 hand-dyed mottleds as shown in Figure 2; sort by color into 18 stacks.

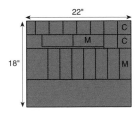

Figure 2

Step 7. Cut (19) 1" by fabric width E strips tan mottled.
Step 8. Cut (38) 1½" by fabric width F strips multicolor batik.
Step 9. Cut eight 1½" by fabric width strips multicolor batik. Join strips on short ends to make one long strip. Cut strip into two 86" I strips and two 67½" J strips.
Step 10. Cut eight 1" by fabric width strips tan mottled. Join strips on short ends to make one long strip. Cut strip

into two 88" K strips and two 68½" L strips.

Step 11. Cut nine 2½" x 6½" M rectangles from each of the hand-dyed mottleds, again referring to Figure 2. Set aside six rectangles for another project.

Step 12. Cut four 6½" x 6½" N squares multicolor batik.

Step 13. Cut nine 1" by fabric width strips tan mottled. Join strips on short ends to make one long strip. Cut strip into two 101" O and two 81½" P strips.

Step 14. Cut nine 2½" by fabric width strips multicolor batik. Join strips on short ends to make one long strip. Cut strip into two 102" Q and two 85½" R strips.

Step 15. Prepare a template for the leaf shape using pattern given. Trace nine leaf shapes onto the fusible web; reverse pattern and trace nine reversed leaves.

Step 16. Cut out shapes, leaving a margin around each one. Fuse one shape to the wrong side of each hand-dyed mottled; cut out shapes on traced lines. Remove paper backing.

Step 17. Cut (10) 2¼" by fabric width strips multicolor batik for binding.

Completing the Blocks

Step 1. Draw a line from corner to corner on the wrong side of each B square.

Step 2. Place a B square right sides together with a C square; stitch ¼" on each side of the marked line as shown in Figure 3.

Figure 3

Step 3. Cut the stitched unit apart on drawn line to make two B-C units, again referring to Figure 3. Repeat for all B-C squares to make 18 B-C units of each hand-dyed mottled.

Step 4. Join four B-C units as shown in Figure 4; repeat. Press seams in one direction.

Figure 4

Step 5. Sew a pieced strip to opposite sides of A as shown in Figure 5; press seams away from A.

Figure 5

Step 6. Join five B-C units with a D square as shown in Figure 6; press seams in one direction. Repeat for two pieced strips.

Figure 6

Step 7. Sew a pieced strip to the remaining sides of the pieced unit referring to the block drawing for positioning of strips; press seams away from A.

Step 8. Center a leaf on A, matching the leaf color to the C triangles and referring to the block drawing for positioning; fuse in place.

Step 9. Machine-stitch a blanket or buttonhole stitch around the leaf shape using all-purpose

thread to match fabric to complete one block. Repeat for 18 blocks. ***Note:*** *Half of the blocks use reverse leaf shapes.*

Completing the Top

Step 1. Sew an E strip between two F strips with right sides together along length; press seams toward F. Repeat for 19 strip sets.

Step 2. Subcut 16 strip sets into (48) 12½" E-F sashing strips as shown in Figure 7.

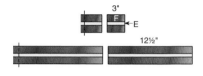

Figure 7

Step 3. Subcut the remaining three strip sets into (31) 3" E-F sashing squares, again referring to Figure 7.

Step 4. Referring to Figure 8 for positioning of leaf blocks, arrange the blocks in diagonal rows with the E-F sashing strips.

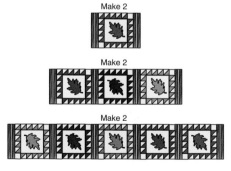

Figure 8

Step 5. Join blocks and strips in diagonal rows; press seams away from blocks.

Step 6. Join E-F sashing strips and sashing squares to make sashing rows as shown in Figure 9; press seams toward sashing strips.

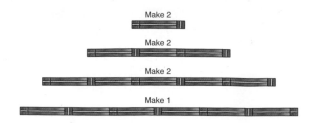

Make 2

Make 2

Make 2

Make 1

Figure 9

Step 7. Join the block rows with the sashing rows and the G and H triangles to complete the pieced center; press seams away from block rows. ***Note:*** *Refer to the Placement Diagram for placement of sashing rows to create a woven look.*

Step 8. Sew an I strip to opposite sides and a J strip to the top and bottom of the pieced center; press seams toward I and J.

Step 9. Sew a K strip to opposite sides and an L strip to the top and bottom of the pieced center; press seams toward K and L.

Step 10. Join 44 M pieces in random order to make a side border strip; repeat for two strips. Press seams in one direction.

Step 11. Sew a strip to opposite sides of the pieced center; press seams toward M strips.

Step 12. Join 34 M pieces in random order to make a top strip;

press seams in one direction. Repeat for a bottom strip. Sew an N square to each end of each strip; press seams away from N.

Step 13. Sew an M-N strip to the top and bottom of the pieced center; press seams toward M-N strips.

Step 14. Sew an O strip to opposite sides and a P strip to the top and bottom of the pieced center; press seams toward O and P.

Step 15. Sew a Q strip to opposite sides and an R strip to the top and bottom of the pieced center; press seams toward Q and R to complete the pieced top.

Step 16. Finish quilt referring to the General Instructions. ◆

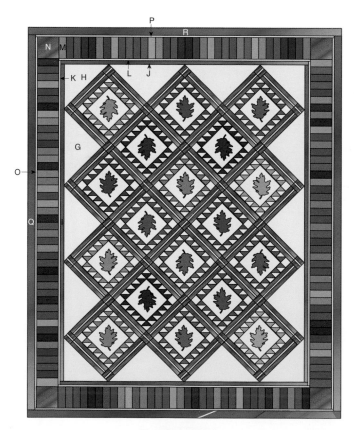

Turning Leaves
Placement Diagram
85" x 105½"

Leaf
Cut 18 hand-dyed mottleds
(reverse half)

AN AUTUMN EVENING

Fiery orange stars shine brightly on the black background of this beautiful quilt.

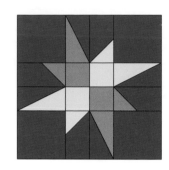

Autumn Evening
12" x 12" Block

DESIGN BY TOBY LISCHKO

Project Specifications
Skill Level: Intermediate
Quilt Size: 85" x 102"
Block Size: 12" x 12"
Number of Blocks: 32

Materials
- ⅝ yard orange/gold mottled for borders
- ¾ yard orange mottled for binding
- 1¼ yards total orange mottleds
- 1⅓ yards total yellow/gold mottleds
- 7½ yards black tonal print
- Backing 91" x 108"
- Batting 91" x 108"
- Neutral color all-purpose thread
- Quilting thread
- Basic sewing tools and supplies

Project Notes
The quilt shown uses a variety of orange and yellow mottleds to create the blocks. If you choose to use scraps or a variety of fabrics, be sure to use the same fabrics in the outside points as the Four-Patch centers. When creating the Four-Patch centers using a variety of fabrics, cut fabric-width strips as directed to total length needed as instructed in the cutting instructions.

Cutting
Step 1. Cut four 2½" by fabric width strips each yellow/gold (A) and orange (B) mottleds.

Step 2. Cut three strips each 4½" by fabric width orange (C) and yellow/gold (CC) mottleds and five strips black tonal print (D). Prepare template for C/CC/D using pattern given; cut 64 each C and CC and 128 D pieces from the strips using the template as shown in Figure 1.

Figure 1

Step 3. Cut eight 4½" by fabric width strips black tonal print; subcut strips into (128) 2½" E rectangles.

Step 4. Cut four 2½" by fabric width strips each yellow/gold (F) and orange (G) mottleds; subcut strips into 64 each 2½" F and G squares.

Step 5. Cut (15) 4½" by fabric width strips black tonal print; subcut strips into (128) 4½" H squares.

Step 6. Cut four 18¼" x 18¼" squares black tonal print; cut each square in half on both diagonals to make 16 I triangles. Set aside two triangles for another project.

Step 7. Cut two 9⅜" x 9⅜" squares black tonal print; cut each square in half on one diagonal to make four J triangles.

Step 8. Cut eight 2" by fabric width strips orange/gold mottled for borders. Join strips on short ends to make one long strip; press seams open. Cut strip into two 90" K strips and two 73" L strips.

Step 9. Cut (10) 7½" by fabric width strips black tonal print. Join strips on short ends to make one long strip; press seams open. Cut strip into two 106" M strips and two 90" N strips.

Step 10. Cut (10) 2¼" by fabric width strips orange mottled for binding.

Piecing the Blocks

Note: *Choose one orange and one yellow/gold per block.*

Step 1. Sew an A strip to a B strip with right sides together along length; press seam in one direction. Repeat for four strip sets. Subcut strip sets into (64) 2½" A-B segments as shown in Figure 2.

Figure 2

Step 2. Join two A-B segments to make an A-B unit as shown in Figure 3; press seams in one direction. Repeat for 32 A-B units.

Figure 3

Step 3. To piece one block, sew C to D as shown in Figure 4; repeat for two C-D units. Press seams toward D. Repeat to make two CC-D units.

Figure 4

Step 4. Mark a line from corner to corner on the wrong side of all F and G squares.

Step 5. Place an F square on one end of E as shown in Figure 5; stitch on the marked line, trim seams and press F to the right side, again referring to Figure 5. Repeat to make 64 each E-F and E-G units as shown in Figure 6.

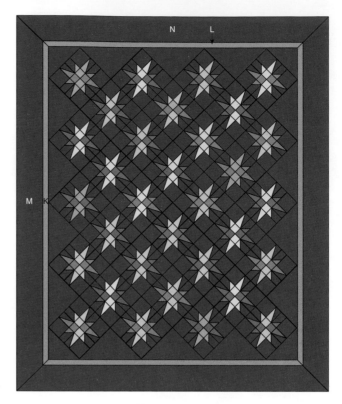

An Autumn Evening
Placement Diagram
85" x 102"

Figure 5

Figure 6

Step 6. To complete one block, join a C-D unit with an E-F unit as shown in Figure 7; repeat for two units. Press seams toward E-F. Repeat with CC-D and E-G to make two units.

Figure 7

Step 7. Arrange the pieced units in rows with an A-B unit and H as shown in Figure 8; join in rows. Press seams toward A-B and H.

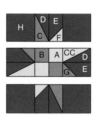

Figure 8

Step 8. Join the rows to complete one block; press seams in one direction. Repeat for 32 blocks.

Completing the Top

Step 1. Arrange the blocks in diagonal rows with the I and J triangles referring to Figure 9; join in rows. Press seams in adjacent rows in opposite directions.

Step 2. Center and sew a K strip to opposite long sides and L strips to the top and bottom, mitering corners; trim mitered seams to ¼" and press seams open as shown in Figure 10.

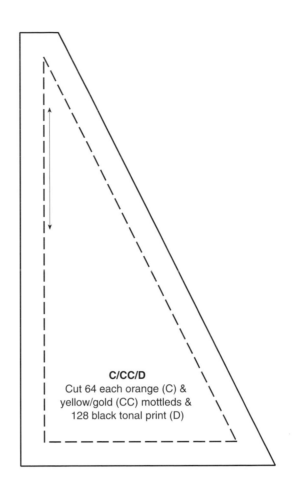

Figure 9

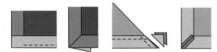

Figure 10

Step 3. Center and sew an M strip to opposite long sides and N strips to the top and bottom, mitering corners; trim mitered seams to ¼" and press seams open as in Step 2.

Step 4. Finish quilt referring to the General Instructions. ✦

C/CC/D
Cut 64 each orange (C) &
yellow/gold (CC) mottleds &
128 black tonal print (D)

PRAIRIE LILY WALL QUILT

Harvest your autumn-colored scraps to create the warm glow in this little accent quilt.

DESIGN BY JODI G. WARNER

Prairie Lily
8" x 8" Block

Project Specifications

Skill Level: Intermediate
Wall Quilt Size: 24" x 24"
Block Size: 8" x 8"
Number of Blocks: 4

Materials

- Wide variety of scraps of tan, orange, dark green and purple
- ⅛ yard gold for sashing and inner border
- ⅜ yard taupe for wide border and binding
- Backing 28" x 28"
- Thin batting 28" x 28"
- Rotary-cutting tools
- All-purpose thread to match patchwork fabrics
- 1 spool contrasting quilting thread
- Basic sewing tools and supplies

Instructions

Step 1. Cut fabrics as directed on templates A–F for one block, cutting two each of two different green fabrics for D and one each of four different purple fabrics for E; repeat for four blocks.

Step 2. Join pairs of F triangles to make squares. Join squares to make block center as shown in Figure 1.

Figure 1

Step 3. Assemble lily units, then join into a frame, adding inner C as shown in Figure 2. Press seams away from background tan patches. Join to center square unit and appliqué E pieces in place referring to block drawing.

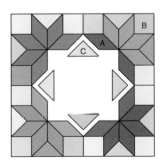

Figure 2

Step 4. Cut two bias strips ¾" x 6½" for stems. Press under ¼" on each long edge. Center stems over diagonal seams of center square as shown in block drawing and baste in place. Appliqué each folded edge. Appliqué each leaf in place. Repeat for four blocks.

Step 5. From gold, cut three strips each 1¼" x 17¼" , two strips each 1¼" x 18¾" and two strips each 1¼" x 8½" . Add to Prairie Lily blocks as shown in Figure 3.

Step 6. Cut two strips each 2⅜" x 18¾" and 2⅜" x 22½" from taupe. Add shorter strips to top and bottom and longer strips to sides.

Step 7. Cut (14) 1½" x 12" strips from a variety of orange scraps. Join along long sides to make one panel. Press seams in one direction. Cut seven 1½" strips across panel. Join strips end-to-end. Separate into four 22-unit border sections. Join one strip to each side of center section. Press seams toward center panel.

Step 8. Cut four purple squares 1½" x 1½" . Add a purple square to each end of remaining two border sections and add to top and bottom of quilt.

Step 9. Mark a ¼" echo line at inside edge of outer borders. Transfer Half-Lattice Quilting Pattern beyond echo line. Prepare for quilting referring to the General Instructions. Quilt on marked lines, at block edges, and in the ditch next to lily patchwork and appliqué designs.

Step 10. Make bias binding and bind quilt to finish referring to the General Instructions. ◆

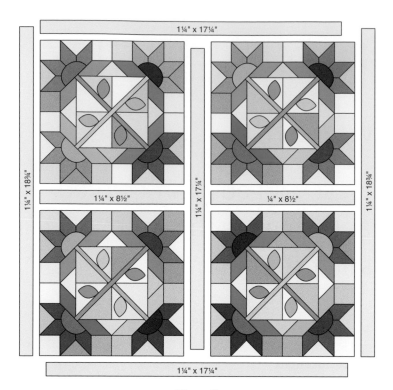

Figure 3

Prairie Lily Wall Quilt
Placement Diagram
24" x 24"

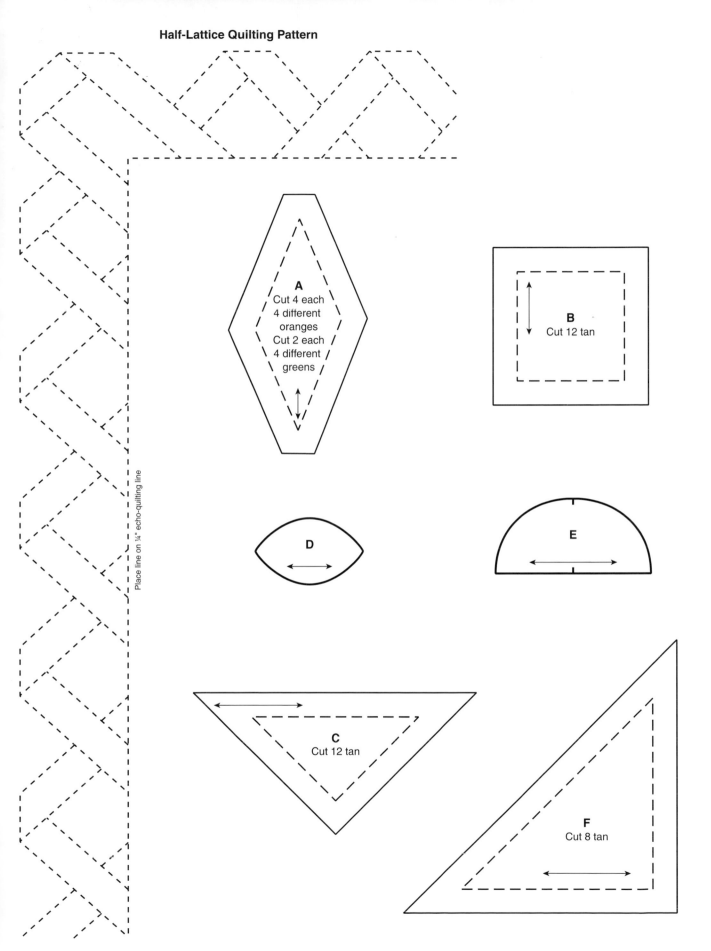

Place line on ¼" echo-quilting line

A
Cut 4 each
4 different
oranges
Cut 2 each
4 different
greens

B
Cut 12 tan

D

E

C
Cut 12 tan

F
Cut 8 tan

SUMMER'S DREAM

The traditional Summer's Dream block seems the perfect choice for a quilt made with a camping print.

Summer's Dream
15" x 15" Block

DESIGN BY SUE HARVEY

Project Specifications

Skill Level: Beginner
Quilt Size: 66½" x 89"
Block Size: 15" x 15"
Number of Blocks: 6

Materials

- ¼ yard tan camp print
- ½ yard each dark green, navy and tan prints
- 1 yard blue print
- 1⅛ yards brown print
- 1⅛ yards vine print
- 2¼ yards green camp print
- 2⅜ yards large camp print
- Backing 73" x 95"
- Batting 73" x 95"
- 9 yards self-made or purchased binding
- All-purpose thread to match fabrics
- Basic sewing tools and supplies, rotary cutter, mat and ruler

Instructions

Step 1. Cut two strips 2½" x 75½" along length of green camp print; set aside for borders.

Step 2. Cut four strips 8¾" by remaining fabric width green camp print; subcut into (15) 8¾" square segments. Cut each square on both diagonals to make A triangles. You will need 58 A triangles.

Step 3. Cut three strips 4¼" by remaining fabric width green camp print; subcut into 4¼" square segments for D. You will need 24 D squares.

Step 4. Cut four strips each vine print and dark green print 2¾" by fabric width; subcut into 2¾" square segments for B. You will need 58 B squares of each fabric.

Step 5. Cut six strips 3⅞" by fabric width vine print; subcut into (58) 3⅞" square segments. Cut each square on both diagonals to make C triangles. You will need 232 C triangles.

Step 6. Mark a diagonal on the wrong side of each vine B square.

Step 7. Place a vine B square right sides together with a dark green B square. Stitch ¼" from each side of the marked line as shown in Figure 1. Cut apart on the marked line and press open to make triangle/squares as shown in Figure 2. Repeat for all B squares.

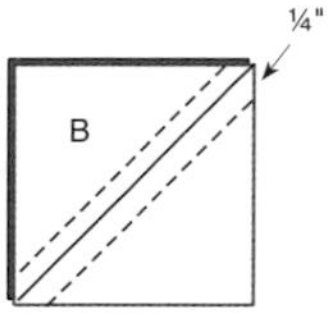

Figure 1

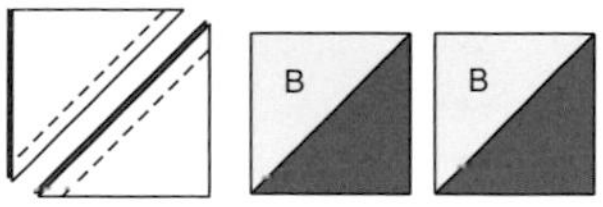

Figure 2

Step 8. Sew C to the dark green sides of each triangle/square as shown in Figure 3.

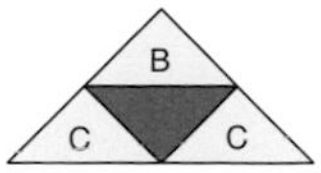

Figure 3

Step 9. Sew a B-C unit to each angled side of A to complete one edge unit as shown in Figure 4; repeat for 58 edge units.

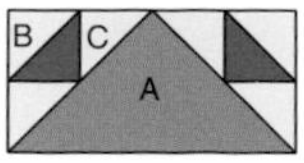

Figure 4

Step 10. Cut seven strips brown print and eight strips blue print 3" by fabric width.

Step 11. Sew a brown print strip between two blue print strips to make an A strip set; repeat for three A strip sets.

Step 12. Sew a blue print strip between two brown print strips to make a B strip set; repeat for two B strip sets.

Step 13. Cut each strip set into 3" segments as shown in Figure 5. You will need 36 A segments and 18 B segments.

Figure 5

Step 14. Sew a B segment between two A segments to complete one Nine-Patch unit as shown in Figure 6; repeat to make 18 Nine-Patch units.

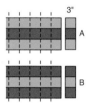

Figure 6

Step 15. To piece one Summer's Dream block, sew an edge unit to opposite sides of a Nine-Patch unit as shown in Figure 7.

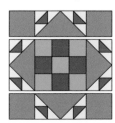

Figure 7

Step 16. Sew D to opposite ends of two edge units; sew to the remaining sides of the Nine-Patch unit to complete one block, again referring to Figure 7. Repeat to make six blocks.

Step 17. Cut 17 squares tan camp print 2" x 2", centering a motif in each square if desired.

Step 18. Cut three strips 2" by fabric width blue print; cut 17 square segments 2" x 2" from one strip.

Step 19. Sew a blue print square to each tan camp print square; press seam toward blue print.

Step 20. Place the pieced unit right sides together with a blue print strip as shown in Figure 8; stitch along edge and trim strip even with pieced unit as shown in Figure 9. Press seam toward strip.

Figure 8   **Figure 9**

Step 21. Cut five strips tan print, six strips navy print and seven strips brown print 2" by fabric width.

Step 22. Place the pieced unit right sides together with a tan print strip as shown in Figure 10; stitch along edge and trim, again referring to Figure 10. Press seam toward strip.

Figure 10

Step 23. Continue adding strips around pieced unit referring to

Figure 11 for order of strips and pressing seams toward strip to complete one Log Cabin unit. Repeat to make 17 Log Cabin units.

Figure 11

Step 24. Sew an edge unit to opposite sides of a Log Cabin unit as shown in Figure 12 to make a sashing unit; repeat for 17 sashing units.

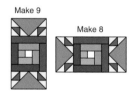

Figure 12

Step 25. Join two blocks with three sashing units to make a block row, beginning and ending with a sashing unit as shown in Figure 13. Repeat for three block rows.

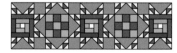

Figure 13

Step 26. Join two sashing units with three Nine-Patch units to make a sashing row, beginning and ending with a Nine-Patch unit as shown in Figure 14. Repeat for four sashing rows.

Figure 14

Step 27. Join sashing rows with block rows to complete the pieced center, beginning and ending with a sashing row and referring to the Placement Diagram for positioning of rows.

Step 28. Sew the green camp print strips cut in Step 1 to opposite long sides of the pieced center. Cut and piece two strips 2½" x 57" green camp print; sew to the top and bottom of the pieced center.

Step 29. Cut two strips 5½" x 79½" along length of large camp print; sew to opposite long sides of the pieced top.

Step 30. Cut and piece two strips 5½" x 67" large camp print; sew to top and bottom to complete the pieced top. **Note:** *Border fabrics used in sample project are directional prints. If your prints are not, you may choose to cut and piece all border strips to reduce fabric requirements or cut all from the length of the fabrics to eliminate piecing.*

Step 31. Sandwich batting between prepared backing and pieced top; pin or baste to hold.

Step 32. Hand- or machine-quilt as desired. **Note:** *The sample shown was professionally machine-quilted.*

Step 33. Trim backing and batting even with top; remove pins or basting.

Step 34. Bind with self-made or purchased binding to finish. ✦

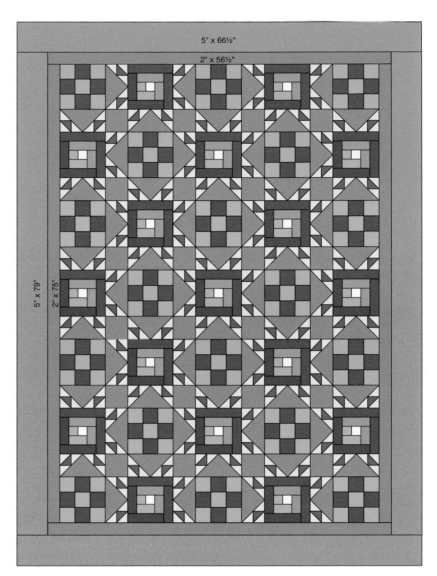

5" x 66½"
2" x 56½"
5" x 79"
2" x 75"

Summer's Dream
Placement Diagram
66¹/₂" x 89"

BOUNTIFUL BASKETS

Make a medallion-style scrappy quilt with these little basket patterns, Four-Patch blocks and strippy bars.

Basket
10" x 10", 8" x 8",
6" x 6" & 4" x 4" Blocks

DESIGN BY DANA DESIGNS AT MOOSE ISLAND QUILTING

Project Specifications
Skill Level: Intermediate
Quilt Size: 90" x 98"
Block Size: 10" x 10" , 8" x 8" ,
6" x 6" and 4" x 4"
Number of Blocks: 81

Materials
- ¾ yard cream print for binding
- 1⅛ yards dark rose print
- 2¾ yards pink gingham check
- 4 yards total dark fabrics (reds, roses and greens)
- 5 yards total light fabrics (creams and pale pinks)
- Backing 96" x 104"
- Batting 96" x 104"
- All-purpose thread to match fabrics
- Quilting thread
- Freezer paper
- Basic sewing tools and supplies

Cutting
Step 1. Cut one 10½" x 10½" light A square; fold and crease to mark horizontal and vertical centers.

Step 2. Cut four dark and four dark rose print 3½" x 3½" B squares.

Step 3. Cut a variety of light and dark fabric-width strips 1" –3" wide for C and F borders.

Step 4. Cut nine light and three pink gingham check 8½" x 8½" D squares; fold and crease to mark horizontal and vertical centers.

Step 5. Cut four 2½" x 2½" dark rose print E squares.

Step 6. Cut 10 dark, 12 light, two dark rose print and four pink gingham check 6½" x 6½" G squares.

Step 7. Cut 60 light, 72 dark rose print and 12 pink gingham check 3½" x 3½" H squares.

Step 8. Cut eight 7½" x 30" I strips pink gingham check.

Step 9. Cut 32 each light and pink gingham check 2¼" x 2¼" J squares.

Step 10. Cut a total of (40) 4½" x 4½" K squares from assorted lights and darks; fold and crease to mark horizontal and vertical centers.

Step 11. Cut eight light and eight dark rose print 3" x 3" L squares.

Step 12. Cut a variety of 3" by fabric width strips from lights and darks for M borders; subcut strips into 136 total 3" x 5½" M rectangles.

Step 13. Cut (16) 4" x 4" N squares pink gingham check.

Step 14. Prepare templates for basket appliqués; cut freezer-paper shapes for each basket shape as directed on each pattern for number to cut.

Step 15. Press a freezer-paper shape to the wrong side of fabrics as directed on patterns for color; cut around shapes, adding a ¼" seam allowance all around as shown in Figure 1.

Figure 1

Step 16. Hand-baste seam allowance over freezer paper; press with iron to prepare for appliqué.

Step 17. Cut (10) 2¼" by fabric width strips cream print for binding.

Completing Appliqué Blocks

Step 1. Center and pin the WW basket shape on the A square; machine-stitch in place using a buttonhole stitch and cream all-purpose thread.

Step 2. Repeat Step 1 with XX basket shapes on D squares, YY basket shapes on G squares and ZZ basket shapes on K squares.

Step 3. Trim background away under basket shapes; remove basting stitches and gently pull out freezer-paper shapes.

Completing the Top

Step 1. Sew several C strips together with right sides together along length; press seams in one direction. Subcut the strip set into 3½" segments as shown in Figure 2; join segments to make a strip. Continue to make and cut strip sets and join segments to make a 290"-long strip. Cut strip into four 10½" and four 60½" C strips. Set aside longer strips for Step 12.

Figure 2

Step 2. Sew a shorter C strip to opposite sides of the appliquéd A-WW block; press seams toward strips. Sew a dark rose print B square to each end of the remaining shorter C strips; press seams toward C strip. Sew to the remaining sides of the A-WW block; press seams toward C strips.

Step 3. Referring to Figure 3, join two appliquéd D-XX blocks to make a row; press seam in one direction. Repeat for two rows. Sew a row to opposite sides of the pieced center, again referring to Figure 3; press seams toward rows.

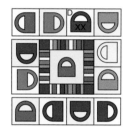

Figure 3

Step 4. Join four appliquéd D-XX blocks to make a row as shown in Figure 4; press seams in one direction. Repeat for two rows. Sew these rows to the top and bottom of the pieced center, again referring to Figure 4; press seams toward rows.

Figure 4

Step 5. Join several F strips with right sides together along length; press seams in one direction. Subcut the strip set into 2½" segments. Join segments to make a strip. Repeat as needed to make a 136"-long strip; press seams in one direction. Cut four 32½" F strips from the strip.

Step 6. Sew an F strip to opposite sides of the pieced center; press seams toward F strips. Sew an E square to each end of the remaining F strips; press seams toward F. Sew these strips to the top and bottom of the pieced center; press seams toward F strips.

Step 7. Join two light or pink gingham check and two dark rose print H squares to make an H unit as shown in Figure 5; press seams toward dark H. Repeat for 36 H units.

Figure 5

Step 8. Join six G-YY blocks to make a G row as shown in Figure 6; repeat for four G rows.

Sew a row to opposite sides of the pieced center; press seams toward row.

Figure 6

Step 9. Sew an H unit to each end of each remaining row as shown in Figure 7; press seams toward rows. Sew these rows to the top and bottom of the pieced center referring to the Placement Diagram; press seams toward rows.

Bountiful Baskets
Placement Diagram
90" x 98"

Figure 7

Step 10. Join eight H units to make an H row as shown in Figure 8; press seams in one direction. Repeat for four H rows. Sew a row to opposite sides of the pieced center referring to the Placement Diagram; press seams toward rows.

Figure 8

Step 11. Sew an appliquéd G-YY block to each end of the remaining two H rows; press seams toward H rows. Sew these rows to the top and bottom of the pieced center; press seams toward rows.

Step 12. Sew a long C strip to opposite sides of the pieced center; press seams toward C. Sew a B square to each end of the remaining two C strips; press seams toward C. Sew a B-C strip to the top and bottom of the pieced center; press seams t oward strips.

Step 13. Join two light and two pink gingham check J squares to make a J unit as shown in Figure 9; press seams toward check J squares and in one direction. Repeat for 16 J units.

Figure 9

Step 14. Join two J units with two N squares as shown in Figure 10; repeat for eight J-N units.

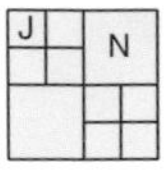

Figure 10

Step 15. Sew I to opposite sides of a J-N unit as shown in Figure 11; repeat for four I-J-N rows.

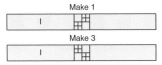

Figure 11

Step 16. Sew an I-J-N row to opposite sides of the pieced center; press seams toward I-J-N rows.

Step 17. Sew a J-N unit to opposite ends of each remaining I-J-N row; press seams away from J-N units. Sew these rows to the top and bottom of the pieced center referring to the Placement Diagram; press seams toward I-J-N rows.

Step 18. Join 20 K-ZZ blocks to make a row referring to the Placement Diagram; press seams in one direction. Repeat for two rows. Sew a row to the top and bottom of the pieced center; press seams toward rows.

Step 19. Join 36 M rectangles to make an M side strip; repeat for two M side strips. Press seams in one direction. Center and sew an M side strip to opposite sides of the pieced center; trim excess even with quilt top at both ends as necessary; press seams toward strips.

Step 20. Join 32 M rectangles to make the top M strip; press seams in one direction. Repeat for the bottom strip.

Step 21. Join four L squares to make a corner unit; repeat for four corner units. Sew a corner unit to each end of the top and bottom M strips; press seams toward M strips. Sew these strips to the top and bottom of the pieced center to complete the pieced top; press seams toward M strips.

Step 22. Finish the quilt referring to the General Instructions. ◆

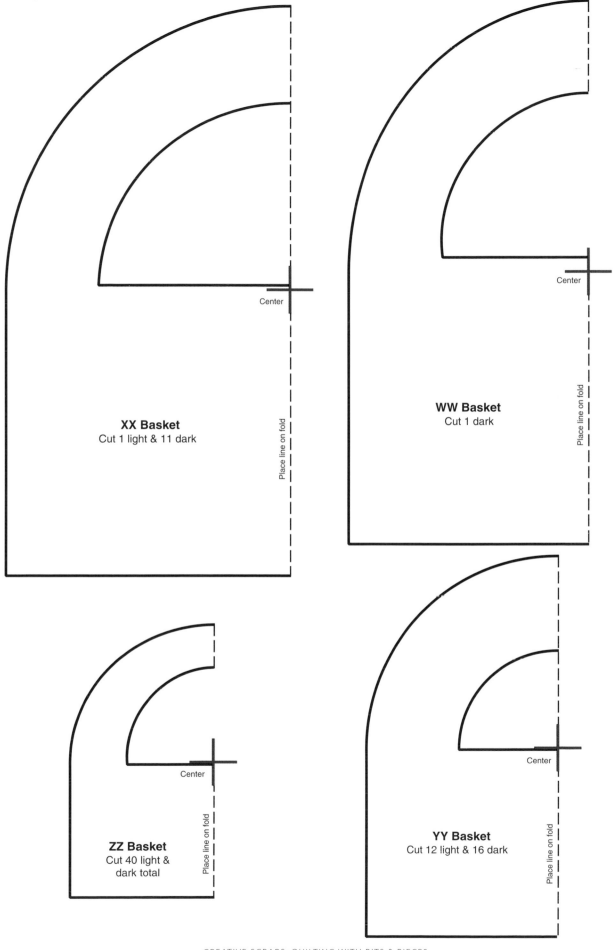

XX Basket
Cut 1 light & 11 dark

Center

Place line on fold

WW Basket
Cut 1 dark

Center

Place line on fold

ZZ Basket
Cut 40 light &
dark total

Center

Place line on fold

YY Basket
Cut 12 light & 16 dark

Center

Place line on fold

STARS & STRIPES

Solid colors create the colorful blocks, and strippy borders are set together with a black tone-on-tone background to make this striking Amish-looking quilt.

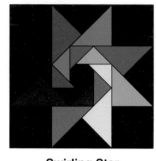

Swirling Star
11" x 11" Block

DESIGN BY DOROTHY MILLIGAN

Project Specifications

Skill Level: Intermediate
Quilt Size: 48" x 61½"
Block Size: 11" x 11"
Number of Blocks: 7

Materials

- ⅜ yard each lime green, bright yellow, orange, red, purple, blue, teal and green solids
- 2½ yards black tone-on-tone
- Backing 54" x 68"
- Batting 54" x 68"
- Neutral color all-purpose thread
- White hand-quilting thread
- Basic sewing tools and supplies

Project Note

The sample quilt uses a few more solids than the eight we have listed to complete the project. The blocks are almost identical, but one or two colors change in each one. It is easier to piece eight identical blocks and make border strips in the same color sequence. If you prefer, you may add more colors to your own version of this quilt.

Making Blocks

Step 1. Prepare templates for pieces D–J using patterns given; cut as directed on each piece for one block. Repeat for seven blocks.

Step 2. To piece one block, begin in the center with H. Pin I to H, matching corner seams and referring to Figure 1 for color positioning.

Figure 1

Step 3. Beginning at the end of the seam allowance, using a ¼" seam, stitch ½" along the H-I seam as shown in Figure 2. Sew E to the H-I unit referring to Figure 3 for color positioning; press seam toward E.

Figure 2   **Figure 3**

Step 4. Continue to add I and E pieces referring to Figure 4 for

positioning. Finish stitching the remaining seam on the beginning I piece.

Figure 4

Step 5. Sew F to a black tone-on-tone J referring to Figure 5; repeat for four F-J units. Press seams away from F.

Figure 5

Step 6. Starting at the block top, sew D onto the first E, stitching 1½" along the edge of E as shown in Figure 6. Sew an F-J unit to the I-D edge of the unit. Continue around the center in this manner, adding D and then F-J units. Complete the seam of the first D along the last F-J edge. Press seams away from the center H-E-I unit.

Figure 6

Step 7. Sew in G at each corner to complete one block as shown in Figure 7; repeat for seven blocks.

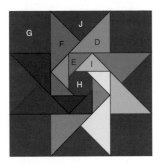

Figure 7

Completing Quilt Center

Step 1. Cut 14 strips each 1½" x 11½" and 1½" x 13½" black tone-on-tone.

Step 2. Sew a shorter strip to opposite sides and longer strips to the top and bottom of each pieced block referring to Figure 8; press seams toward strips.

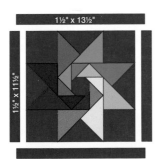

Figure 8

Step 3. Cut six 5" x 13½" M rectangles and four 13½" x 13¾" N rectangles black tone-on-tone.

Step 4. Join two N rectangles, two pieced blocks and one M rectangle to make Rows 1 and 3 as shown in Figure 9. Join

three pieced blocks and four M rectangles to make Row 2, again referring to Figure 9. Press seams away from pieced blocks.

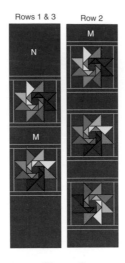

Figure 9

Step 5. Using the pattern given, round each corner on outside N pieces as shown in Figure 10. Transfer matching dots for border pieces to quilt top.

Figure 10

Step 6. Cut four 1½" by fabric width strips each solid-color fabric. Join one strip of each color in any color order along length with right sides together to create a strip set as shown in Figure 11; repeat for four strip sets; press seams in one direction.

Figure 11

Step 7. Cut one end of each strip set at a 45-degree angle as shown in Figure 12; subcut strip sets into 2¾"-wide segments, again referring to Figure 12. You will need 28 segments.

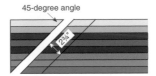

Figure 12

Step 8. Join six segments to create a long strip; repeat for two strips. Join the block rows with the strips; press seams toward strips. Trim excess strip at ends even with rows as shown in Figure 13.

Figure 13

Step 9. Join five segments to create another long strip; repeat for two strips. Remove seven pieces from one end of each strip. Prepare template for O. Place the O template on the beginning and ending segments of each strip and mark the matching dots. Sew a strip to opposite sides of the pieced center referring to the Placement Diagram, matching dots on N to dots on end pieces.

Step 10. Repeat Step 9 to create top and bottom border strips using three segments in each strip and removing only one piece from one end of each strip. Sew a strip to the top and bottom of the pieced center.

Step 11. Prepare templates for pieces P–W using pattern pieces given. Cut pieces P and W from fabrics different than those at the ends of the border strips. Cut remaining pieces to vary color placement around corners.

Step 12. Join one each P–W pieces to make a corner unit as shown in Figure 14; set in a corner unit at each corner, completing seams between end pieces and attaching to N.

Figure 14

Finishing the Quilt
Step 1. Mark a quilting design in each N piece using the pattern given. Mark three consecutive lines around the pattern referring to Figure 15 for positioning. Mark 1" diagonal lines at a 45-degree angle on each M piece.

Figure 15

Step 2. Sandwich batting between completed top and prepared backing piece; pin or baste layers together to hold flat.

Step 3. Quilt on marked lines and in the ditch of block and border seams using white hand-quilting thread. When quilting is complete, trim backing and batting even with quilt top edges; remove pins or basting.

Step 4. Cut 2¼"-wide bias strips black tone-on-tone and join on short ends to make a 6-yard strip. Fold the strip with wrong sides together along length; press.

Step 5. Pin raw edges of the folded strip to the raw edges of the quilt top; stitch all around, overlapping beginning and end. Turn to the back side and hand-stitch in place to finish. ✦

Stars & Stripes
Placement Diagram
48" x 61½"

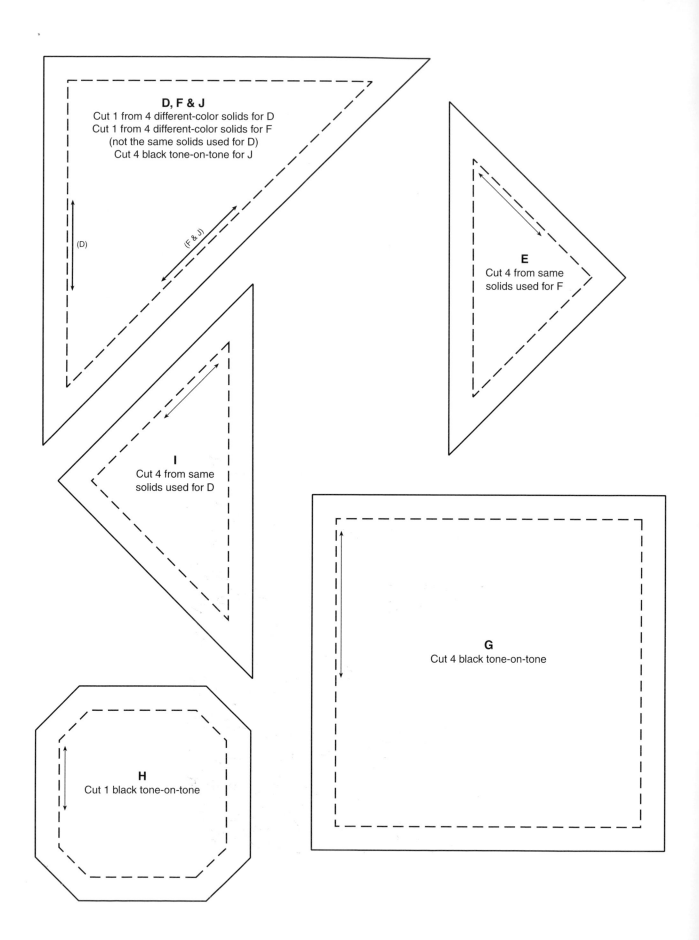

D, F & J
Cut 1 from 4 different-color solids for D
Cut 1 from 4 different-color solids for F
(not the same solids used for D)
Cut 4 black tone-on-tone for J

(D)

(F & J)

E
Cut 4 from same
solids used for F

I
Cut 4 from same
solids used for D

G
Cut 4 black tone-on-tone

H
Cut 1 black tone-on-tone

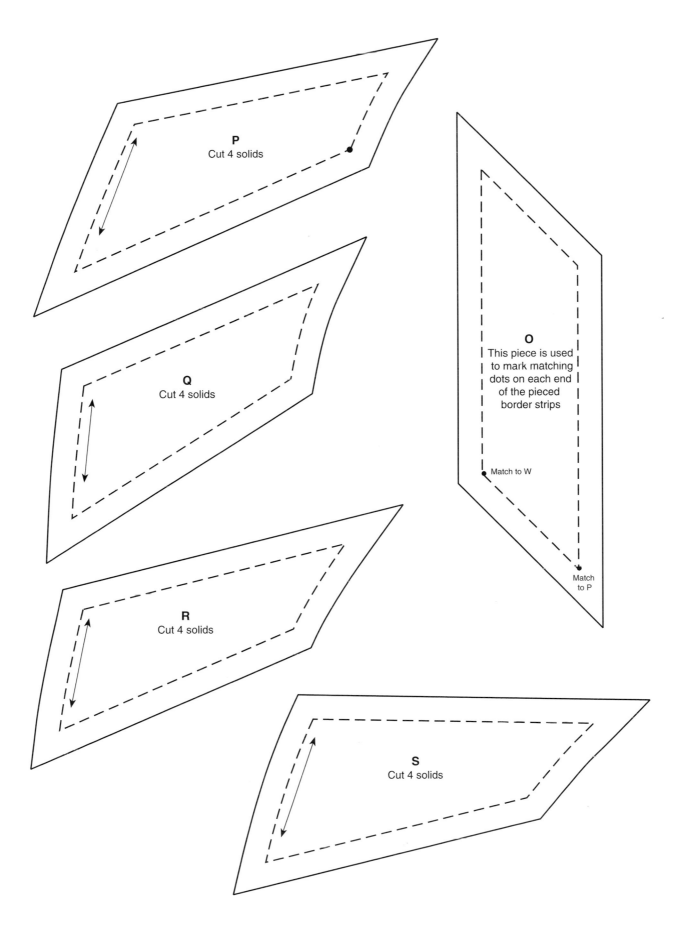

P
Cut 4 solids

Q
Cut 4 solids

R
Cut 4 solids

S
Cut 4 solids

O
This piece is used to mark matching dots on each end of the pieced border strips

Match to W

Match to P

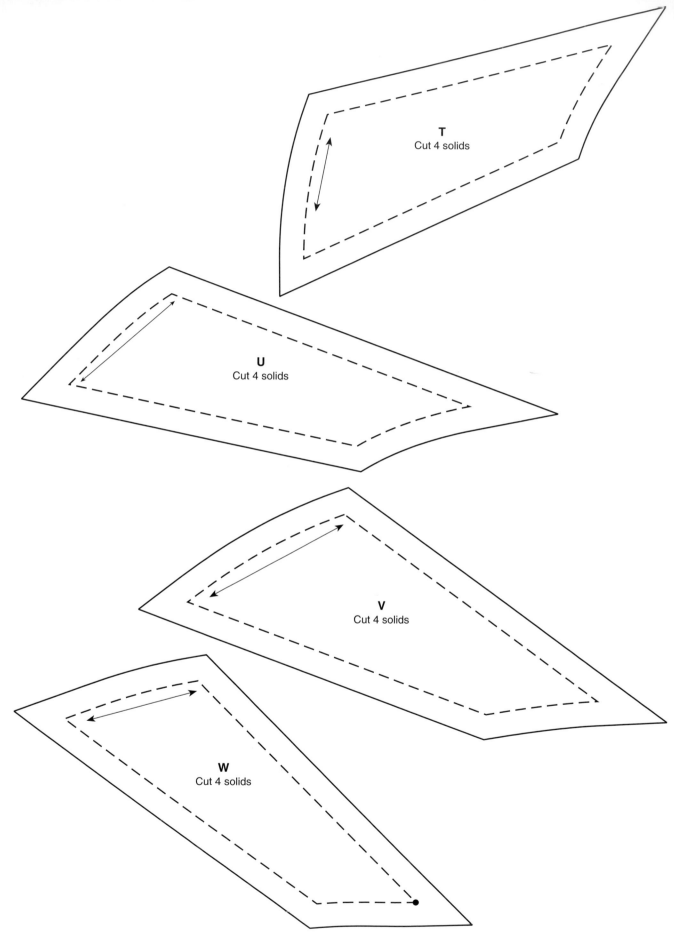

T
Cut 4 solids

U
Cut 4 solids

V
Cut 4 solids

W
Cut 4 solids

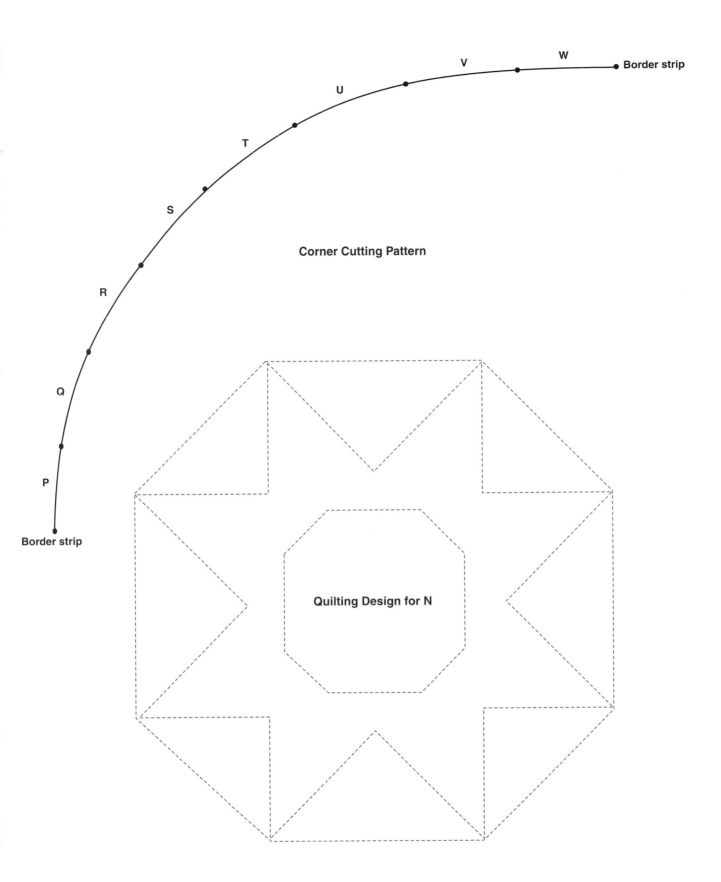

Border strip

W

V

U

T

S

R

Q

P

Border strip

Corner Cutting Pattern

Quilting Design for N

SCRAPWORK DIAMONDS

Quick-cut, quick-pieced half-triangle squares yield a resulting dark beauty with minimal effort.

DESIGN BY JANET JONES WORLEY

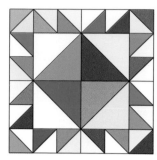

Scrapwork Diamonds
12" x 12" Block

Project Specifications
Skill Level: Intermediate
Quilt Size: 69" x 93"
Block Size: 12" x 12"
Number of Blocks: 24

Materials
- Wide variety of assorted beige print scraps
- Wide variety of assorted dark print scraps
- ¾ yard brick red for inner border
- 3 yards dark blue paisley print for outer borders and binding
- Backing 75" x 99"
- Batting 75" x 99"
- Rotary-cutting tools
- All-purpose thread to blend with fabrics
- 2 spools natural quilting thread
- Basic sewing tools and supplies

Instructions
Step 1. From assorted beige print scraps, cut 48 squares 4⅞" x 4⅞" and 240 squares 2⅞" x 2⅞".

Draw a diagonal line from corner to corner on the wrong side of each square.

Step 2. From assorted dark print scraps, cut 48 squares 4⅞" x 4⅞" and 240 squares 2⅞" x 2⅞".

Step 3. Place a 4⅞" beige print square and a dark square right sides together. Sew ¼" seam on each side of traced line. Cut apart on marked line as shown in Figure 1. Press open for two half-triangle squares. Repeat with all 4⅞" squares and 2⅞" squares.

Figure 1

Step 4. Sew two small squares together as shown in Figure 2. Sew joined squares to one side of larger half-triangle square as shown in Figure 3.

Step 5. Join three small squares as shown in Figure 4. Sew strip to top of unit as shown in Figure 5. Note color placement.

Figure 2

Figure 3

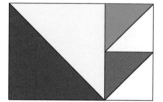

Figure 4

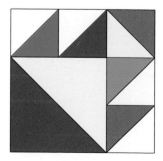

Figure 5

Step 6. Join four units as shown in Figure 6 for one block. Repeat for a total of 24 pieced blocks.

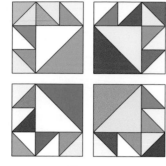

Figure 6

Step 7. Join four blocks to make a row; repeat to make six rows. Press seams in adjoining rows in opposite directions. Join the rows to complete the pieced center; press seams in one direction.

Step 8. From brick red print, cut two strips each 3" x 53½" and 3" x 72½" , piecing if necessary. Sew longer strips to sides of quilt and shorter strips to top and bottom.

Step 9. From dark blue paisley print, cut two strips each 8½" x 77½" and 8½" x 69½" along length of fabric. Sew longer strips to sides of quilt and shorter strips to top and bottom.

Step 10. Prepare for quilting referring to the General Instructions. Quilt as desired by hand or machine.

Step 11. Cut 9½ yards of bias binding 2¼" wide as shown in the General Instructions. Bind to finish.✦

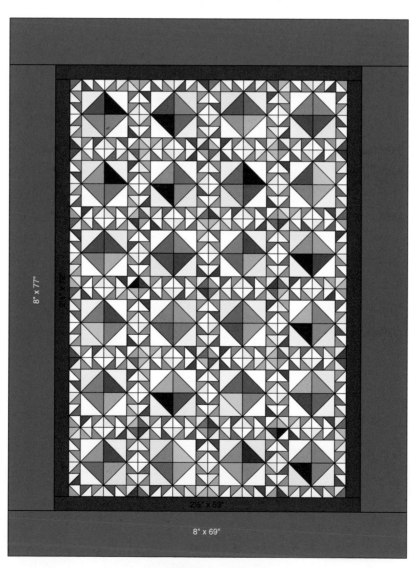

Scrapwork Diamonds
Placement Diagram
69" x 93"

BY THE SEASHORE

The colors of the ocean combine with the Storm at Sea pattern to make a lovely monochromatic quilt.

DESIGN BY HOLLY DANIELS

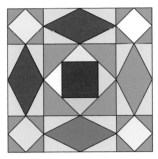

Storm at Sea
16" x 16" Block

Ocean Waves
16" x 16" Block

Project Notes

All the fabrics used in this quilt are blue or aqua. Choose a variety of light and dark fabrics to provide contrast in the blocks. Maintain a scrappy look by using pieces of each fat quarter in each block.

Project Specifications

Skill Level: Beginner
Quilt Size: 98" x 98"
Block Sizes: 16" x 16"
Number of Blocks: 25

Materials

- 18 light blue/aqua fat quarters
- 21 dark blue/aqua fat quarters
- 2½ yards blue mottled
- Batting 104" x 104"
- Backing 104" x 104"
- 11⅓ yards self-made or purchased binding
- All-purpose thread to match fabrics
- Clear nylon monofilament
- Basic sewing tools and supplies, rotary cutter, mat and ruler

Ocean Waves Blocks

Step 1. Cut 13 squares light blue/aqua 6⅛" x 6⅛" for A.

Step 2. Cut 26 squares dark blue/aqua 4⅞" x 4⅞". Cut each square in half on one diagonal to make B triangles; you will need 52 B triangles.

Step 3. Cut 45 strips each 2⅞" x 21" light (C) and dark (D) blue/aqua fabrics.

Step 4. Layer one C and D strip with right sides together; press. Subcut strips into 2⅞" square segments to make seven squares per strip; you will need 312 layered squares. Cut 52 squares on one diagonal through both layers to make 104 each light (C) and dark (D) triangles; set aside.

Step 5. Draw a line across the diagonal on the light square of the remaining 260 layered squares. Sew ¼" on each side of the drawn line as shown in Figure 1; cut along the line and press triangles to the right side to make 520 C-D units.

Figure 1   **Figure 2**

Step 6. Sew two C triangles to a C-D unit as shown in Figure 2; repeat for 52 C-C-D units. Press seams toward C triangles.

Step 7. Sew a C-C-D unit to each side of A to complete a block center referring to Figure 3; press seams toward A. Repeat for 13 block-center units.

Figure 3

Step 8. Sew two D triangles to a C-D unit as shown in Figure 4; repeat for 52 D-C-D units. Press seams toward D. Add B to each unit to complete 52 corner units, again referring to Figure 4. Press seams toward B.

Figure 4

Step 9. Join eight C-D units to make a side unit as shown in Figure 5; repeat for 52 side units.

Figure 5

Step 10. Sew a side unit to opposite sides of a center unit as shown in Figure 6; press seams toward side units.

Figure 6

Step 11. Sew a corner unit to opposite ends of two side units as shown in Figure 7; press seams toward side units. Sew to opposite sides of the center/side unit to complete one Ocean Waves block as shown in Figure 8; press seams toward side/corner units. Repeat for 13 blocks.

Figure 7

Figure 8

Storm at Sea Blocks

Step 1. Cut 12 squares dark blue/aqua 4½" x 4½" for E.

Step 2. Cut 24 squares 3¾" x 3¾" light blue/aqua; cut each square in half on one diagonal to make F triangles. You will need 48 F pieces.

Step 3. Sew F to each side of E as shown in Figure 9; press seams toward F. Repeat for 12 E-F units; trim each unit to 6¾" x 6¾".

Figure 9

Step 4. Cut 24 squares 4⅞" x 4⅞" dark blue/aqua; cut each square in half on one diagonal for G.

Step 5. Sew G to each side of an E-F unit as shown in Figure 10; press seams toward G. Repeat for 12 E-F-G units; trim each unit to 8½" x 8½".

Figure 10

Step 6. Cut 48 squares 3⅜" x 3⅜" light blue/aqua for H.

Step 7. Cut 96 squares dark blue/aqua 2⅞" x 2⅞"; cut each square on one diagonal to make 192 J triangles.

Step 8. Sew J to each side of H as shown in Figure 11; repeat for 48 H-J units. Press seams toward J.

Figure 11

Step 9. Prepare templates for pieces K and L using pattern

pieces given; cut as directed on each piece.

Step 10. Sew L and LR to K as shown in Figure 12; repeat for 48 L-K units.

Figure 12

Step 11. To piece one block, sew an L-K unit to opposite sides of an E-F-G unit as shown in Figure 13; press seams away from center unit.

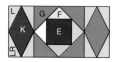

Figure 13

Step 12. Sew an H-J unit to each end of two K-L units as shown in Figure 14. Sew these units to opposite sides of the previously pieced unit to complete one Storm at Sea block as shown in Figure 15; press seams away from center unit. Repeat for 12 blocks.

Figure 14

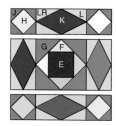

Figure 15

Completing the Quilt

Step 1. Join two Storm at Sea blocks with three Ocean Waves blocks to make a row as shown in

Figure 16; repeat for three rows. Press seams in one direction.

Step 2. Join three Storm at Sea blocks with two Ocean Waves blocks to make a row, again referring to Figure 16; repeat for two rows. Press seams in one direction.

Make 3

Make 2

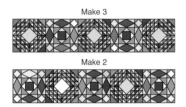

Figure 16

Step 3. Join the rows referring to the Placement Diagram for positioning; press seams in one direction.

Step 4. Cut and piece two strips each 9½" x 80½" and 9½" x 98½" blue mottled. Sew the shorter strips to opposite sides and longer strips to the top and bottom of the pieced center; press seams toward strips.

Step 5. Prepare for quilting and quilt as desired referring to the General Instructions. ***Note:*** *The quilt shown was machine-quilted in a meandering design using clear nylon monofilament in the top of the machine and all-purpose thread in the bobbin.*

Step 6. Apply self-made or purchased binding referring to the General Instructions to finish. ✦

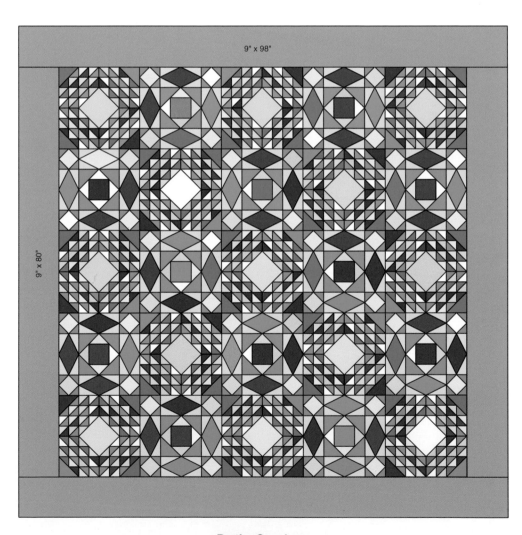

9" x 98"

9" x 80"

By the Seashore
Placement Diagram
98" x 98"

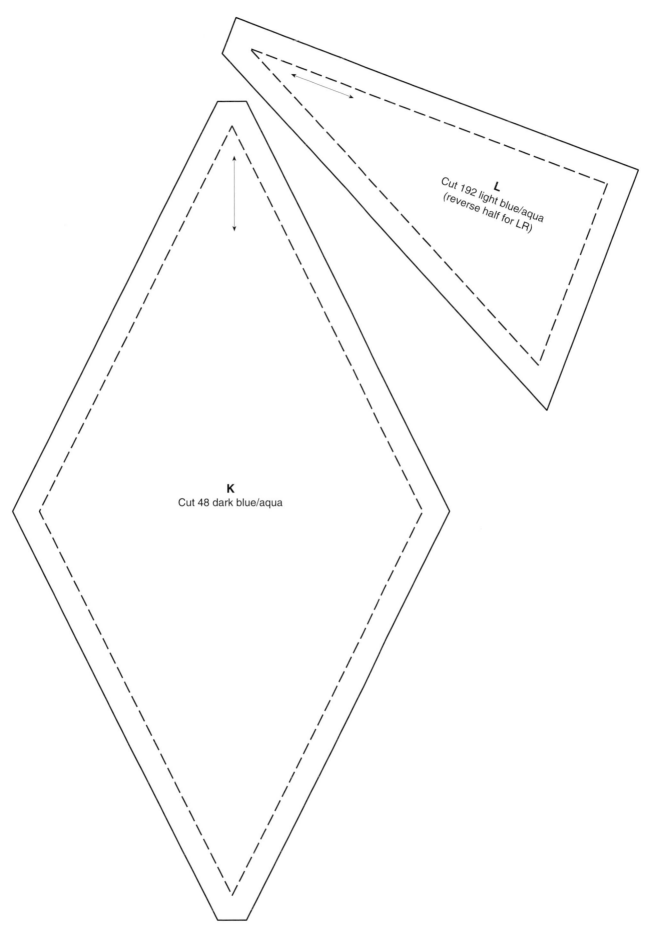

L
Cut 192 light blue/aqua
(reverse half for LR)

K
Cut 48 dark blue/aqua

BEAR PAW JEWELS

Jewel-tone fabrics are used to make the Bear Paw blocks in this quilt. These colors are set off against a black background giving the project an Amish look.

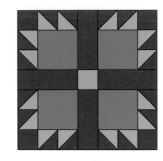

Bear Paw
14" x 14" block

DESIGN BY LUCY A. FAZELY

Project Specifications
Skill Level: Intermediate
Project Size: 46" x 62"
Block Size: 14" x 14"
Number of Blocks: 6

Materials
- ⅓ yard each of 12 jewel-tone prints
- 2 yards black solid
- Backing 52" x 68"
- Batting 52" x 68"
- Black all-purpose thread
- Basic sewing tools and supplies

Instructions
Step 1. Cut 20 strips black solid 2½" by fabric width. Subcut eight of the strips into 2½" segments for B squares; you will need 120 B squares; set aside. Subcut four strips into 6½" segments for C; you will need 24 C segments. Subcut two strips into 14½" segments for D sashing strips; you will need four D strips. Cut and piece the remaining strips to make three

2½" x 46½" strips and two 2½" x 34½" strips.

Step 2. Choose six jewel-tone prints for large squares in each block. Cut four 4½" x 4½" squares from each of these fabrics for A.

Step 3. Cut one 2½" by fabric width strip from each of the remaining six jewel-tone prints; subcut into 2½" square segments for B. You will need 17 B squares from each jewel-tone print.

Step 4. Place one jewel-tone print B square right sides together with a black solid B square. Draw a diagonal line on the print square; sew along line. Trim ¼" beyond seam; press pieces open with seam toward the black solid B as shown in Figure 1. Repeat for 16 B units in each color.

Figure 1

Step 5. Join two same-fabric B units; sew a black solid B to one unit as shown in Figure 2.

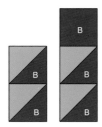

Figure 2

Step 6. Join the pieced units with A to complete one A-B unit as shown in Figure 3; repeat for four units of the same fabrics.

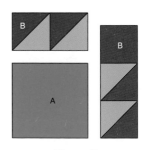

Figure 3

Step 7. Sew two A-B units to C as shown in Figure 4; repeat. Sew the

remaining B square between two C rectangles. Join the pieced units as shown in Figure 5 to complete one block. Repeat for six blocks.

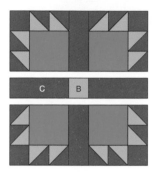

Figure 4

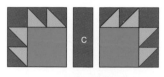

Figure 5

Step 8. Join three blocks with two D sashing strips to make a row as shown in Figure 6; repeat for two rows. Press seams toward strips.

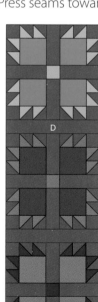

Figure 6

Step 9. Join the rows with three 2½" x 46½" black solid strips; press seams toward strips. Sew a 2½" x 34 ½" strip black solid to the top and bottom; press seams toward strips.

Step 10. Cut two strips of each jewel-tone print 2½" by fabric width. Join one strip of each color along length with right sides together to make a panel; press seams in one direction. Repeat for a second panel in the same color order as the first one.

Step 11. Cut six 6½" segments from each panel as shown in Figure 7. Join two segments to make a border strip as shown in Figure 8; repeat for four border strips.

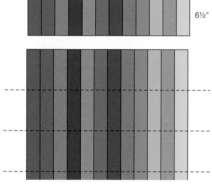

6½"

Figure 7

Figure 8

Step 12. Lay a border strip along each side of the pieced center with the colors flowing in a clockwise direction as shown in Figure 9. Remove the last strips from the top right and bottom

left side border strips. Add these pieces to the side strip adjacent to it, again referring to Figure 9.

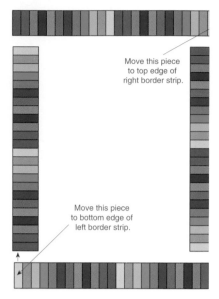

Move this piece to top edge of right border strip.

Move this piece to bottom edge of left border strip.

Figure 9

Step 13. Sew longer strips to longer sides and shorter strips to the top and bottom of the pieced center; press seams toward strips. **Note:** *If the strips do not fit exactly, adjust seam allowance between strips as needed.*

Step 14. Prepare 6½ yards self-made black binding, prepare quilt top for quilting and finish referring to the General Instructions. ◆

Bear Paw Jewels
Placement Diagram
46" x 62"

GARDEN OF EDEN

With the use of machine appliqué, you'll be done with this quilt in no time.

DESIGN BY LUCY A. FAZELY & MICHAEL L. BURNS

Garden of Eden A
14" x 14" Block

Garden of Eden B
14" x 14" Block

Project Specifications

Skill Level: Beginner
Quilt Size: 58" x 58"
Block Size: 14" x 14"
Number of Blocks: 9

Materials

- ⅓ yard rose print
- ⅓ yard light green print
- ½ yard peach print
- ⅔ yard medium green print
- ¾ yard burgundy tonal
- 1⅜ yards cream tonal
- 1⅜ yards dark green tonal
- 1½ yards peach paisley
- Backing 64" x 64"
- Batting 64" x 64"
- Neutral color all-purpose thread
- Clear nylon monofilament
- Quilting thread
- 5½ yards 12"-wide fusible web
- 3⅝ yards 22"-wide fabric stabilizer
- Basic sewing tools and supplies

Cutting

Step 1. Cut three 14½" by fabric width strips cream tonal; subcut strips into five 14½" A squares.

Step 2. Cut two 14½" by fabric width strips dark green tonal; subcut strips into four 14½" B squares.

Step 3. Cut two 2½" x 42½" C strips burgundy tonal.

Step 4. Cut three 2½" by fabric width strips burgundy tonal. Join strips on short ends to make one long strip; subcut strip into two 46½" D strips.

Step 5. Cut six 6½" by fabric width strips peach paisley. Join strips on short ends to make one long strip; press seams open. Subcut strip into two 46½" E strips and two 58½" F strips.

Step 6. Prepare templates for each appliqué shape using full-size patterns given. Trace shapes onto the paper side of the fusible web, leaving ⅛" between shapes and referring to patterns for number to cut.

Step 7. Cut out shapes, leaving a margin around each one; remove liner. Fuse shapes to the wrong side of fabrics as directed on pattern for color.

Step 8. Cut out shapes on traced lines; remove paper backing.

Step 9. Cut nine 14" x 14" squares fabric stabilizer.

Step 10. Cut six 2¼" by fabric width strips dark green tonal for binding.

Completing the Blocks

Step 1. Fold and crease A and B squares to mark horizontal, vertical and diagonal centers as shown in Figure 1.

Figure 1

Step 2. To complete an A block, fold and crease a burgundy tonal large circle to find the center. Center the circle on an A square using the creased lines as guides.

Step 3. Arrange four stem motifs on the diagonal creases of A, centering the center stem on the crease and tucking ends under the large circle; fuse stem and circle shapes in place.

Step 4. Arrange a ring and small circle on the large circle; fuse in place.

Step 5. Place a bud base and bud at the tip of each stem, placing the burgundy tonal bud on the center stem and the peach paisley buds on the side stems; fuse in place to complete one A block. Repeat for five A blocks.

Step 6. Repeat Steps 2–5 with peach print large circles, rose print rings, medium green print small circles and stems, light green print bud bases and peach and rose print buds to complete four B blocks.

Step 7. When all blocks are complete, pin a square of stabilizer to the wrong side of each block.

Step 8. Using clear nylon monofilament and a narrow zigzag stitch, stitch around each shape to secure.

Step 9. When stitching is complete, remove fabric stabilizer.

Completing the Top

Step 1. Join one B block with two A blocks to make a row; press seams toward B block. Repeat for two rows.

Step 2. Join one A block with two B blocks to make a row; press seams toward B blocks.

Step 3. Join the rows referring to the Placement Diagram for positioning of rows; press seams in one direction.

Step 4. Sew a C strip to opposite sides and a D strip to the top and bottom of the pieced center; press seams toward strips.

Step 5. Sew an E strip to opposite sides and an F strip to the top and bottom of the pieced center to complete the quilt top; press seams toward E and F strips.

Step 6. Finish quilt referring to the General Instructions. ✦

Garden of Eden
Placement Diagram
58" x 58"

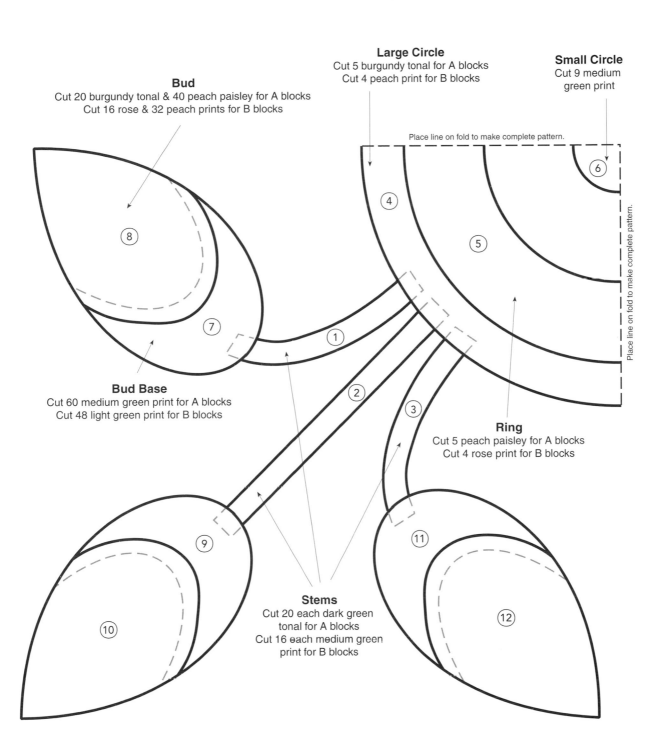

Bud
Cut 20 burgundy tonal & 40 peach paisley for A blocks
Cut 16 rose & 32 peach prints for B blocks

Large Circle
Cut 5 burgundy tonal for A blocks
Cut 4 peach print for B blocks

Small Circle
Cut 9 medium green print

Place line on fold to make complete pattern.

Place line on fold to make complete pattern.

Bud Base
Cut 60 medium green print for A blocks
Cut 48 light green print for B blocks

Ring
Cut 5 peach paisley for A blocks
Cut 4 rose print for B blocks

Stems
Cut 20 each dark green
tonal for A blocks
Cut 16 each medium green
print for B blocks

TEABERRY TWIST

Tea-and berry-colored fabrics twist when they meet along the edges of these blocks.

DESIGN BY KARLA SCHULTZ

Teaberry Twist
16" x 16" Block

Project Specifications
Skill Level: Intermediate
Quilt Size: 63" x 79"
Block Size: 16" x 16"
Number of Blocks: 12

Materials
- ¾ yard gold check
- ¾ yard green tonal
- 1⅛ yards brown print
- 1¼ yards red tonal
- 1⅝ yards light gray print
- 1⅞ yards dark blue tonal
- Backing 69" x 85"
- Batting 69" x 85"
- All-purpose thread to match fabrics
- Basic sewing tools and supplies

Cutting
Step 1. Cut three 2⅝" by fabric width strips each gold check (A) and green tonal (B). Subcut strips into (48) 2⅝" squares of each fabric. Cut each square in half on one diagonal to make 96 each A and B triangles.
Step 2. Cut three 2¼" by fabric width strips dark blue tonal; subcut strips into (48) 2¼" C squares.
Step 3. Cut two 4" by fabric width strips red tonal; subcut strips into (12) 4" D squares.
Step 4. Cut one 7½" by fabric width strip brown print; subcut strip into (24) 1" E strips.
Step 5. Cut one 8½" by fabric width strip brown print; subcut strip into (24) 1" F strips.
Step 6. Cut four 6½" by fabric width strips light gray print; subcut strips into (24) 6½" G squares. Cut each square in half on one diagonal to make 48 G triangles.
Step 7. Cut eight 2⅞" by fabric width strips light gray print (H) and four strips each red tonal (I) and brown prints (J); subcut strips into 2⅞" squares. You will need 96 H and 48 each I and J squares. Cut each square in half on one diagonal to make 192 H and 96 each I and J triangles.
Step 8. Cut three 4⅞" by fabric width strips gold check; subcut strips into (24) 4⅞" K squares.

Cut each square in half on one diagonal to make 48 K triangles.
Step 9. Cut two 2½" by fabric width strips each brown (L) and light gray (M) prints; subcut strips into (24) 2½" squares of each fabric.
Step 10. Cut four 2⅞" by fabric width strips dark blue tonal; subcut strips into (48) 2⅞" N squares. Cut each square in half on one diagonal to make 96 N squares.
Step 11. Cut six 2½" by fabric width strips green tonal; join strips on short ends to make one long strip. Subcut the strip into two 48½" O and two 68½" P strips.
Step 12. Cut seven 6" by fabric width strips dark blue tonal; join strips on short ends to make one long strip. Subcut the strip into two 52½" Q and two 79½" R strips.
Step 13. Cut eight 2¼" by fabric width strips red tonal for binding.

Piecing the Blocks
Step 1. To piece one block, sew A to B along the diagonal; press

seam toward B. Repeat for eight A-B units.

Step 2. Join two A-B units to make a strip as shown in Figure 1; repeat for four A-B strips. Press seams toward B.

Make 2

Make 2

Figure 1

Step 3. Referring to Figure 2, sew an A-B strip to two opposite sides of D; press seams toward D. Sew C to each end of the remaining two A-B strips; press seams toward C. Sew the A-B-C units to the A-B-D unit; press.

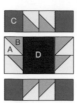

Figure 2

Step 4. Sew an E strip to opposite sides and the F strips to the top and bottom of the pieced unit; press seams toward E and F.

Step 5. Sew a G triangle to each side of the pieced unit as shown in Figure 3; press seams toward G.

Figure 3

Step 6. Sew H to I along the diagonal; press seam toward I. Repeat for eight units.

Step 7. Join two H-I units with N as shown in Figure 4; press seams toward N. Repeat for two units, again referring to Figure 4. Sew L to one unit referring to Figure 5; press seam toward L.

Make 1   Make 1

Figure 4

Figure 5

Step 8. Sew the H-I-N unit to one short side of K; press seams toward K. Add the H-I-N-L unit to the remaining short side of K as shown in Figure 6 to complete one brown unit; repeat for two brown triangle units.

Figure 6

Step 9. Repeat Steps 6–8 with H and J triangles and M squares to complete two red triangle units as shown in Figure 7.

Figure 7

Step 10. Sew the triangle units to the pieced center unit as shown in Figure 8 to complete one block; press seams away from center unit. Repeat for 12 blocks.

Figure 8

Completing the Top

Step 1. Arrange the blocks in four rows of three blocks each referring to the Placement Diagram for positioning of blocks. Join blocks in rows; join rows to complete the pieced center; press seams in one direction.

Step 2. Sew an O strip to the top and bottom of the pieced center; press seams toward O. Sew a P strip to opposite long sides; press seams toward P.

Step 3. Sew a Q strip to the top and bottom of the pieced center; press seams toward Q. Sew an R strip to opposite long sides to complete the pieced top; press seams toward R.

Finishing the Quilt

Step 1. Sandwich the batting between the completed top and prepared backing; pin or baste layers together to hold.

Step 2. Hand- or machine-quilt as desired. When quilting is complete, trim batting and backing even with top; remove pins or basting.

Step 3. Join binding strips on short ends to make one long strip. Fold the strip in half along length with wrong sides together; press.

Step 4. Sew binding to quilt edges, mitering corners and overlapping ends. Fold binding to the back side and stitch in place to finish. ✦

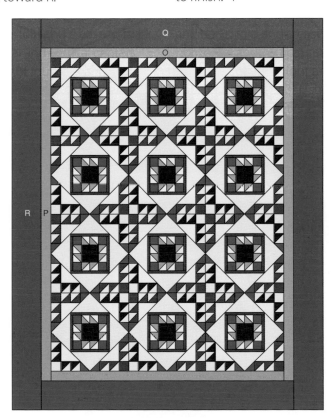

Teaberry Twist
Placement Diagram
63" x 79"

RED & WHITE FRUSTRATION

Dress up your holidays with this two-color quilt using red-and-white fabrics.

Red & White Frustration
8" x 8" Block

DESIGN BY TOBY LISCHKO

Project Specifications
Skill Level: Advanced
Quilt Size: 50⅝" x 61⅞"
Block Size: 8" x 8"
Number of Blocks: 32

Materials
- 2½ yards total white-with-red prints
- 5 yards total red prints
- Backing 57" x 68"
- Batting 57" x 68"
- Neutral color all-purpose thread
- Quilting thread
- Basic sewing tools and supplies

Cutting
Step 1. Prepare templates for A and B using patterns given; cut as directed on each piece.
Step 2. Cut (16) 4¾" by fabric width strips red prints; subcut strips into (128) 4¾" C squares.
Step 3. Cut (14) 4½" x 4½" D squares red prints.
Step 4. Cut (28) 6⅞" x 6⅞" squares red prints. Cut each square on both diagonals to make 112 E triangles.

Step 5. Cut six 2¼" by fabric width strips red prints for binding.

Completing the Blocks
Step 1. Sew B to A and BR to AR as shown in Figure 1; press seams toward A and AR. Repeat for 128 each A-B and AR-BR units.

Figure 1

Step 2. To piece one block, sew an A-B unit to an AR-BR unit to make a quarter unit as shown in Figure 2; repeat for four quarter units.

Figure 2

Step 3. Join two quarter units to complete a half unit; repeat for two half units. Join the half units to complete a circle unit, clipping seams in the center and pressing

seams in a clockwise direction as shown in Figure 3.

Figure 3

Step 4. Turn under the edge of the circle unit ¼" all around; baste to hold and press.
Step 5. Join four C squares; press seams counterclockwise, splitting center seam to press in opposite directions as shown in Figure 4.

Figure 4

Step 6. Center a circle unit on the C unit; baste in place. Hand- or machine-stitch circle unit in place. Remove basting stitches; press.
Step 7. Trim stitched block to 8½" x 8½" square with edges of circle ¼" from center side seams of C as shown in Figure 5.

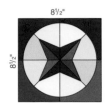

8½"

8½"

Figure 5

Step 8. Carefully trim excess C squares away from under circle shape, leaving a ¼" seam allowance as shown in Figure 6 to complete one block; repeat for 32 blocks.

Figure 6

Completing the Top

Step 1. Sew E to two adjacent sides of D to make a side unit as shown in Figure 7; press seams toward E. Repeat for 14 side units.

Figure 7

Step 2. Join two E triangles as shown in Figure 8 to complete a corner unit; press seam in one direction. Repeat for four corner units.

Figure 8

Step 3. Arrange the blocks in diagonal rows with the side and corner units referring to Figure 9. Join to make rows; press seams in adjacent rows in opposite directions.

Figure 9

Step 4. Join 17 E pieces as shown in Figure 10 to make a top border strip; press seams in one direction.

Repeat for bottom border strip. Sew a strip to the top and bottom of the pieced center referring to the Placement Diagram for positioning of strips.

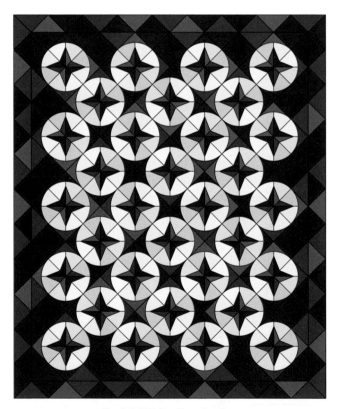

Figure 10

Step 5. Repeat Step 4 with 21 E pieces to make two side border strips. Sew a strip to opposite sides of the pieced center.

Step 6. Join seams of E strips at corners to complete the top; press seams in one direction.

Step 7. Finish quilt referring to the General Instructions. ✦

Red & White Frustration
Placement Diagram
50⅝" x 61⅞"

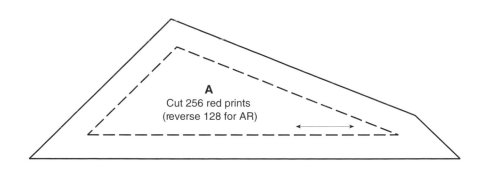

A
Cut 256 red prints
(reverse 128 for AR)

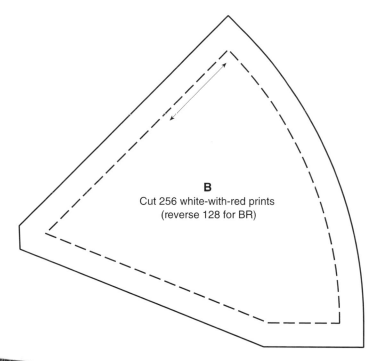

B
Cut 256 white-with-red prints
(reverse 128 for BR)

POMEGRANATE FOUR-PATCH

Learn to machine scribble stitch to accomplish Baltimore elegance in quick time!

DESIGN BY JODI G. WARNER

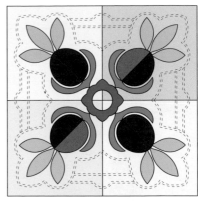

Pomegranate
14" x 14" Block

Project Specifications
Skill Level: Intermediate
Quilt Size: 39" x 39"
Block Size: 14" x 14"
Number of Blocks: 4

Materials
- Four different light sage green fat quarters for Four-Patch background squares
- ½ yard navy print for sashing and narrow borders
- 4½" x 35½" strips of four different sage greens for outer borders
- Scraps of four deep reds, deep navy, dark green and medium sage green for appliqué
- 22" x 22" square of dark sage green for binding
- Backing 45" x 45"
- Thin batting 45" x 45"
- Rotary-cutting tools
- All-purpose thread to match fabrics
- 1 yard fusible web
- Spring darning foot attachment for sewing machine
- Small spring embroidery hoop (optional)

- 1 spool each natural and olive green quilting thread
- Basic sewing tools and supplies

Instructions
Note: *Refer to Scribble-Stitch Machine-Appliqué Instructions on page 199.*
Step 1. From light sage green fat quarters, cut 16 squares 7½" x 7½". Using one square of each color, piece a Four-Patch block. Repeat for four blocks.
Step 2. From four deep red scraps, cut four strips each 1¾" x 7". Pair strips in most pleasing combinations. Sew four identical pairs of each combination. Press seams open.
Step 3. Trace appliqué shapes on paper side of fusible web as directed on templates. Cut out roughly ¼" outside traced lines. Following manufacturer's directions, fuse to selected fabrics. Pomegranate shapes should be centered on seams of paired red strips. Cut out on traced lines.
Step 4. Referring to block diagram, arrange appliqué pieces

on each block; fuse. Scribble-stitch around each appliqué piece with closely matched thread. Stitch around center collar with moderate-width continuous loops as shown in Figure 1. Stitch calyx with variable zigzag as shown in Figure 2, then leaf clusters with feather stitch as shown in Figure 3. Stitch pomegranates with ¼"-wide continuous loops.

Figure 1

Figure 2

Figure 3

Step 5. From navy print, cut two strips each 1½" x 14½" and 1½" x 31½" . Cut three strips 1½" x 29½" . Arrange and sew blocks and sashing as shown in Figure 4, pressing seam allowances toward navy strips as each is joined.

Step 6. Add four sage green border strips to quilt Log Cabin style around the center as shown in Figure 5. Press seam allowances toward navy borders.

Step 7. Transfer quilting lines to appliquéd blocks. Mark a 1½" on-point grid on sage green borders.

Step 8. Prepare for quilting referring to the General Instructions.

Step 9. Quilt in the ditch around appliqué shapes, next to narrow border seams and on marked lines with olive green quilting thread. Quilt on marked grid on sage green border with natural quilting thread.

Step 10. From the 22" x 22" square of dark sage green fabric, prepare 4¾ yards of 2¼"-wide binding as shown in the General Instructions. Bind to finish. Add a sleeve for hanging, if desired. ✦

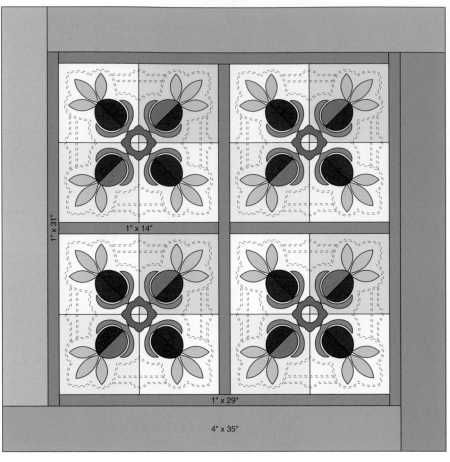

Pomegranate Four-Patch
Placement Diagram
39" x 39"

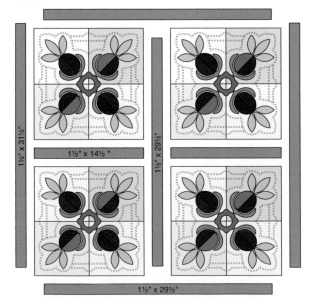

Figure 4

Figure 5

Scribble-Stitch Machine-Appliqué Instructions

Step 1. Trace appliqué shapes onto the paper side of lightweight fusible transfer web. Turn non-symmetrical shapes over to trace them as reverse image on the paper, so they will face the right direction from the fabric front.

Step 2. Cut out each shape roughly ¼" beyond the traced lines. Trim excess fusing from the interior of each shape, leaving a ⅜" margin with fusing and paper inside traced lines.

Step 3. Follow manufacturer's directions to fuse each shape to the wrong side of selected fabrics. Consider grain line or fabric patterning as shapes are positioned before applying heat.

Step 4. Carefully trim each shape on traced lines. Remove paper backing.

Step 5. Position shapes on right side of selected background fabric according to design layout, overlapping edges as required. When arrangement is complete, fuse shapes in place.

Step 6. Determine the best order for completing the scribble stitching; stitch first around shapes which are overlapped by other edges.

Step 7. Thread the machine top and bobbin with color coordinated to the first appliqués. Drop the feed dogs. Attach the spring darning foot. If desired, center the background fabric in an inverted hoop to help stabilize it.

Step 8. Select a stitching pattern. Many variations are possible, including a variable zigzag, continuous loops and feather stitch. Insert the needle through the work and draw the bobbin thread through to help avoid tangling on the underside. Hold threads out of the way, take a few stitches in place to lock, then begin free-motion stitching along the edge of the appliqué. Scribble stitching should overlap the raw edge barely, as well as extending into the body of the appliqué approximately ¼".

Step 9. At the end of the stitching run, take a few stitches in place to lock, then raise the presser foot and remove the work form the machine. Trim thread ends neatly, or pull them to the underside. Complete scribble stitching in sequence for remaining edges, changing thread color as needed. ✦

**Pomegranate Four-Patch
Appliqué Pattern**
($\frac{1}{4}$ block)

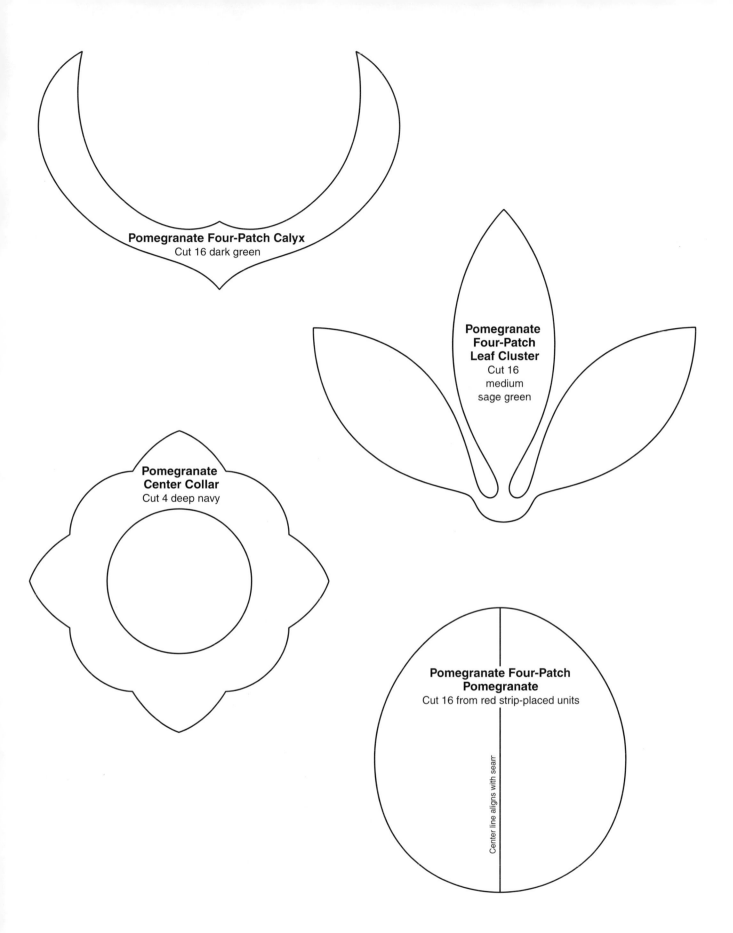

Pomegranate Four-Patch Calyx
Cut 16 dark green

**Pomegranate
Four-Patch
Leaf Cluster**
Cut 16
medium
sage green

**Pomegranate
Center Collar**
Cut 4 deep navy

**Pomegranate Four-Patch
Pomegranate**
Cut 16 from red strip-placed units

Center line aligns with seam

HOLLY, WOOD & VINE

A combination of holly and vine prints inspired the unique name of this delightful bed-size quilt.

Holly Stars
15" x 15" Block

DESIGN BY JULIE WEAVER

Project Specifications
Skill Level: Intermediate
Quilt Size: 90" x 106"
Block Size: 15" x 15"
Number of Blocks: 20

Materials
- ⅓ yard each 2 different green prints
- ½ yard red tonal
- ⅔ yard each 4 different red prints
- 1¾ yards small black floral
- 1⅞ yards black print
- 3⅜ yards cream tonal
- 3⅛ yards large black floral
- Backing 96" x 112"
- Batting 96" x 112"
- Neutral color all-purpose thread
- Quilting thread
- Basic sewing tools and supplies

Cutting
Step 1. Cut two 4½" by fabric width strips from each green print; subcut strips into (10) 4½" A squares each fabric.

Step 2. Cut (10) 2½" by fabric width strips small black floral; subcut strips into (160) 2½" B squares. Draw a line from corner to corner on each B square.

Step 3. Cut (15) 2½" by fabric width strips cream tonal; subcut strips into (240) 2½" C squares.

Step 4. Cut four 2½" by fabric width strips from each red print; subcut two strips of each fabric into (40) 1½" D rectangles. Subcut the remaining two strips of each fabric into (20) 2½" E squares.

Step 5. Cut two 8½" by fabric width strips black print; subcut strips into (40) 1½" F strips.

Step 6. Cut two 10½" by fabric width strips black print; subcut strips into (40) 1½" G strips.

Step 7. Cut (12) 2⅞" by fabric width strips cream tonal; subcut strips into (160) 2⅞" H squares. Draw a line from corner to corner on the wrong side of each H square.

Step 8. Cut three 2⅞" by fabric width strips from each red print; subcut strips into (40) 2⅞" I squares each fabric.

Step 9. Cut one 14½" by fabric width strip cream tonal; subcut strip into (40) 1" J strips.

Step 10. Cut one 15½" by fabric width strip cream tonal; subcut strip into (40) 1" K strips.

Step 11. Cut one 15½" by fabric width strip small black floral; subcut strip into (25) 1½" L sashing strips.

Step 12. Cut (10) 1½" by fabric width strips small black floral; join strips on short ends to make one long strip. Subcut strip into six 65½" M sashing strips.

Step 13. Cut eight 1" by fabric width strips cream tonal; join strips on short ends to make one long strip. Subcut strip into two 81½" N strips and two 66½" O strips.

Step 14. Cut eight 1½" by fabric width strips red tonal; join strips on short ends to make one long strip. Subcut strip into two 82½" P strips and two 68½" Q strips.

Step 15. Cut nine 11½" by fabric width strips large black floral; join strips on short ends to make one long strip. Subcut strip into two 84½" R strips and two 90½" S strips.

Step 16. Cut (10) 2¼" by fabric width strips black print for binding.

Piecing the Blocks

Step 1. To piece one block, select matching red print D, E and I pieces. Sew D to opposite sides of C as shown in Figure 1; press seams toward D. Repeat for four C-D units.

Figure 1

Step 2. Place a B square on the D end of one C-D unit as shown in Figure 2. Stitch on the marked line, trim seam allowance to ¼" and press B to the right side, again referring to Figure 2. Repeat on the opposite end of the C-D unit to complete a B-C-D unit as shown in Figure 3. Repeat for four units.

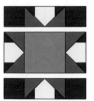

Figure 2

Figure 3

Step 3. Sew a B-C-D unit to opposite sides of A as shown in Figure 4; press seams toward A.

Figure 4

Step 4. Sew E to each B end of the two remaining B-C-D units as shown in Figure 5; press seams toward E.

Figure 5

Step 5. Sew a B-C-D-E unit to opposite sides of the A-B-C-D unit as shown in Figure 6 to complete the block center; press seams toward A-B-C-D.

Figure 6

Step 6. Sew F to opposite sides and G to the top and bottom of the block center; press seams toward F and G.

Step 7. Place an H square right sides together with an I square; stitch ¼" on each side of the marked line as shown in Figure 7. Cut apart on the marked line to complete two H-I units, again referring to Figure 7. Repeat for 16 H-I units.

Figure 7

Step 8. Join four H-I units with C as shown in Figure 8; repeat for four units. Press seams toward C.

Figure 8

Step 9. Sew a C-H-I unit to the F sides of the pieced center as shown in Figure 9; press seams toward F.

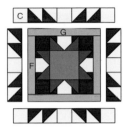

Figure 9

Step 10. Sew a C square to each end of the remaining two C-H-I units; press seams toward C. Sew these units to the remaining sides of the pieced center, again referring to Figure 9; press seams toward G strips.

Step 11. Sew J to opposite sides and K to the top and bottom of the pieced unit to complete one block as shown in Figure 10; press seams toward J and K. Repeat for 20 blocks, five of each fabric combination.

Figure 10

Completing the Top

Step 1. Arrange the blocks in five rows of four blocks each with one of each combination in each row, placing blocks of different fabrics in a pleasing arrangement. Join the blocks with five L strips to make a row; press seams toward L. Repeat for five rows.

Step 2. Join the rows with six M strips, beginning and ending with a strip; press seams toward M.

Step 3. Sew an N strip to opposite long sides and O strips to the top and bottom of the pieced center; press seams toward N and O.

Step 4. Sew a P strip to opposite long sides and Q strips to the top and bottom of the pieced center; press seams toward P and Q.

Step 5. Sew an R strip to opposite long sides and S strips to the top and bottom of the pieced center; press seams toward R and S to complete the top.

Finishing the Quilt

Step 1. Sandwich batting between the completed top and prepared backing; pin or baste to hold layers together.

Step 2. Quilt as desired by hand or machine; remove basting or pins.

Step 3. When quilting is complete, trim batting and backing even with quilt top.

Step 4. Join the binding strips on short ends to make one long strip. Fold the strip in half along length with wrong sides together; press.

Step 5. Sew binding to quilt edges, mitering corners and overlapping ends. Fold binding to the back side and stitch in place. ✦

Holly, Wood & Vine
Placement Diagram
90" x 106"

OH, CHRISTMAS TREE

Use lots of scraps to make this pretty pieced tree design.

DESIGN BY JULIE WEAVER

Project Specifications
Skill Level: Beginner
Quilt Size: 32" x 44"

Materials
- ⅛ yard total gold tonal scraps
- ⅛ yard total brown tonal scraps
- ¼ yard white tonal for borders
- ¾ yard red mottled for borders and binding
- ¾ yard total green tonal scraps
- 1 yard total white/cream tonal scraps
- Backing 38" x 50"
- Batting 38" x 50"
- All-purpose thread to match fabrics
- Quilting thread
- Basic sewing tools and supplies

Cutting
Step 1. Cut (124) 2⅞" x 2⅞" A squares white/cream tonal scraps; draw a line from corner to corner on the wrong side of 69 squares.
Step 2. Cut four 2⅞" x 2⅞" B squares brown tonal scraps; draw a line from corner to corner on the wrong side of two squares.
Step 3. Cut (96) 2⅞" x 2⅞" C squares green tonal scraps; draw a line from corner to corner on the wrong side of 42 squares.
Step 4. Cut eight 2⅞" x 2⅞" D squares gold tonal scraps; draw a line from corner to corner on the

wrong side of three squares.
Step 5. Cut two 1½" x 24½" F strips and four 1½" x 36½" H strips white tonal.
Step 6. Cut four 2" x 24½" E strips and two 2" x 36½" G strips red mottled.
Step 7. Cut four 2¼" by fabric width strips red mottled for binding.

Piecing the Units
Step 1. To piece an A-A unit, referring to Figure 1, place a marked A right sides together with an unmarked A; stitch ¼" on each side of the marked line. Cut apart on the marked line; press seam to one side on each unit. Repeat 55 times to make 110 A-A units.

Figure 1

Step 2. Referring to Figure 2, repeat Step 1 with four D squares to make four D-D units, three each D and A squares to make six A-D units, one each D and C squares to make two C-D units, four B squares to make four B-B units, 11 each C and A squares to make 22 A-C units and 84 C squares to make 84 C-C units.

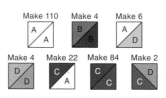

Figure 2

Completing the Top
Step 1. Arrange and join the pieced units in rows referring to Figure 3, and number row sequence; press seams in adjacent rows in opposite directions.

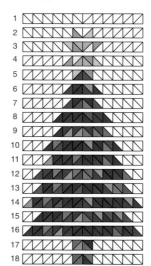

Figure 3

Step 2. Join the rows in numbered sequence; press seams in one direction.
Step 3. Sew an H strip between two G strips; repeat for two G-H-G strips. Press seams toward G. Repeat with F between two E strips to make two E-F-E strips.

Step 4. Sew G-H-G strips to opposite long sides of the pieced center; press seams toward strips.

Step 5. Join four C-C units to make a corner unit as shown in Figure 4; press seams in one direction.

Figure 4

Step 6. Sew a C corner unit to the ends of an E-F-E strip; press seams toward E-F-E. Repeat for two strips.

Step 7. Sew a strip to the top and bottom of the pieced center; press seams toward strips.

Finishing the Quilt

Step 1. Sandwich batting between the completed top and prepared backing; pin or baste to hold layers together.

Step 2. Quilt as desired by hand or machine; remove pins or basting.

Step 3. When quilting is complete, trim batting and backing even with quilt top.

Step 4. Join the binding strips on short ends to make one long strip. Fold the strip in half along length with wrong sides together; press.

Step 5. Sew binding to quilt edges, mitering corners and overlapping ends. Fold binding to the back side and stitch in place. ◆

Oh, Christmas Tree
Placement Diagram
32" x 44"

CHRISTMAS PUZZLE

Color placement creates the look of an interlocking design in this pretty holiday quilt.

DESIGN BY KARLA SCHULZ

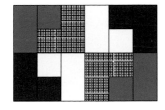

Christmas Puzzle
12" x 8" Block

Project Specifications
Skill Level: Beginner
Quilt Size: 78" x 98"
Block Size: 12" x 8"
Number of Blocks: 50

Materials
- 1⅝ yards dark red tonal
- 2⅛ yards dark green tonal
- 2½ yards cream tonal
- 4¼ yards holiday check
- Backing 84" x 104"
- Batting 84" x 104"
- All-purpose thread to match fabrics
- Quilting thread
- Basic sewing tools and supplies

Cutting
Step 1. Cut seven 4½" by fabric width strips each holiday check (A), dark red tonal (B), cream tonal (C) and dark green tonal (D); subcut strips into (100) 2½" rectangles each A, B, C and D.
Step 2. Cut seven 2½" by fabric width strips each holiday check (E), dark red tonal (F), cream tonal (G) and dark green tonal (H).
Step 3. Cut eight 3½" by fabric width strips cream tonal; join strips on short ends to make one long

strip. Subcut strip into two 60½" I strips and two 86½" J strips.
Step 4. Cut two 6½" x 66½" K strips and two 6½" x 98½" L strips along the length of the holiday check.
Step 5. Cut nine 2¼" by fabric width strips dark green tonal for binding.

Completing the Blocks
Step 1. Sew an H strip to an E strip with right sides together along length; press seams toward H. Repeat for seven strip sets. Subcut strip sets into (100) 2½" E-H units as shown in Figure 1. Repeat with F and G strips to make 100 F-G units, again referring to Figure 1.

Figure 1

Step 2. Sew A to one side and D to the opposite side of an E-H unit as shown in Figure 2; repeat for 100 units. Press seams toward E-H.

Figure 2

Step 3. Sew B to one side and C to the opposite side of an F-G unit as shown in Figure 3; repeat for 100 units. Press seams toward B and C.

Figure 3

Step 4. Join one B-F-G-C unit with one D-E-H-A unit as shown in Figure 4; press seams toward A. Repeat for 100 units.

Figure 4

Step 5. Join two pieced units to complete one block as shown in Figure 5; repeat for 50 blocks. Press seams in one direction.

Figure 5

Completing the Top
Step 1. Join five blocks on the short ends to make a row as shown in Figure 6; repeat for 10 rows. Press seams in one direction.

Figure 6

Step 2. Join rows with seams of adjacent rows pressed in opposite directions; press seams in one direction.

Step 3. Sew an I strip to the top and bottom and J strips to opposite sides of the pieced center; press seams toward I and J.

Step 4. Sew a K strip to the top and bottom and L strips to opposite sides of the pieced center; press seams toward K and L.

Finishing the Quilt

Step 1. Sandwich batting between the completed top and prepared backing; pin or baste to hold layers together.

Step 2. Quilt as desired by hand or machine; remove pins or basting.

Step 3. When quilting is complete, trim batting and backing even with quilt top.

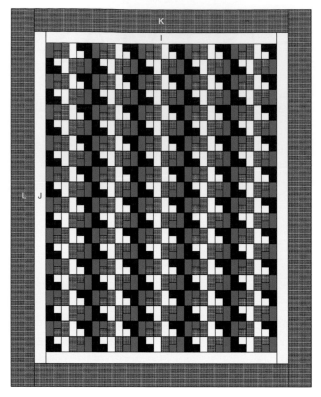

Christmas Puzzle
Placement Diagram
78" x 98"

Step 4. Join the binding strips on short ends to make one long strip. Fold the strip in half along length with wrong sides together; press.

Step 5. Sew binding to quilt edges, mitering corners and overlapping ends. Fold binding to the back side and stitch in place. ✦

CHRISTMAS WREATHS

Use a pieced wreath-design block to create a quilt for the holidays or any time of the year.

Christmas Wreath
20" x 20" Block

DESIGN BY KARLA SCHULZ

Project Specifications
Skill Level: Intermediate
Quilt Size: 86" x 106"
Block Size: 20" x 20"
Number of Blocks: 12

Materials
- 1½ yards red tonal
- 1¾ yards coordinating stripe
- 2⅝ yards cream print
- 3⅜ yards medium green print
- 3⅜ yards dark green print
- Backing 92" x 112"
- Batting 92" x 112"
- Neutral color all-purpose thread
- Quilting thread
- Basic sewing tools and supplies.

Cutting
Step 1. Cut six 4½" by fabric width strips medium green print; subcut strips into (48) 4½" A squares.
Step 2. Cut three 4⅞" by fabric width strips medium green print; subcut strips into (24) 4⅞" squares. Cut each square in half on one diagonal to make 48 C triangles.
Step 3. Cut four 2⅞" by fabric

width strips medium green print; subcut strips into (48) 2⅞" squares. Cut each square in half on one diagonal to make 96 D triangles.
Step 4. Cut (18) 2½" by fabric width strips medium green print; subcut strips into (288) 2½" E squares. Mark a line from corner to corner on the wrong side of each square.
Step 5. Cut three 5¼" by fabric width strips each red tonal (H) and medium green print (I); subcut strips into (24) 5¼" squares each fabric. Cut each square on both diagonals to make 96 each H and I triangles.
Step 6. Cut five 3¾" by fabric width strips red tonal; subcut strips into (48) 3¾" squares. Cut each square in half on one diagonal to make (96) B triangles.
Step 7. Cut two 4½" by fabric width strips red tonal; subcut strips into (12) 4½" K squares.
Step 8. Cut six 6½" by fabric width strips cream print; subcut strips into (96) 2½" F rectangles.

Step 9. Cut six 4½" by fabric width strips cream print; subcut strips into (96) 2½" J rectangles.
Step 10. Cut three 2½" by fabric width strips dark green print; subcut strips into (48) 2½" G squares.
Step 11. Cut eight 2½" by fabric width strips cream print. Join strips on short ends to make one long strip; press seams open. Subcut strips into two 60½" L strips and two 84½" M strips.
Step 12. Cut eight 3½" by fabric width strips coordinating stripe. Join strips on short ends to make one long strip; press seams open. Subcut strips into two 64½" N strips and two 90½" O strips.
Step 13. Cut two 8½" x 106½" P strips and two 8½" x 70½" Q strips along the length of the dark green print.
Step 14. Cut (10) 2¾" by fabric width strips coordinating stripe for binding.

Completing the Blocks
Step 1. To piece one block, sew B to

two adjacent sides of A as shown in Figure 1; press seams toward B. Repeat for four A-B units.

Figure 1

Step 2. Add C to the A-B units; press seams toward C. Add D to the B sides as shown in Figure 2; press seams toward D.

Figure 2

Step 3. Referring to Figure 3, place E on one corner of F; stitch on the marked line. Trim seam to ¼"; press E to the right side to complete an E-F unit. Repeat for

four E-F and four E-F reversed units, again referring to Figure 3.

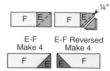

E-F   E-F Reversed
Make 4   Make 4

Figure 3

Step 4. Sew G to the F end of each E-F reversed unit as shown in Figure 4; press seams toward G.

Figure 4

Step 5. Sew an E-F and E-F-G unit to an A-B-C-D unit to complete a corner unit as shown in Figure 5; repeat for four corner units. Press seams toward E-F units.

Figure 5

Step 6. Sew H to I on the short sides; press seams toward H. Repeat for eight units.

Step 7. Join two H-I units as shown in Figure 6; repeat for four units. Press seams in one direction.

Figure 6

Step 8. Referring to Figure 7, place an E square on one end of J; stitch on the marked line. Trim seam to ¼" and press E to the right side. Repeat with a second E on the opposite end of J to complete an E-J unit, again referring to Figure 7. Repeat for eight E-J units.

Figure 7

Step 9. Sew an E-J unit to opposite sides of an H-I unit to complete a side unit as shown in Figure 8; repeat for four side units. Press seams toward I I-I units.

Figure 8

Step 10. Sew a side unit to opposite sides of K to make the center row; press seams toward K.

Step 11. Sew a side unit between two corner units to make a row; repeat for two rows. Press seams toward corner units.

Step 12. Sew a row to the top and bottom of the center row to complete one block as shown in Figure 9; press seams toward center row. Repeat for 12 blocks.

Figure 9

Completing the Top

Step 1. Join three blocks to make a row; press seams in one direction. Repeat for four rows.

Step 2. Join the rows to complete the pieced center; press seams in one direction.

Step 3. Sew an L strip to the top and bottom and M strips to opposite sides of the pieced center; press seams toward L and M.

Step 4. Sew an N strip to the top and bottom and O strips to opposite sides of the pieced center; press seams toward N and O.

Step 5. Sew a Q strip to the top and bottom and P strips to opposite sides of the pieced center; press seams toward Q and P.

Step 6. Finish quilt referring to the General Instructions, stitching binding to the back of the quilt and turning to the front to make a wider binding on the front side. ✦

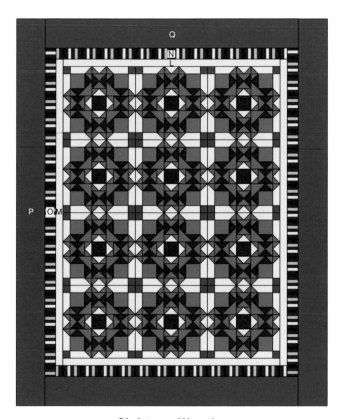

Christmas Wreaths
Placement Diagram
86" x 106"

TIC-TAC-TOE

Add triangles to the corners of strippy squares and then add sashing for results that look like a Tic-Tac-Toe game.

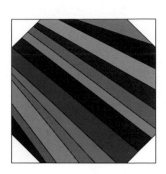

Strippy Scrap
10" x 10" Block

DESIGN BY JULIE WEAVER

Project Specifications
Skill Level: Beginner
Quilt Size: 64" x 78"
Block Size: 10" x 10"
Number of Blocks: 20

Materials
- 20 (11" x 11") squares paper or muslin for foundations
- Scraps of a variety of medium-to-dark flannel for blocks
- 1⅜ yards rust mottled flannel
- 2¼ yards total assorted cream flannel scraps
- 2¼ yards rust tonal flannel
- Backing 70" x 84"
- Batting 70" x 84"
- Neutral color all-purpose thread
- Quilting thread
- Basic sewing tools and supplies

Cutting
Step 1. Cut medium-to-dark flannel scraps that vary from 1"–2" wide and up to 16½" long.
Step 2. Cut (356) 2½" x 2½" B squares and (30) 4½" x 4½" C squares from assorted cream flannel scraps.

Step 3. Cut (17) 4½" by fabric width strips rust tonal; subcut strips into (49) 10½" D rectangles.
Step 4. Cut (10) 2½" by fabric width strips rust mottled; subcut strips into (22) 4½" E rectangles and (18) 10½" F rectangles.
Step 5. Cut two 2⅞" x 2⅞" G squares each rust mottled and cream scraps; cut each square in half to make G triangles.
Step 6. Cut eight 2¼" by fabric width strips rust mottled for binding.

Piecing Blocks
Step 1. Place a long 1"–2" strip right side up on the diagonal on a foundation square as shown in Figure 1. Select a second strip and place right sides together on the first strip as shown in Figure 2; do not line up raw edges. Sew in place; trim strip 1 seam allowance away from behind strip 2 to reduce bulk. Press strip 2 to the right side. ***Note:** Sewing the strips in a slightly off manner adds to the interest of the block and gives the quilt a strippy look.*

Figure 1

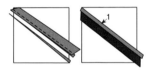

Figure 2

Step 2. Select another strip and sew to the opposite side of strip 1 as for strip 2. Trim and press.
Step 3. Continue adding strips until the entire foundation is covered as shown in Figure 3.

Figure 3

Step 4. Trim square to 10½" x 10½" for A; repeat for 20 A squares.
Step 5. If using paper foundations, remove paper at this time.
Step 6. Draw a line from corner to corner on the wrong side of each B square.

Step 7. Pin and stitch a B square to each corner of A, sewing on the marked line as shown in Figure 4; trim seam to ¼" and press B to the right side to complete one Strippy Scrap block. Repeat for 20 blocks.

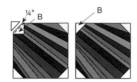

Figure 4

Completing the Top

Step 1. Sew a B square to each corner of D as in Step 7 of Piecing Blocks to complete a B-D unit as shown in Figure 5; repeat for 49 units.

Figure 5

Step 2. Sew a B square to two corners of each E and F rectangle to make B-E and B-F units as shown in Figure 6.

Figure 6

Step 3. Join four blocks with two B-F and five B-D units to make a block row as shown in Figure 7; repeat for five block rows. Press seams toward B-D units.

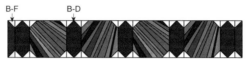

Figure 7

Step 4. Join two B-E units with four B-D units and five C squares to make a sashing row referring to Figure 8; repeat to make six sashing rows. Press seams toward C.

Figure 8

Step 5. Sew a cream G to a rust mottled G to make a G unit as shown in Figure 9; repeat for four G units.

Figure 9

Step 6. Join two G units with five B-E units and four B-F units to make a top row as shown in Figure 10; repeat for bottom row. Press seams away from B-E units.

Figure 10

Step 7. Arrange top and bottom rows with block and sashing rows referring to the Placement

Diagram for positioning of rows; join to complete the pieced top. Press seams toward sashing rows.

Finishing the Quilt
Step 1. Sandwich the batting between the completed top and prepared backing piece; pin or baste to hold.
Step 2. Hand- or machine-quilt as desired.
Step 3. Trim batting and backing even with the quilted top.
Step 4. Join the binding strips on short ends with a diagonal seam to make a long strip; press seams toward one side.
Step 5. Press the strip in half along length with wrong sides together to complete the binding strip. Bind edges of quilt to finish. ✦

Tic-Tac-Toe
Placement Diagram
64" x 78"

CHECKERBOARD FOUR-PATCH

Red and green metallic prints add a richness to this Christmas quilt.

DESIGN BY SANDRA L. HATCH

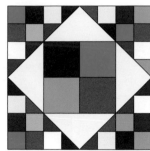

Checkerboard Four-Patch
16" x 16" Block

Project Specifications
Skill Level: Beginner
Quilt Size: 88" x 104"
Block Sizes: 16" x 16"
Number of Blocks: 20

Materials
- 10 fat quarters cream and off-white prints and tone-on-tones
- 12 fat quarters red-with-metallic prints
- 13 fat quarters green-with-metallic prints
- ¾ yard cream print for borders
- ¾ yard red print for borders
- 2¾ yards red-and-green metallic directional print or 1⅜ yards non-directional print for outside border strips
- Batting 94" x 110"
- Backing 94" x 110"
- 11 yards self-made or purchased binding
- All-purpose thread to match fabrics
- Gold machine-quilting thread
- Basic sewing tools and supplies, rotary cutter, mat and ruler

Instructions

Note: The instructions will refer to fabrics by color, not by listed name in the Materials list.

Step 1. Cut two 4½" x 96½" strips red-and-green metallic border print along length of fabric.

Note: The print used on the quilt is a one-way design, requiring the strips be cut along the length of the fabric. If your fabric is not a directional print, strips may be cut across the width of the fabric and pieced for the sides. Cut and piece two 4½" x 88½" strips red-and-green metallic border print. Set aside border strips. Remainder of border fabric may be used in piecing blocks.

Step 2. Cut (10) 4½" x 22" strips each red and green fat quarters.

Note: Cut one strip each from 10 different red and green fat quarters.

Step 3. Sew a green strip to a red strip with right sides together along length; press seams toward green print strips. Subcut strip sets into 4½" segments as shown in Figure 1; you will need 40 segments.

4½"

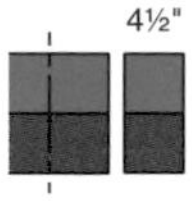

Figure 1

Step 4. Join two segments as shown in Figure 2 to make a Four-Patch unit; repeat for 20 Four-Patch units. Press seams in one direction.

Figure 2

Step 5. Cut 40 squares off-white or cream fat quarters 6⅝" x 6⅝". Cut each square in half on one diagonal to make A triangles. You will need 80 A triangles.

Step 6. Sew four same-fabric A triangles to each Four-Patch unit as shown in Figure 3; press seams toward A.

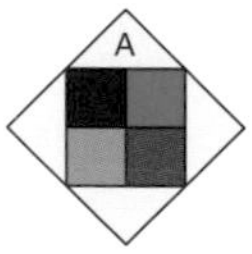

Figure 3

Step 7. Cut 21 strips 2½" x 22" each green and red fat quarters. Sew a green strip to a red strip with right sides together along length; press seams toward green print strips. Repeat for 21 strip sets.

Step 8. Subcut strip sets into 2½" segments as shown in Figure 4; you will need 168 segments.

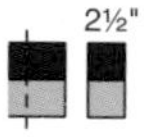

2½"

Figure 4

Step 9. Join two segments to make a Four-Patch unit as shown in Figure 5; press seams in one direction. You will need 84 Four-Patch units; set aside 80 for blocks and four for borders.

Figure 5

Step 10. Cut 20 strips 2½" x 22" off-white or cream fat quarters; subcut strips into 2½" squares for B. You will need 160 B squares.

Step 11. Cut 23 strips red fat quarters 2⅞" x 22"; subcut strips into 2⅞" square segments. Cut each square in half on one diagonal to make C triangles. You will need 320 C triangles.

Step 12. Sew two C triangles to adjacent sides of B as shown in Figure 6; repeat for 160 B-C units.

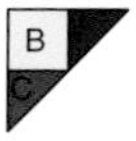

B
C

Figure 6

Step 13. Sew a B-C unit to two adjacent sides of a Four-Patch unit as shown in Figure 7; repeat for 80 units.

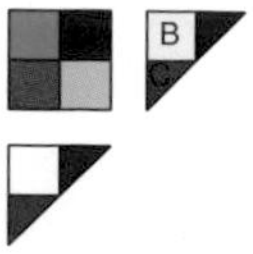

B
C

Figure 7

Step 14. Sew a B-C/Four-Patch unit to each side of an A unit to complete one block as shown in Figure 8; repeat for 20 blocks.

A

Figure 8

Step 15. Join four blocks to make a row; repeat for five rows. Press seams in one direction. Join the rows to complete the pieced center; press seams in one direction.

Step 16. Cut and piece two strips each cream and red print border fabrics 2½" x 64½" and 2½" x 80½". Sew a 64½" cream print strip to a 64½" red print strip with right sides together along length; press seam toward red print strip. Repeat for two strips. Sew these strips to the top and bottom of the pieced center; press seams toward strips.

Step 17. Sew an 80½" cream print strip to an 80½" red print strip with right sides together along length; press seam toward

red print strip. Repeat for two strips. Sew a Four-Patch unit set aside in Step 9 to each end of each strip; sew these strips to opposite long sides of the pieced center. Press seams toward strips.

Step 18. Cut 20 strips 4½" x 22" green fat quarters; subcut into 4½" square segments for D. You will need 80 D squares. Join 22 D squares to make a side strip; repeat for two side strips. Press seams in one direction. Sew a strip to opposite long sides of the pieced center; press seams toward strips.

Step 19. Cut four squares 4½" x 4½" from red fat quarters. Join 18 green squares to make a strip; add a red square to each end to make the top strip. Repeat for bottom strip. Press seams in one direction; sew a strip to the top and bottom of the pieced center; press seams toward strips.

Step 20. Sew the 96½" strips cut in Step 1 to opposite long sides and the 88½" strips to the top and bottom of the pieced center; press seams toward strips.

Step 21. Prepare for quilting and quilt as desired referring to the General Instructions. **_Note:_** _The quilt shown was professionally machine-quilted in a meandering pattern using gold machine-quilting thread._

Step 22. Apply self-made or purchased binding referring to the General Instructions to finish. ◆

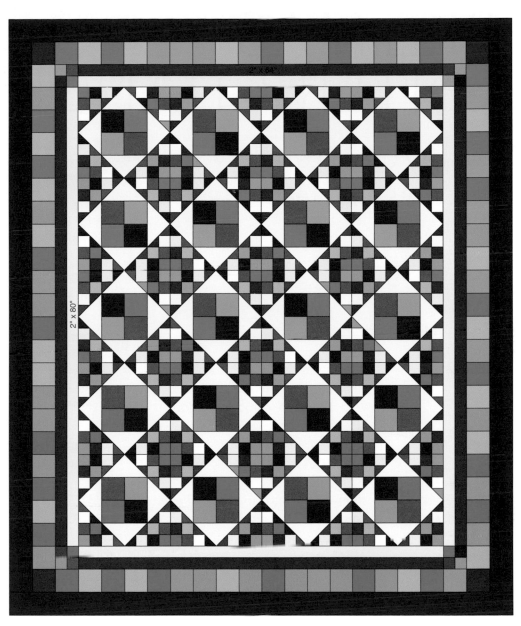

Checkerboard Four-Patch
Placement Diagram
88" x 104"

CHRISTMAS COUNTER-CHANGE

Select a variety of scraps in Christmas colors and cream to make this very simple Four-Patch design.

DESIGN BY JODI G. WARNER

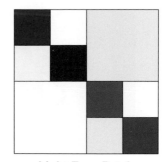

Light Four-Patch
5" x 5" Block

Dark Four-Patch
5" x 5" Block

Project Specifications
Skill Level: Beginner
Quilt Size: 59" x 69"
Block Size: 5" x 5"
Number of Blocks: 99

Materials
- 7" x 15" scraps 25 different red/burgundy, green and cream fabrics
- ¼ yard green tonal
- ⅜ yard cream print
- 1½ yards burgundy print
- Backing 65" x 75"
- Batting 65" x 75"
- Neutral color all-purpose thread
- Quilting thread
- Basic sewing tools and supplies

Cutting
Step 1. From each red/burgundy and green scrap, cut two 3" x 3" A squares and one 1¾" x 14" B strip.
Step 2. From each cream scrap, cut four 3" x 3" C squares and two 1¾" x 14" D strips.
Step 3. Cut five 1¾" by fabric width strips cream print. Join strips on short ends to make one long strip; press seams to one side. Subcut strip into two 55½" F strips and two 48" G strips.
Step 4. Cut six 1¼" by fabric width strips green tonal. Join strips on short ends to make one long strip; press seams to one side. Subcut strip into two 58" H strips and two 49½" I strips.
Step 5. Cut six 5½" by fabric width strips burgundy print. Join strips on short ends to make one long strip; press seams to one side. Subcut strip into four 59½" J strips.
Step 6. Cut seven 2¼" by fabric width burgundy print for binding.

Piecing Blocks
Step 1. Sew a D strip to a B strip to make a strip set; press seams toward B. Subcut strip set into eight 1¾" B-D segments as shown in Figure 1. Repeat with all B and D strips.
Step 2. To make Dark Four-Patch

blocks, sew a green/cream B-D segment to a red/cream B-D segment as shown in Figure 2; repeat for 100 units.

Figure 1

Figure 2

Step 3. Sew a red/burgundy A to a B-D unit as shown in Figure 3; repeat for 50 units. Repeat with

a green A and a B-D unit, again referring to Figure 3 to make 50 units. Press seams toward A.

Figure 3

Step 4. Join one unit of each color combination to complete one Dark Four-Patch block referring to Figure 4; repeat for 50 blocks. Press seams in one direction.

Figure 4

Step 5. To make Light Four-Patch blocks, join two red/cream B-D segments as shown in Figure 5; repeat for 49 units. Join two green/cream B-D segments, again referring to Figure 5; repeat for 49 units.

Figure 5

Step 6. Sew a C square to each B-D unit as shown in Figure 6; press seams toward C. Join the units to complete one Light Four-Patch block as shown in Figure 7; repeat for 49 blocks.

Figure 6

Figure 7

Completing the Top
Step 1. Join four Light Four-Patch blocks and five Dark Four-Patch blocks to make a row referring to Figure 8; press seams toward Dark Four-Patch blocks. Repeat for six rows.
Step 2. Join four Dark Four-Patch blocks and five Light Four-Patch blocks to make a row, again referring to Figure 8; press seams toward Dark Four-Patch blocks. Repeat for five rows.

Step 3. Join the rows referring to the Placement Diagram to complete the pieced top; press seams in one direction.
Step 4. Sew an F strip to opposite sides and a G strip to the top and bottom of the pieced center; press seams toward strips.
Step 5. Sew an H strip to opposite sides and an I strip to the top and bottom of the pieced center; press seams toward H and I strips.

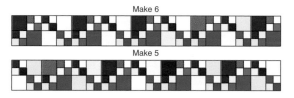

Figure 8

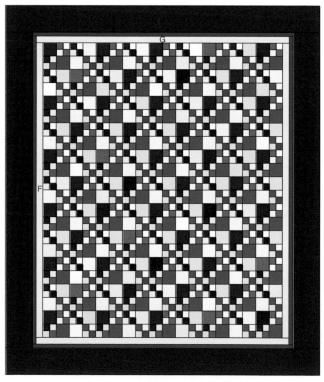

Christmas Counter-Change
Placement Diagram
59" x 69"

Step 6. Sew a J strip to opposite sides and to the top and bottom of the pieced center; press seams toward J strips.

Finishing the Quilt

Step 1. Sandwich the batting between the completed top and prepared backing piece; pin or baste to hold.

Step 2. Hand- or machine-quilt as desired. ***Note:*** *The quilting design given was machine-quilted in the J border strips on the sample quilt.*

Step 3. Trim batting and backing even with the quilted top.

Step 4. Join the binding strips on short ends with a diagonal seam to make a long strip; press seams toward one side.

Step 5. Press the strip in half along length with wrong sides together to complete the binding strip. Bind edges of quilt to finish. ✦

Border Quilting Design

HAVE A HAPPY SCRAPPY CHRISTMAS

This quilt has all the right features—fast, easy, scrappy and Christmas bright!

DESIGN BY LUCY A. FAZELY

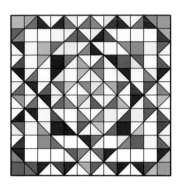

Happy Scrappy Christmas
36" x 36" Block

Project Specifications
Skill Level: Beginner
Quilt Size: 80" x 80"
Block Size: 36" x 36"
Number of Blocks: 4

Materials
- Green print scraps totaling 2 yards
- Red print scraps totaling 2½ yards
- White-on-white print scraps totaling 4½ yards
- 2¼ yards green print for borders (1⅛ yards if pieced)
- 30" x 30" square of green print binding fabric
- Backing 86" x 86"
- Batting 86" x 86"
- Rotary-cutting tools
- All-purpose thread to blend with fabrics
- 1 spool white quilting thread
- Basic sewing tools and supplies

Instructions
Step 1. Cut the following number of 3½" x 3½" squares: 208 green print, 272 red print and 496 white-on-white print.

Step 2. Draw a diagonal line on the reverse side of 368 white-on-white squares.

Step 3. Place a white-on-white square on a red print square, right sides together. Stitch on marked line. Press and trim seam to ¼". Repeat to make 224 red and white half-square triangles as shown in Figure 1.

Figure 1

Step 4. Repeat Step 3 using green print squares to make 144 green and white half-square triangles as shown in Figure 2.

Figure 2

Step 5. Draw a diagonal line on the reverse side of 32 red print squares. Right sides together, place a red square on a green square and stitch as in Step 3. Repeat for 32 red and green half-square triangles as shown in Figure 3.

Figure 3

Step 6. Arrange squares as shown in Figure 4. Sew squares into rows; then sew rows together. Repeat for 16 sections.

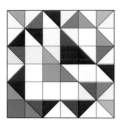

Figure 4

Step 7. Sew four sections together to make a block as shown in the Block Diagram. Sew four blocks together as shown in the Placement Diagram.

Step 8. From green print border fabric, make two border strips each 4½" x 72½" and 4½" x 80½", piecing as necessary. Sew the shorter strips to the top and bottom of the quilt and the longer strips to the sides.

Step 9. Prepare for quilting, referring to the General Instructions. Quilt as desired by hand or machine.

Step 10. Make 9¼ yards of 2½"-wide continuous bias binding, referring to the General Instructions. Bind quilt to finish. ✦

Have a Happy Scrappy Christmas
Placement Diagram
80" x 80"

CHRISTMAS LOG CABIN

The secondary patterns formed in this Log Cabin layout create a wonderful visual experience.

DESIGN BY RUTH M. SWASEY

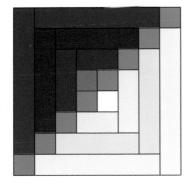

Christmas Log Cabin
12" x 12"

Project Specifications

Skill Level: Beginner
Quilt Size: 87" x 99"
Block Size: 12" x 12"
Number of Blocks: 42

Materials

- 2½ yards small red print for inner border and binding
- 2⅝ yards red-and-green print for outer border (1 yard if pieced)
- 1¼ yards dark green Christmas print for pieced border and secondary green pattern in blocks
- Variety of light background Christmas prints for logs totaling 3 yards
- Variety of red background Christmas prints for logs totaling 3 yards
- Backing 93" x 105"
- Batting 93" x 105"
- Rotary-cutting tools
- All-purpose thread to blend with fabrics
- 2 spools red quilting thread
- Basic sewing tools and supplies

Instructions

Step 1. From the dark green fabric for secondary pattern, cut eight squares 2" x 2". From red background scraps and light background scraps, cut one each 2" x 2", 2" x 3½", 2" x 5", 2" x 6½", 2" x 8", 2" x 9½" and 2" x 11".

Step 2. Sew four 2" x 2" squares together to make a Four-Patch square as shown in Figure 1. Sew one dark green 2" x 2" square to one end of each red strip. Sew one 2" x 3½" white background strip to top of Four-Patch square. Continue adding strips in a counterclockwise direction as shown in Figure 2. Repeat for 42 blocks.

Figure 1

Step 3. Referring to the Placement Diagram, carefully lay out rows as shown to create secondary patterns. Sew blocks together in rows and sew rows together.

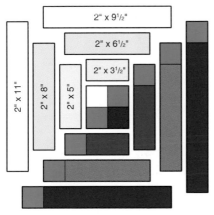

Figure 2

Step 4. From small red print, cut two border strips each 3½" x 78½" and 3½" x 84½". Sew the longer strips to the sides of the quilt and the shorter strips to the top and bottom.

Step 5. From dark green secondary pattern fabric and light background scraps, cut 114 squares each 2" x 2". Sew two strips of 60 squares each and two strips of 54 squares each, alternating green and light, for borders. Sew the longer strips to the sides of the quilt and the shorter strips to the top and bottom.

Step 6. From red-and-green outer border print, cut two strips each 3½" x 87½" and 3½" x 93½" (piecing if necessary). Sew the longer strips to the sides of the quilt and the shorter strips to the top and bottom.

Step 7. Prepare for quilting, referring to the General Instructions. Quilt as desired by hand or machine.

Step 8. Prepare 11 yards of 2½"-wide bias binding, referring to the General Instructions. Bind to finish. ✦

Christmas Log Cabin
Placement Diagram
87" x 99"

POSY PATCH

Frayed edges form the petals in this garden of pastel posies.

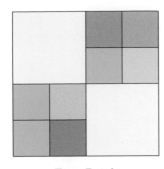

Four-Patch
8" x 8" Block

DESIGN BY SUE HARVEY

Project Specifications
Skill Level: Beginner
Quilt Size: 56" x 72"
Block Size: 8" x 8"
Number of Blocks: 18

Materials
- 17 pastel 1930s print fat quarters
- 3½ yards yellow print
- Batting 62" x 78"
- Backing 62" x 78"
- All-purpose thread to match fabrics
- Pastel-variegated machine-quilting thread
- 1 skein 6-strand yellow embroidery floss
- Basting spray
- Basic sewing tools and supplies, rotary cutter, mat and ruler, yo-yo template and embroidery needle

Instructions
Step 1. Cut four strips 8½" by fabric width yellow print; subcut into 17 squares 8½" x 8½" for flower background squares.
Step 2. Cut two strips each 2½" x 44½", 2½" x 56½", 4½" x 56½" and 4½" x 64½" along remaining length of the yellow print; set aside for borders.

Step 3. Cut 36 squares 4½" x 4½" yellow print for A.
Step 4. From each pastel print fat quarter, cut two strips 2½" x 22" and one strip 2¼" x 22"; set aside the 2¼" strips for binding.
Step 5. Join two randomly selected 2½" strips along length to make a strip set; repeat to make 17 strip sets. Cut each strip set into 2½" segments as shown in Figure 1.

Figure 1

Step 6. Join two segments to make a Four-Patch unit as shown in Figure 2; repeat for 36 Four-Patch units. Set aside remaining segments for the pieced border.

Figure 2

Step 7. Sew an A square to one side of each Four-Patch unit as shown in Figure 3.

Figure 3

Step 8. Join two pieced strips to complete one Four-Patch block as shown in Figure 4; repeat for 18 blocks.

Figure 4

Step 9. Trace one each 6½", 4½" and 2½" circles on one pastel print fat quarter using the purchased yo-yo template. **Note:** *If not using a purchased yo-yo template, make a template for each size circle.*
Step 10. Cut out the circles to form flower shapes as shown in Figure 5; repeat with all pastel print fat quarters.

Figure 5

Step 11. Lightly apply basting spray to the wrong side of a 6½" flower shape; center it on a flower background square and smooth in place. Repeat to center a 4½" flower shape and a 2½" flower shape on the larger flower shape

as shown in Figure 6, using a different print for each size.

Figure 6

Step 12. Repeat Step 11 to make 17 flower units.

Step 13. Using pastel-variegated machine-quilting thread in the top of the machine and all-purpose thread in the bobbin, topstitch ½" inside the edge of each flower shape as shown in Figure 7.

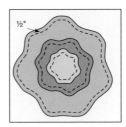

Figure 7

Step 14. Join two flower units with three Four-Patch blocks to make a row as shown in Figure 8; repeat for four rows.

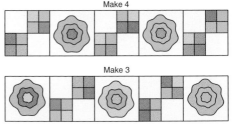

Make 4

Make 3

Figure 8

Step 15. Join three flower units with two Four-Patch blocks to

make a row, again referring to Figure 8; repeat for three rows.

Step 16. Join the rows to complete the pieced center referring to the Placement Diagram for positioning of rows.

Step 17. Sew the 2½" x 56½" yellow print border strips to opposite long sides of the pieced center and the 2½" x 44½" yellow print border strips to the top and bottom; press seams toward strips.

Step 18. Join 15 segments set aside in Step 6 to make a border strip as shown in Figure 9; repeat. Sew a strip to opposite long sides of the pieced center.

Step 19. Join 12 segments to make a border strip, again referring to Figure 9; repeat. Sew a strip to the top and bottom of the pieced center.

Figure 9

Step 20. Sew the 4½" x 64½" yellow print border strips to opposite long sides of the pieced center and the 4½" x 56½" strips to the top and bottom to complete the top; press seams toward strips.

Step 21. Prepare for quilting and quilt referring to the General Instructions. ***Note:*** *The sample shown was professionally machine-quilted.*

Step 22. Trim edges even. Join the 2¼" binding strips set aside in Step 4 on short

ends to make a long strip as shown in Figure 10. Press strip in half along length with wrong sides together; bind edges of quilt referring to the General Instructions.

Figure 10

Step 23. Cut a 2½" circle from each pastel print fat quarter. Hand- or machine-baste ½" inside the edge of each circle using pastel-variegated machine-quilting thread; pull thread to draw edge tightly to the center, knot thread and flatten to make a yo-yo, leaving the raw edge exposed at top of yo-yo as shown in Figure 11.

Figure 11

Step 24. Use a 6" length of 6-strand yellow embroidery floss to attach a yo-yo to the center of each flower, bringing the ends of the embroidery floss up through the center of the yo-yo and knotting tightly; trim ends ⅛"–¼" beyond yo-yo.

Step 25. Wash and dry quilt to fray edges of flowers. ◆

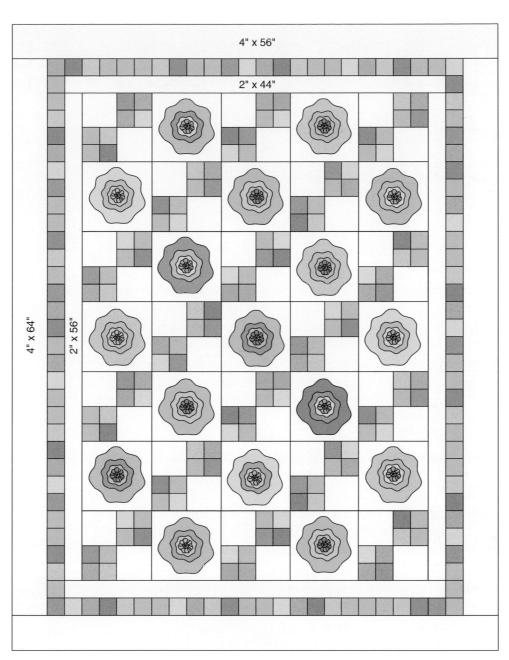

Posy Patch
Placement Diagram
56" x 72"

LOLLIPOP FLOWERS

Soft chenille flower heads make this a cuddly toddler-size quilt.

DESIGN BY SUE HARVEY

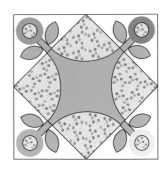

Lollipop Flowers
12" x 12" Block

Project Specifications
Skill Level: Intermediate
Quilt Size: 48" x 60"
   (including scallops)
Block Size: 12" x 12"
Number of Blocks: 12

Materials
- 2¼ yards floral print
- 1¼ yards each white print and green tone-on-tone
- Batting 54" x 66"
- Backing 54" x 66"
- White all-purpose thread
- White machine-quilting thread
- Light green rayon thread
- 1½ yards fusible web
- 4 yards tear-away fabric stabilizer
- 1 package each Blue Moon, Banana, Grape Soda and Raspberry Chenille By The Inch
- Chenille Brush
- Chenille Cutting Guide
- Spray bottle
- 6" x 6" square lightweight plastic
- Basic sewing tools and supplies

Project Note
Fabric stabilizer is used behind each block to machine-appliqué the curved pieces, stems and leaves and to stitch the chenille strips in place. I prefer to use a solid piece of stabilizer behind the block

rather than two or more pieces. To do this, (12) 12" x 12" squares of stabilizer, or 4 yards, are needed with approximately 10" leftover from the stabilizer width. This can be used for other projects. To use several smaller pieces of stabilizer behind each block, purchase only 2½ yards.

Making A-B Units
Step 1. Cut five strips 4¼" by fabric width floral print; subcut into 48 squares 4¼" x 4¼" for A.

Step 2. Cut three strips 9" by fabric width green tone-on-tone; subcut into 12 squares 9" x 9" for B.

Step 3. Prepare template for D; trace 48 D pieces on the paper side of the fusible web. Cut out each piece.

Step 4. Place a D piece on the wrong side of an A square, aligning edges of D with edges of A as shown in Figure 1; fuse in place.

Figure 1

Step 5. Trim the A square even with outer curved edge of D as shown in Figure 2; repeat with all A squares. Remove paper backing from D pieces.

Figure 2

Step 6. Place an A piece on one corner of B, aligning corner and edges of A with corner and edges of B as shown in Figure 3; fuse in place.

Figure 3

Step 7. Trim away the unfused green tone-on-tone section under the A piece as shown in Figure 4. Repeat on all corners of each B square to complete 12 A-B units.

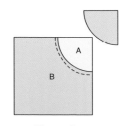

Figure 4

Making C Units

Step 1. Cut four strips 6⅞" by fabric width white print; subcut into 6⅞" square segments. Cut each square in half on one diagonal to make 48 C triangles.

Step 2. Cut one strip 3½" by fabric width floral print and three strips 3¼" x 18" fusible web. Apply fusible web to the wrong side of the floral print strip.

Step 3. Cut one strip 9" by fabric width green tone-on-tone and three strips 8½" x 18" fusible web. Apply fusible web to the wrong side of the green tone-on-tone strip.

Step 4. Cut one strip 2" by fabric width from the fused green tone-on-tone strip; subcut into ½" segments for stems. You will need 48 stems; remove paper backing.

Step 5. Prepare templates for the flower center and leaf pieces. Trace 48 flower center pieces on the paper side of the fused floral print strip; cut out each piece and remove paper backing.

Step 6. Trace 96 leaf pieces on the paper side of the fused green tone-on-tone strip; cut out each piece and remove paper backing.

Step 7. Arrange one stem, one flower center and two leaf pieces on each C triangle, centering the stem piece on the long side of the triangle as shown in Figure 5; fuse pieces in place.

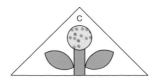

Figure 5

Completing the Blocks

Step 1. Center and sew a C unit to each side of an A-B unit as shown in Figure 6; press seams toward C. Repeat for 12 A-B-C units.

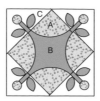

Figure 6

Step 2. Cut 12 squares 12" x 12" fabric stabilizer; pin one square on the wrong side of each unit.

Step 3. Using light green rayon thread in the top of the machine and white all-purpose thread in the bobbin, machine buttonhole-stitch along the curved A edges and the stem and leaf pieces. Do not stitch around the flower center pieces.

Step 4. Prepare 70" of each color of chenille strips, referring to manufacturer's instructions.

Step 5. Stitch a purple chenille strip around the edge of one flower center piece on an A-B-C unit, overlapping ends of strip about ¼"; trim strip.

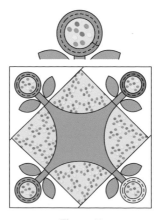

Figure 7

Step 6. Repeat with remaining colors on each of the remaining flower center pieces to complete one block as shown in Figure 7. Repeat with all A-B-C units to make 12 blocks, placing the chenille strips in the same color order on each block. Do not brush the chenille strips.

Completing the Top

Step 1. Join three blocks to make a row as shown in Figure 8; repeat for four rows. Press seams in two rows in one direction and in the remaining rows in the opposite direction.

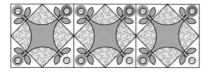

Figure 8

Step 2. Join rows to complete the pieced center, alternating pressed rows to offset seams; press seams in one direction.

Step 3. Cut (and piece) two strips each 1½" x 38½" and 1½" x 48½" white print. Sew the longer strips to opposite long sides and shorter strips to the top and bottom of the pieced center; press seams toward strips.

Step 4. Cut and piece two strips each 3½" x 44½" and 3½" x 50½" floral print. Sew the longer strips to opposite long sides and shorter strips to the top and bottom of the pieced center; press seams toward strips.

Step 5. In the center of the lightweight plastic square, mark a circle that is ⅛" inch larger in circumference than the flower center piece; cut out circle.

Step 6. Place opening of the plastic square over one flower circle with edges of plastic under chenille strip as shown in Figure 9; vigorously brush chenille strip. Spray lightly with water; brush until strip is fluffy. *Note: The plastic square protects the buttonhole stitches and surrounding fabric from the stiff bristles of the brush and prevents fuzz from coating the white print fabric around each flower.*

Figure 9

Finishing the Quilt

Step 1. Sandwich the batting between the completed top and prepared backing piece; pin or baste to hold layers together.

Step 2. Quilt as desired by hand or machine, stopping stitches 1" from the outer edge of the floral print border. ***Note:*** *The sample shown was professionally machine-quilted using white machine-quilting thread.*

Step 3. Trim batting and backing even with quilted top; remove pins or basting. Fold the backing edge down away from the quilt edge; pin or baste in place.

Step 4. Cut seven strips 4½" by fabric width floral print. Fold each strip in half across width with right sides together; subcut into 2½" segments. You will need 50 segment pairs.

Step 5. Prepare a template for E. Trace E on one side of each segment pair, aligning the straight edge of E with a long edge of the segment as shown in Figure 10.

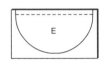

Figure 10

Step 6. Stitch each pair on the marked line; trim seam

allowance, turn right side out and press flat to complete scallop shapes.

Step 7. Pin 14 scallop shapes along one long side of the quilted top, beginning and ending ¼" from corners as shown in Figure 11; stitch in place through top and batting layers only. Repeat on the opposite side. Arrange and stitch 11 scallop shapes each on the top and bottom edges.

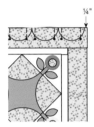

Figure 11

Step 8. Trim batting close to stitching line. Fold the scallop pieces out and the seam allowance to the back of the quilt; press lightly.

Step 9. Release the backing fabric; turn raw edge in ¼" and press. Pin in place around scallop edge. Hand- or machine-stitch in place.

Step 10. Hand- or machine-quilt ½" from edge of floral print border to finish. ◆

Lollipop Flowers
Placement Diagram
48" x 60"
(including scallops)

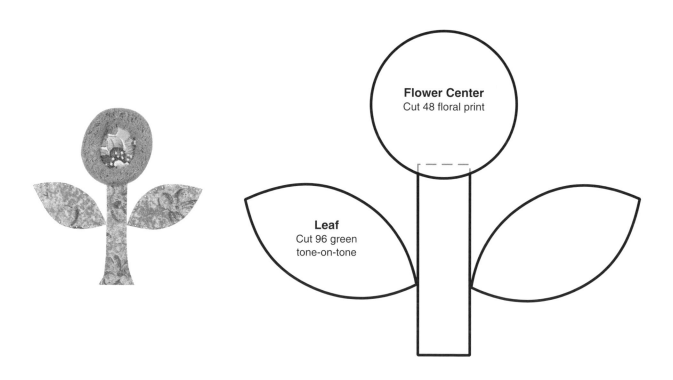

Flower Center
Cut 48 floral print

Leaf
Cut 96 green
tone-on-tone

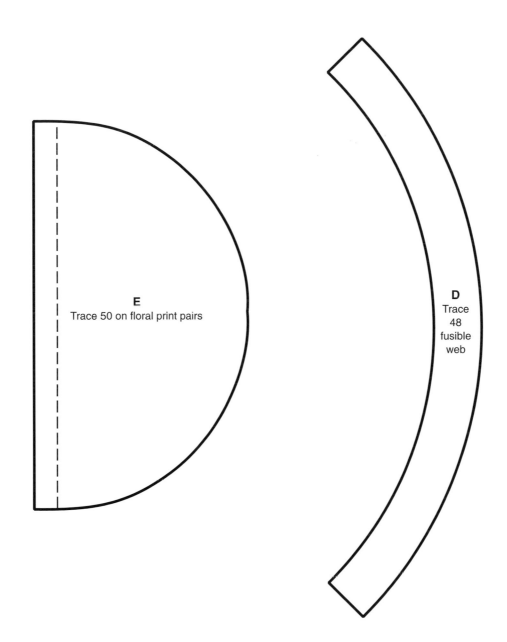

E
Trace 50 on floral print pairs

D
Trace
48
fusible
web

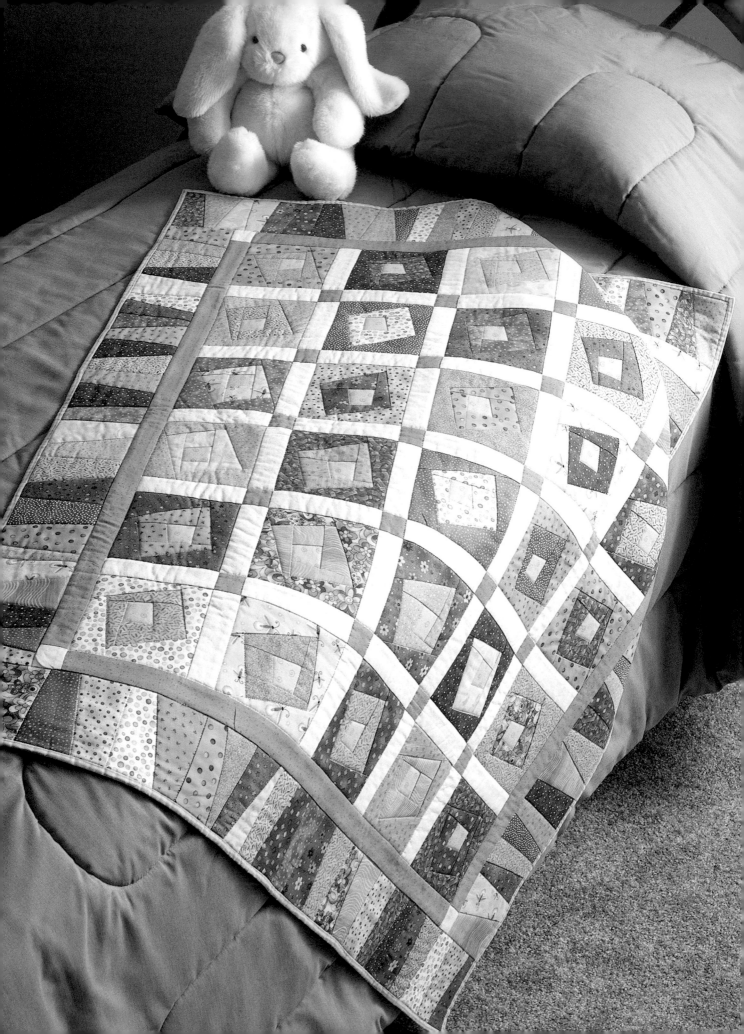

CRAZY LOGS KID'S QUILT

Off-center Log Cabin blocks, using an assortment of bright, colorful children's prints, give this quilt a true scrappy look.

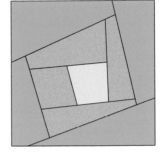

Crazy Logs
5" x 5" Block

DESIGN BY CONNIE KAUFFMAN

Project Specifications
Skill Level: Beginner
Quilt Size: 40½" x 46¾"
Block Size: 5" x 5"
Number of Blocks: 30

Materials
- Fat quarters 15–20 bright prints
- ⅛ yard yellow tone-on-tone
- ⅓ yard aqua mottled
- ½ yard yellow stripe for binding
- ½ yard white-on-white print
- Backing 47" x 53"
- Batting 47" x 53"
- Neutral color all-purpose thread
- Quilting thread
- Basic sewing tools and supplies

Making Blocks
Step 1. Cut 30 squares yellow tone-on-tone 2" x 2" for block centers.
Step 2. Cut four 2" x 18" and four 2¾" x 18" strips from each bright print.

Step 3. Make 30 copies of the Crazy Log paper-piecing pattern. Pre-fold all lines on each pattern.
Step 4. Pin a 2" x 2" yellow tone-on-tone square right side up on the unmarked side of one paper pattern, covering the center No. 1 space.
Step 5. Choose one 2" x 18" strip bright print for pieces 2, 3, 4 and 5. Pin the strip right sides together with piece 1; turn paper over and stitch on the marked line between pieces 1 and 2. **Note:** *The fabric strips will be underneath the paper.*
Step 6. Turn paper over; press piece 2 flat and trim excess strip beyond the line between pieces 2 and 3 as shown in Figure 1.

Figure 1

Step 7. Continue to add pieces 3, 4 and 5 in the same manner using

the same 2"-wide strip as shown in Figure 2.

Figure 2

Step 8. Select a 2¾" x 18" strip of another bright print for pieces 6–9. Sew strips to completed unit as in Steps 5–7 to complete one block. Repeat for 30 blocks. Trim blocks even with foundation patterns.

Completing the Top
Step 1. Cut three strips white-on-white print 5½" by fabric width; subcut strips into 1¾" A sashing strips. You will need 49 A strips.
Step 2. Cut one strip aqua mottled 1¾" by fabric width; subcut strip into 1¾"-square segments for B. You will need 20 B squares.
Step 3. Join five Crazy Log blocks with four A strips to make a block

row referring to Figure 3; press seams toward A. Repeat for six rows.

Figure 3

Step 4. Join five A strips with four B squares to make a sashing row as shown in Figure 4; press seams toward A. Repeat for five rows.

A B

Figure 4

Step 5. Join the block rows with the sashing rows to complete the pieced center; press seams toward sashing rows.

Step 6. Cut four 1¾" x 1¾" C squares white-on-white print. Cut two 1¾" x 30½" D strips and two 1¾" x 36¾" E strips aqua mottled.

Step 7. Sew a D strip to the top and bottom of the pieced center; press seams toward D. Sew C to each end of each E strip; press seams toward E. Sew a C-E strip to opposite long sides of the pieced center; press seams toward strips.

Step 8. Prepare 20 copies of the border paper-piecing pattern. Using the leftover bright print strips, cover paper sections as for making blocks. **Note:** *It may be necessary to cut more strips*.

Step 9. Join five pieced sections

to complete a side border strip; repeat for two side strips. Sew a strip to opposite sides of the pieced center; press seams toward the E strips. Trim strips even with quilt center. Repeat with five sections on the top and bottom.

Step 10. Remove all paper foundations.

Finishing the Quilt

Step 1. Prepare quilt top for quilting and quilt.

Step 2. When quilting is complete, trim batting and backing edges even with quilted top.

Step 3. Prepare 5¼ yards yellow stripe binding and bind edges of quilt to finish. ◆

Crazy Logs Kid's Quilt
Placement Diagram
40½" x 46¾"

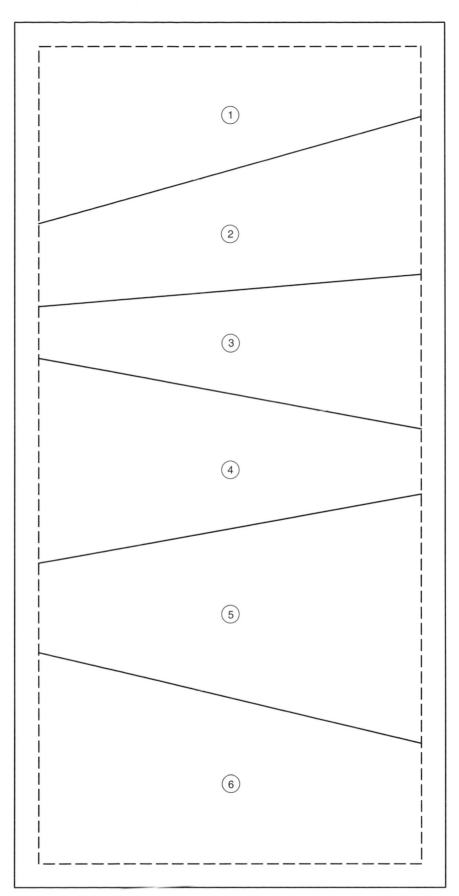

Border Paper-Piecing Pattern
Make 20 copies

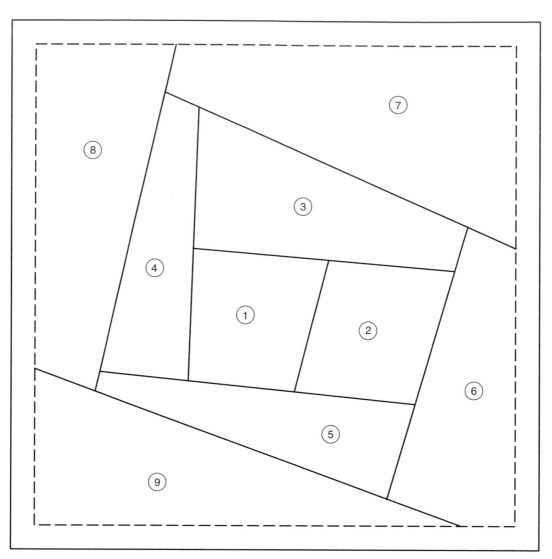

Crazy Log Paper-Piecing Pattern
Make 30 copies

POLKA-DOT PARTY

Bright polka-dots make this quilt a cheerful addition to any room.

DESIGN BY CONNIE KAUFFMAN

Crossed Dots
6" x 6" Block

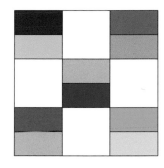

Dot Nine-Patch
6" x 6" Block

Project Specifications
Skill Level: Beginner
Quilt Size: 42" x 42"
Block Size: 6" x 6"
Number of Blocks: 25

Materials
- 1 fat quarter each 6 or more polka-dot fabrics
- 1 fat quarter each 5 bright fabrics
- ⅜ yard white tonal
- ½ yard white background with dots (white dot)
- ½ yard green background with dots (green dot)
- 1 yard purple background with dots (purple dot)
- Backing 48" x 48"
- Batting 48" x 48"
- Neutral color all-purpose thread
- Quilting thread
- Basic sewing tools and supplies

Cutting
Step 1. Cut four 2½" by fabric width strips white tonal; subcut strips into (52) 2½" A squares.
Step 2. Cut (65) 1½" x 2½" B rectangles from the polka-

dot fabrics. Repeat to cut 65 B rectangles from the five bright fabrics.
Step 3. Cut six 7¼" x 7¼" squares each purple dot (C) and white dot (D); cut each square in half on both diagonals to make 24 each C and D triangles.
Step 4. Cut two 3½" x 30½" E strips and two 3½" x 36½" F strips green dot.
Step 5. Cut approximately 20 G strips each polka-dot and bright fabrics 2" x 7"–2" x 11" for pieced outside borders.
Step 6. Cut five 2¼" by fabric width strips purple dot for binding.

Piecing Blocks
Step 1. Join one each polka-dot and bright B rectangles on the 2½" sides to make a B unit; repeat for 65 B units.
Step 2. To complete one Dot Nine-Patch block, join two B units with A to make a row as shown in Figure 1; repeat for two rows. Press seams toward B units.
Step 3. Join one B unit with two A squares to make a row, again

referring to Figure 1; press seams toward B unit.

Make 2

Make 1

^ B

Figure 1

Step 4. Join the rows to complete one Dot Nine-Patch block as shown in Figure 2; press seams in one direction. Repeat for 13 blocks.

Figure 2

Step 5. To piece one Crossed Dots block, sew C to D as shown in Figure 3; repeat for two C-D units. Press seams toward C.

Figure 3

Step 6. Join two C-D units to complete one Crossed Dots block as shown in Figure 4; press seams in one direction. Repeat for 12 blocks.

Figure 4

Completing the Top

Step 1. Join three Dot Nine-Patch blocks with two Crossed Dots blocks to make a row referring to Figure 5; press seams toward Crossed Dots blocks. Repeat for three rows.

Step 2. Join three Crossed Dots blocks with two Dot Nine-Patch blocks to make a row, again referring to Figure 5; press seams toward Crossed Dots blocks. Repeat for two rows.

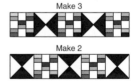

Make 3

Make 2

Figure 5

Step 3. Join the rows referring to the Placement Diagram; press seams in one direction.

Step 4. Sew E strips to opposite

sides and F strips to the top and bottom of the pieced center; press seams toward strips.

Step 5. Join the G strips on short ends to make one long strip, alternating polka-dot and bright strips; press seams in one direction.

Step 6. Cut two strips each 36½" (G) and 42½" (I) and four strips 39½" (H).

Step 7. Sew G to opposite sides and H to the top and bottom of the pieced center; press seams toward E and F. Sew H to opposite sides and I to the top and bottom of the pieced center; press seams toward H and I.

Finishing the Quilt

Step 1. Sandwich the batting between the completed top and prepared backing piece; pin or baste to hold.

Step 2. Hand- or machine-quilt as desired.

Step 3. Trim batting and backing even with the quilted top.

Step 4. Join the binding strips on short ends with a diagonal seam to make a long strip; press seams toward one side.

Step 5. Press the strip in half along length with wrong sides together to complete the binding strip. Bind edges of quilt to finish. ✦

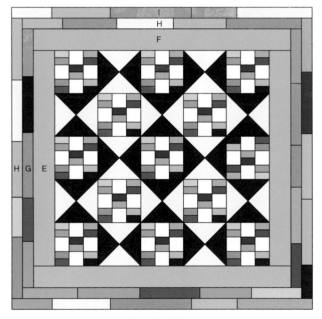

Polka-Dot Party
Placement Diagram
42" x 42" Block

SCRAP-PATCH HEARTS

Create a scrappy look with lots of love using 1930s reproduction prints.

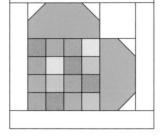

Scrap-Patch Heart
8" x 8" Block

DESIGN BY JULIE WEAVER

Project Specifications
Skill Level: Beginner
Quilt Size: 44⅛" x 55½"
Block Size: 8" x 8"
Number of Blocks: 18

Materials
- ⅜ yard each 20 assorted yellow, blue, pink, green and lavender 1930s reproduction prints (4 each color used in the sample)
- ½ yard green 1930s reproduction print for binding
- 1⅞ yards white dot
- Backing 50" x 61"
- Batting 50" x 61"
- All-purpose thread to match fabrics
- Quilting thread
- Basic sewing tools and supplies

Cutting
Step 1. Cut three 1½" x 10" A strips from each of the 20 reproduction prints for a total of 60 strips.
Step 2. Cut two 2½" x 4½" B rectangles each from 18 of the prints.
Step 3. Cut three 1½" by fabric width strips white dot; subcut strips into (72) 1½" C squares. Draw a line from corner to corner on the wrong side of each square.
Step 4. Cut two 2½" by fabric width strips white dot; subcut strips into (18) 2½" D squares.
Step 5. Cut two 6½" by fabric width strips white dot; subcut strips into (36) 1½" E strips.
Step 6. Cut two 8½" by fabric width strips white dot; subcut strips into (36) 1½" F strips.
Step 7. Cut one 12⅝" by fabric width strip white dot; subcut strip into three 12⅝" squares. Cut each square in half on both diagonals to make 10 G triangles. Set aside two triangles for another project.
Step 8. Cut two 6⅝" x 6⅝" squares white dot; cut each square in half on one diagonal to make four H triangles.
Step 9. Cut four 1½" by fabric width strips white dot; join strips on short ends to make one long strip. Subcut strip into two 46" I strips and two 34⅝" J strips.
Step 10. Cut 2" x 4½" K rectangles

from the prints to total 104. Cut two 2⅛" x 4½" L rectangles and four 2½" x 4½" M rectangles from the prints.
Step 11. Cut four 4½" x 4½" N squares blue print.
Step 12. Cut six 2¼" by fabric width strips green reproduction print for binding.

Piecing the Blocks
Step 1. Select four different A strips; join with right sides together along length to make a strip set. Press seams in one direction; repeat for 15 strip sets.
Step 2. Subcut strip sets into (72) 1½" A segments as shown in Figure 1.

Figure 1   **Figure 2**

Step 3. Select four different A segments; join as shown in Figure 2 to complete one A unit. Press seams in one direction; repeat for 18 A units.

Step 4. Place a C square on two opposite ends of B and stitch on the marked lines as shown in Figure 3; trim seam allowance to ¼" and press B to the right side to complete one B-C unit, again referring to Figure 3. Repeat for 36 B-C units.

Figure 3

Step 5. Select two same-fabric B-C units. Sew a B-C unit to one side of an A unit as shown in Figure 4; press seams toward B-C.

Figure 4

Step 6. Sew D to one end of the remaining same-fabric B-C unit; press seam toward B-C. Sew the B-C-D unit to the A-B-C unit, again referring to Figure 4; press seams toward B-C-D.

Step 7. Sew E to opposite sides and F to the top and bottom of the pieced unit to complete one block as shown in Figure 5; repeat for 18 blocks. Press seams toward E and F.

Figure 5

Completing the Top
Step 1. Arrange the blocks in diagonal rows with G and H triangles as shown in Figure 6; join in rows. Press seams

in adjacent rows in opposite directions. Join the rows to complete the pieced center; press seams in one direction.

Figure 6

Step 2. Sew I strips to opposite sides and J strips to the top and bottom of the pieced center; press seams toward I and J.

Step 3. Join 29 K rectangles in random order; add an M rectangle to each end to make a K-M strip. Repeat for two K-M strips. Repeat with 23 K rectangles and one L rectangle to make one K-L strip each for the top and bottom. Press seams in one direction.

Step 4. Center and sew a K-M strip to opposite long sides of the pieced center; press seams toward I strips.

Step 5. Sew an N square to each end of a K-L strip; press seams toward N. Sew a strip to the top and bottom of the pieced center to complete the top; press seams toward J.

Step 6. Finish quilt referring to the General Instructions. ◆

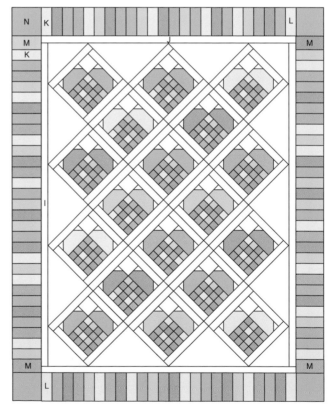

Scrap-Patch Hearts
Placement Diagram
44⅛" x 55½"

BUTTERFLY DANCE DUO

The soft colors used to make the Butterfly blocks in this crib quilt are reminiscent of those used in fabrics of the 1930s.

DESIGNS BY CHRISTINE SCHULTZ

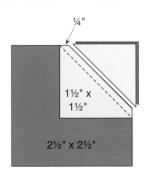

Butterfly
6½" x 6½" Block

Quilt

Project Specifications
Skill Level: Beginner
Quilt Size: 37½" x 52"
Block Size: 6½" x 6½"
Number of Blocks: 24

Materials
- ⅛ yard black solid
- ½ yard green print
- ¾ yard floral print
- ¾ yard assorted scraps or 24 squares 8" x 8" assorted prints
- 1 yard white solid
- Backing 44" x 58"
- Batting 44" x 58"
- 5½ yards self-made or purchased binding
- Neutral color all-purpose thread
- White quilting thread
- Basic sewing tools and supplies, rotary cutter, ruler and mat

Making Butterfly Blocks

Step 1. Cut one 3½" x 28" strip black solid and two 1½" x 28" strips white solid for butterfly bodies.

Step 2. Sew a black solid strip between two white solid strips as shown in Figure 1; press seams toward black solid. Square up one end of the strip; subcut into 1" segments for butterfly bodies as shown in Figure 2.

Figure 1

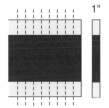

Figure 2

Step 3. To make lower wing, cut a 2½" x 2½" square print and two 1½" x 1½" squares white solid. Fold or mark diagonal line on the back of each white solid square. Lay one of these squares on one corner of a 2½" x 2½" print square; sew on the folded diagonal line as shown in Figure 3; trim away the corner to ¼", again referring to Figure 3. Press seam toward white solid.

Figure 3

Step 4. Repeat on opposite corner to complete a lower wing unit as shown in Figure 4; repeat for two lower wing units.

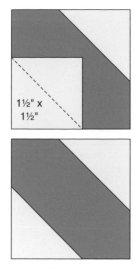

Figure 4

Step 5. To make upper wing, cut a print square 3½" x 3½" and three white solid squares 1½" x 1½". Fold or mark diagonal lines on the wrong side of the three small squares. Lay them on three adjacent corners of the print square, right sides together; sew on the diagonals as shown in Figure 5. Trim away corners as for lower wing units and press seams toward white solid to complete one upper wing unit as shown in Figure 6. Repeat for two upper wing units.

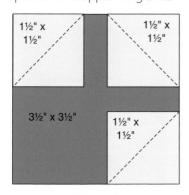

Figure 5

Step 6. Cut two rectangles white solid 1½" x 2½". Sew a rectangle to one side of a lower wing unit as shown in Figure 7; repeat to make a reverse piece, again referring to Figure 7.

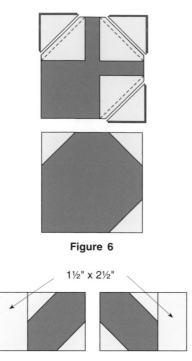

Figure 6

Figure 7

Step 7. Join an upper wing unit with a lower wing unit as shown in Figure 8; repeat with reverse pieces. Join the two pieced units with a body segment made in Step 2 as shown in Figure 9. Press seams away from body segment.

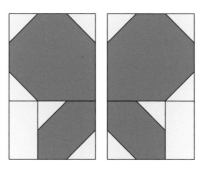

Figure 8

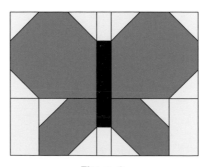

Figure 9

Step 8. Cut two strips white solid 1¼" x 7". Sew one strip to the top and one to the bottom of each pieced butterfly unit to complete one block as shown in Figure 10.

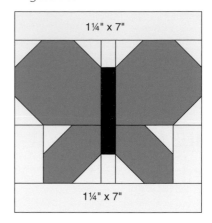

Figure 10

Step 9. Repeat Steps 3–8 to make 24 Butterfly blocks using assorted prints.

Completing Quilt Center
Step 1. Join four blocks as shown in Figure 11; repeat for six four-block units. Press seams in one direction.

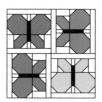

Figure 11

Step 2. Cut four strips green print 2" x 13½". Join three four-block units with two strips to make a row as shown in Figure 12; repeat for two rows. Press seams in one direction.

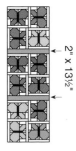

Figure 12

Step 3. Cut three strips green print 2" x 42½"; join the two pieced units with the strips, beginning and ending with a strip as shown in Figure 13. Press seams toward strips.

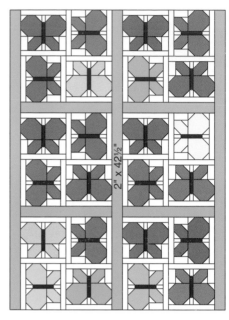

Figure 13

Step 4. Cut two strips green print 2" x 31"; sew to the top and bottom of the pieced section. Press seams toward strips.

Step 5. Cut and piece two strips each floral print 4" x 45½" and 4" x 38". Sew the longer strips to opposite long sides and shorter strips to the top and bottom; press seams toward strips.

Finishing the Quilt

Step 1. Sandwich batting between completed top and prepared backing; pin or baste layers together to hold flat. Quilt as desired by hand or machine. **Note:** *The quilt shown was hand-quilted in the blocks as shown in Figure 14. Borders were quilted as shown in Figure 15 using the quilting designs given.*

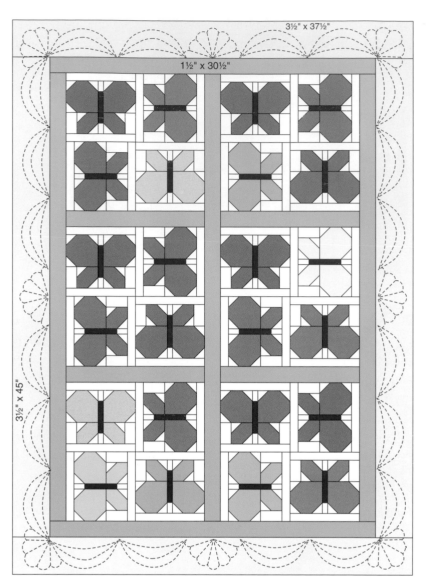

Butterfly Dance Duo Crib Quilt
Placement Diagram
37½" x 52"

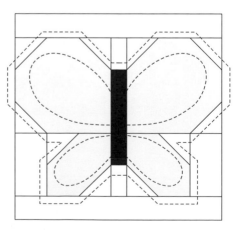

Figure 14

Figure 15

Step 2. When quilting is complete, trim edges even. Bind with self-made or purchased binding to finish.

Pillow

Project Specifications
Pillow Size: 13" x 13" without ruffle
Block Size: 6½" x 6½"
Number of Blocks: 4

Materials
- 4 squares 8" x 8" assorted prints for butterflies
- 3½" x 6" strip black solid
- ¼ yard white solid
- ¾ yard green print
- 15" x 15" square muslin
- Batting 15" x 15"
- Neutral color all-purpose thread
- White quilting thread
- 12" pillow form
- Basic sewing tools and supplies, rotary cutter, ruler and mat

Instructions
Step 1. Cut two strips 1½" x 6" white solid for butterfly bodies. Make four Butterfly blocks using assorted prints and referring to Steps 2–8 for Making Butterfly Blocks.

Step 2. Join four blocks to make pillow top referring to the Placement Diagram for positioning of blocks.

Step 3. Sandwich batting between pillow top and 15" x 15" muslin square; pin or baste layers together. Quilt as desired by hand or machine. When quilting is complete, trim edges even; remove pins or basting.

Step 4. Cut three strips green print 6" by fabric length; join together on short ends and trim to make a 102"-long strip. Join on short ends to make a tube; press seams open.

Step 5. Fold tube in half with wrong sides together; gather along raw edges to make a ruffled strip 54" in circumference.

Step 6. Fold ruffle to mark four equidistant points in the length; pin these to the four corners of the pillow top. Pin-baste the ruffle to the center of each side of the pillow top as shown in Figure 16. Continue pinning all around. Machine-baste ruffle in place.

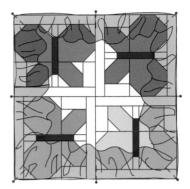

Figure 16

Step 7. Cut a 13½" x 13½" backing square from green print. Pin backing square to the ruffle/pillow top with right sides together. Stitch all around just inside ruffle stitching line, leaving an 8" opening on one side.

Step 8. Turn right side out through opening. Insert pillow form through opening. Hand-stitch opening closed to finish. ◆

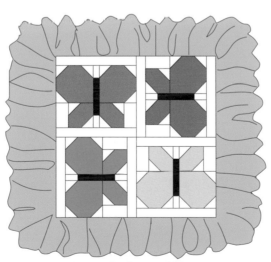

Butterfly Dance Pillow
Placement Diagram
13" x 13" without ruffle

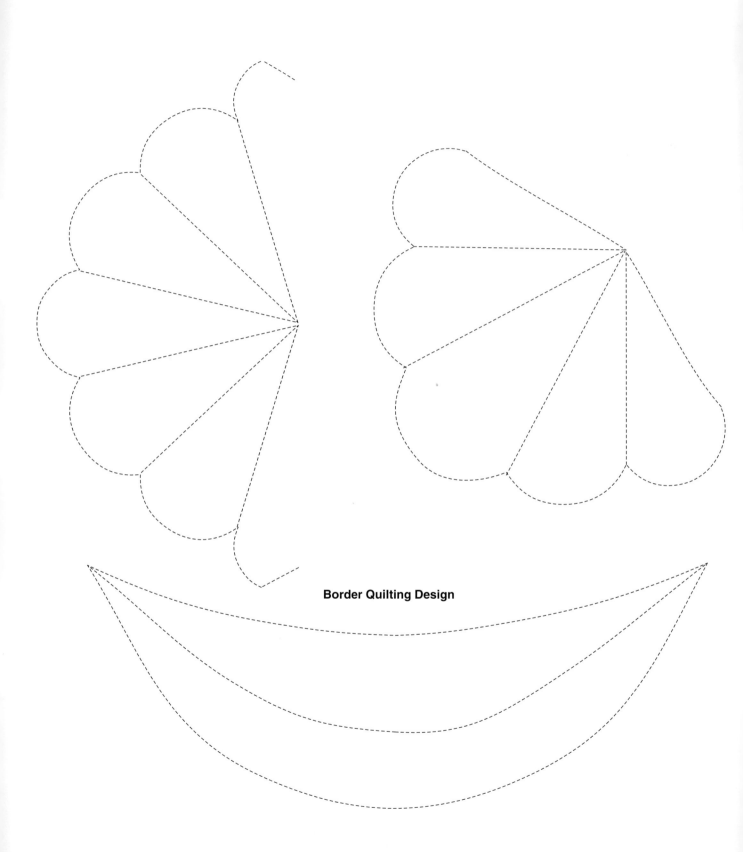

Border Quilting Design

PATCHWORK FUN

Not only is this quilt bright and fabulously fun—it's quick and easy, too!

DESIGN BY LUCY A. FAZELY

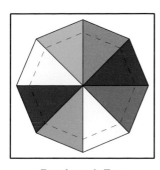

Patchwork Fun
12" x 12" Block

Project Specifications
Skill Level: Beginner
Quilt Size: 72" x 96"
Block Size: 12" x 12"
Number of Blocks: 35

Materials
- 4¼ yards white-on-white print
- 3¾ yards bleached white muslin
- Wide variety of bright scraps for piecing or 35 squares 13½" x 13½"
- 2⅜ yards bright blue print for border and bindings
- Backing 78" x 102"
- Batting 78" x 102"
- Rotary-cutting tools
- All-purpose thread to blend with fabrics
- 1 spool white quilting thread
- Basic sewing tools and supplies

Instructions
Step 1. From white-on-white print, cut 35 squares 12½" x 12½". From bleached white muslin, cut 35 squares 11¼" x 11¼".
Step 2. From bright scraps, use template to cut 280 triangle shapes. Or, if using 13½" squares, cut each in half top to bottom, then left to right as shown in

Figure 1. Cut each resulting square in half diagonally. Trim end of each triangle with template and rotary cutter as shown in Figure 2.

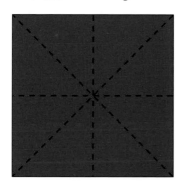

Figure 1

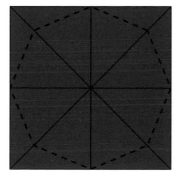

Figure 2

Step 3. Stitch triangles randomly in pairs as shown in Figure 3. Press all seams in the same direction. Sew two pairs together as shown in Figure 4, again pressing all seams in the same direction.

Sew two sets of four together as shown in Figure 5, again pressing all seams in the same direction. Repeat for 35 complete circles.
Step 4. Place each circle on one bleached white muslin square, right sides together. Stitch around circle ¼" from outer edge. Trim muslin even with circle.

Figure 3

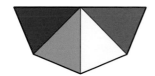

Figure 4

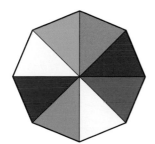

Figure 5

Step 5. Carefully cut a 1" slit in center of muslin only. Turn piece right side out. Press edges flat.

Step 6. Center one patchwork circle on each 12½" white-on-white print square. Pin in place. Stitch around piece 1" from edge of circle as shown in Figure 6.

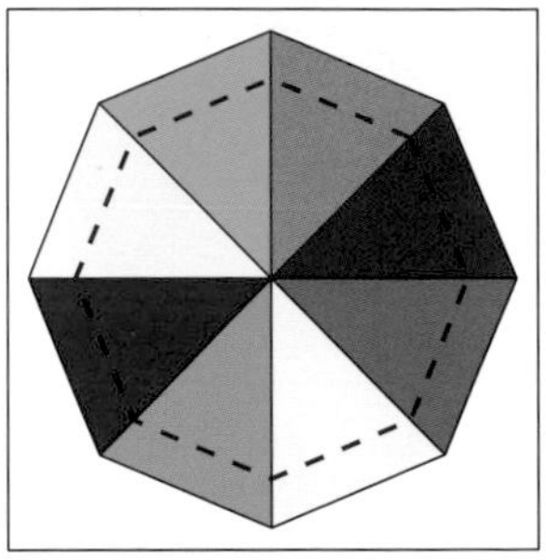

Figure 6

Step 7. Referring to Placement Diagram, arrange blocks in seven rows of five blocks each. Stitch blocks into rows and then sew rows together.

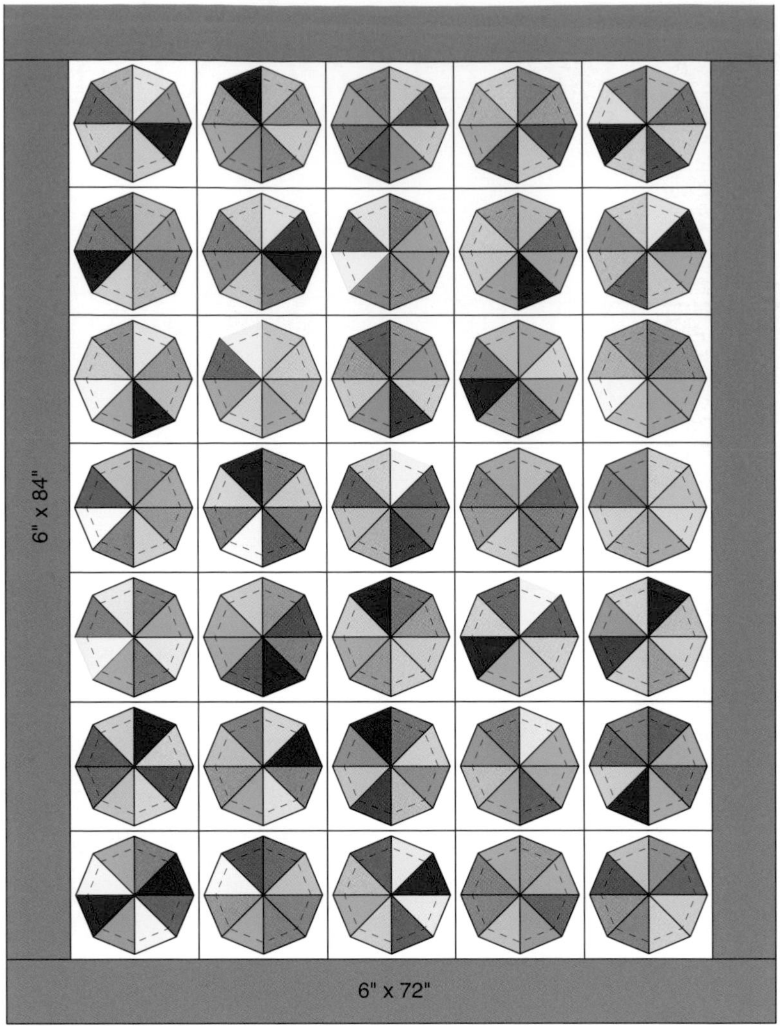

Patchwork Fun
Placement Diagram
72" x 96"

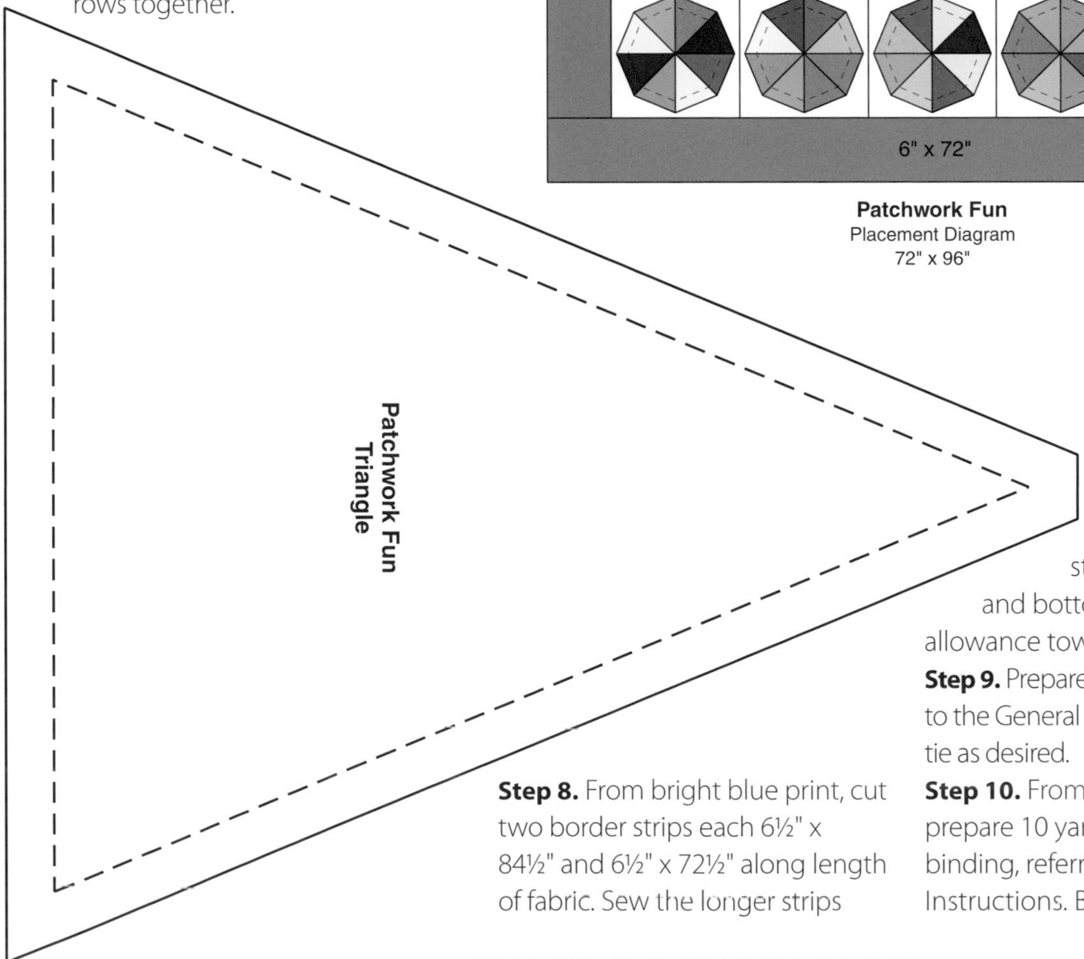

Patchwork Fun
Triangle

to two opposite sides of the quilt. Sew the shorter strips to the top and bottom. Press seam allowance toward borders.

Step 9. Prepare for quilting, referring to the General Instructions. Quilt or tie as desired.

Step 8. From bright blue print, cut two border strips each 6½" x 84½" and 6½" x 72½" along length of fabric. Sew the longer strips

Step 10. From bright blue print, prepare 10 yards of 2½"-wide binding, referring to the General Instructions. Bind to finish. ◆

STARS & SWIRLS TODDLER QUILT

Choose bright-color print fat quarters to create this scrappy looking quilt.

DESIGN BY HOLLY DANIELS

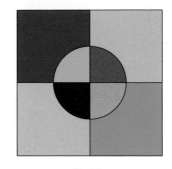

Swirls
8" x 8" Block

Project Specifications
Skill Level: Intermediate
Quilt Size: 48" x 56"
Block Size: 8" x 8"
Number of Blocks: 20

Materials
- 11 different bright-color fat quarters
- 1⅛ yards blue print
- Backing 54" x 62"
- Batting 54" x 62"
- Neutral color all-purpose thread
- Clear nylon monofilament
- Basic sewing tools and supplies

Instructions
Step 1. Prepare templates using pattern pieces given.
Step 2. Layer two to four fat-quarter pieces and press.
Step 3. Cut (12) 4½" x 4½" squares for A and (12) 2½" x 2½" squares for B from each layered fat quarter section referring to Figure 1 for best use of fabric. Keep squares in layers.

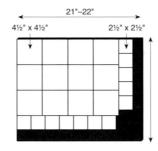

21"–22"

4½" x 4½"   2½" x 2½"

Figure 1

Step 4. Place the A template on each stack of A squares and cut; repeat with B pieces. You will need 124 each A and B pieces.
Step 5. Randomly select one A and one B piece. Fold each piece, crease and pin to mark the centers as shown in Figure 2.

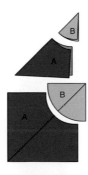

Figure 2

Step 6. Pin B to A right sides together, matching centers as shown in Figure 3.

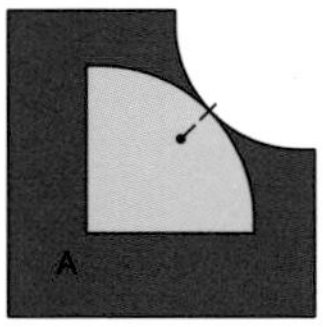

Figure 3

Step 7. Pin B to A at each edge and ease the fullness between, inserting pins as necessary as shown in Figure 4. Stitch, removing pins as you sew. Clip seam as shown in Figure 5; press seam toward A. Repeat for 124 A-B units.

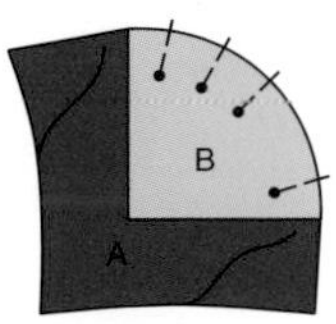

Figure 4

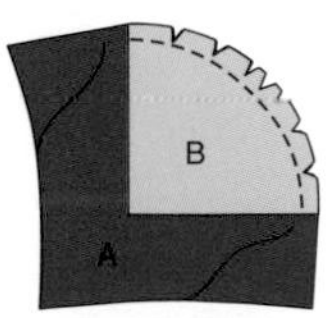

Figure 5

Step 8. Join four A-B units as shown in Figure 6 to complete one Swirls block; repeat for 20 blocks.

Figure 6

Step 9. Join four blocks to make a row; press seams in one direction. Repeat for five rows.

Step 10. Join the rows to complete the quilt center; press seams in one direction.

Step 11. Cut two strips each 2½" x 36½" and 2½" x 40½" blue print. Sew the longer strips to opposite sides and the shorter strips to the top and bottom of the quilt center; press seams toward strips.

Step 12. Join 11 A-B units as shown in Figure 7 to make a Y strip; repeat for two Y strips. Join 11 A-B units to make a Z strip, again referring to Figure 7; repeat for two Z strips. Press seams in one direction. Sew a Z strip to opposite long sides of the pieced center, referring to the Placement Diagram for positioning; press seams toward blue print strips. Sew the Y strips to the top and bottom; press seams toward blue print strips.

Step 13. Cut and piece two strips each 2½" x 48½" and 2½" x 52½" blue print. Sew the longer strips to opposite sides and the shorter strips to the top and bottom of the quilt center; press seams toward strips.

Step 14. Sandwich batting between completed top and prepared backing; pin or baste to hold.

Step 15. Quilt as desired by hand or machine. **Note:** *The quilt shown was machine-quilted using the swirling star design given using clear nylon monofilament in the top of the machine and all-purpose thread in the bobbin.*

Step 16. When quilting is complete, remove pins or basting; trim backing and batting even with quilt top.

Step 17. Cut six strips blue print 2¼" by fabric width; join on short ends to make one long strip for binding. Fold the strip in half along length with wrong sides together; press. Sew binding to quilt edges, mitering corners and overlapping ends. Turn binding to the back side; hand- or machine-stitch in place to finish. ◆

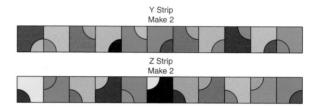

Figure 7

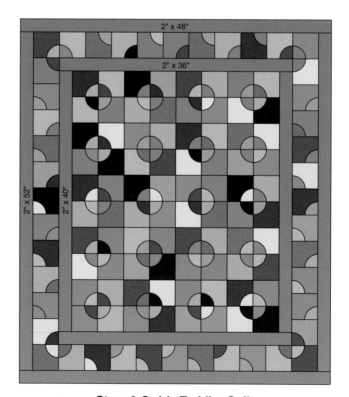

Stars & Swirls Toddler Quilt
Placement Diagram
48" x 56"

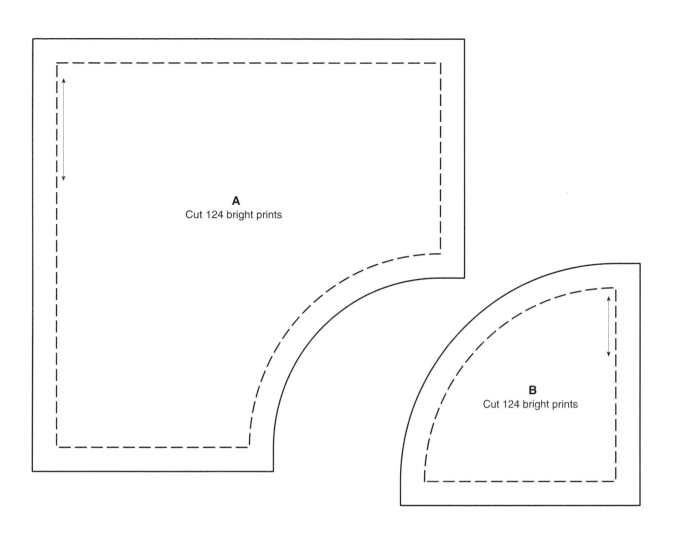

A
Cut 124 bright prints

B
Cut 124 bright prints

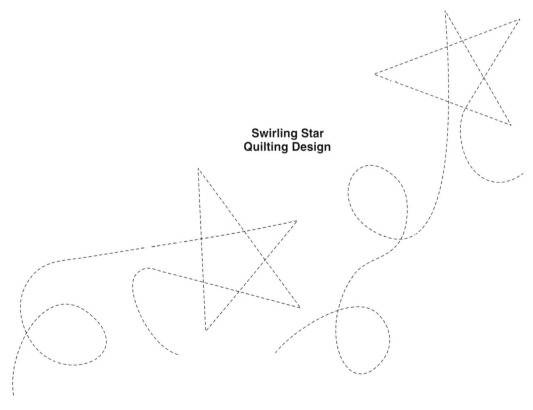

**Swirling Star
Quilting Design**

FARM ANIMAL BABY QUILT

Reproduction prints create a pretty baby quilt in a style Grandmother would love.

DESIGN BY CHRIS MALONE

Applique Block
6" x 6" Block

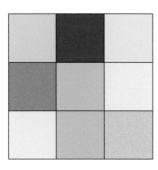

Nine-Patch
6" x 6" Block

Project Specifications

Skill Level: Beginner
Quilt Size: 25" x 49"
Block Size: 6" x 6"
Number of Blocks: 21

Materials

- Assorted 1930s reproduction pink, blue, green, yellow and red scraps
- Dark green solid scrap for appliqué
- ¼ yard blue solid
- ⅓ yard green print for binding
- ⅜ yard muslin
- ½ yard pink print
- Backing 31" x 55"
- Batting 31" x 55"
- Neutral color and black all-purpose thread
- Quilting thread
- Black 6-strand embroidery floss
- ½ yard fusible web
- ¾ yard fabric stabilizer
- Basic sewing tools and supplies

Cutting

Step 1. Prepare templates for appliqué shapes using full-size patterns given. *Note: Patterns are given in reverse for fusible appliqué.*

Step 2. Trace shapes as directed onto the paper side of the fusible web. Cut out shapes, leaving a margin around each one.

Step 3. Fuse shapes to the wrong side of scrap fabrics as directed on each piece for color. Cut out shapes on traced lines; remove paper backing.

Step 4. Cut 10 muslin A squares 6½" x 6½".

Step 5. Cut 10 squares fabric stabilizer 6½" x 6½".

Step 6. Cut 99 scrap B squares 2½" x 2½".

Step 7. Cut two 1¼" x 42½" C strips and two 1¼" x 20" D strips blue solid.

Step 8. Cut (and piece) two 3¼" x 44" E strips and two 3¼" x 25½" F strips pink print.

Step 9. Cut four 2¼" by fabric width strips green print for binding.

Completing Appliqué Blocks

Step 1. Fold A squares in quarters and lightly press to mark centers. Center one appliqué motif on each A square; fuse shapes in place in numerical order.

Step 2. Pin a fabric stabilizer square behind each fused square.

Step 3. Machine blanket-stitch around each shape using black all-purpose thread; remove fabric stabilizer.

Step 4. Using 2 strands black embroidery floss, stem-stitch detail lines and make straight-stitch X's for eyes.

Completing Nine-Patch Blocks

Step 1. Select nine different B squares. Join three squares to

make a row; press seams in one direction. Repeat for three rows.

Step 2. Join the rows with seams of adjacent rows going in opposite directions to complete one Nine-Patch block as shown in Figure 1; repeat for 11 blocks.

Figure 1

Completing the Top

Step 1. Arrange Nine-Patch blocks with Appliqué blocks in seven rows of three blocks each referring to the Placement Diagram for positioning of blocks.

Step 2. Join blocks in rows; press seams of adjacent rows in opposite directions. Join rows to complete the pieced center; press seams in one direction.

Step 3. Sew a C strip to opposite long sides and D strips to the top and bottom of the pieced center; press seams toward strips.

Step 4. Sew an E strip to opposite long sides and F strips to the top and bottom of the pieced center; press seams toward strips.

Finishing the Quilt

Step 1. Sandwich the batting between the completed top and prepared backing; pin or baste layers together to hold.

Step 2. Hand- or machine-quilt as desired. When quilting is complete, trim batting and backing even with top; remove pins or basting.

Step 3. Join the previously cut binding strips on short ends to make one long strip. Fold the strip in half along length with wrong sides together; press.

Step 4. Sew binding to quilt edges, mitering corners and overlapping ends. Fold binding to the back side and stitch in place to finish. ✦

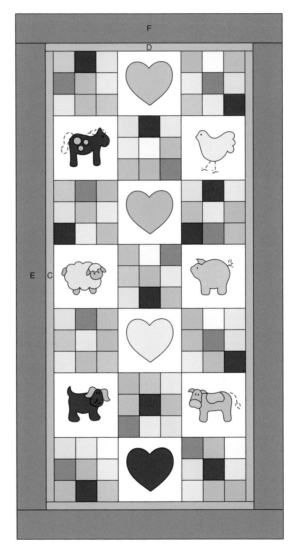

Farm Animal Baby Quilt
Placement Diagram
25" x 49"

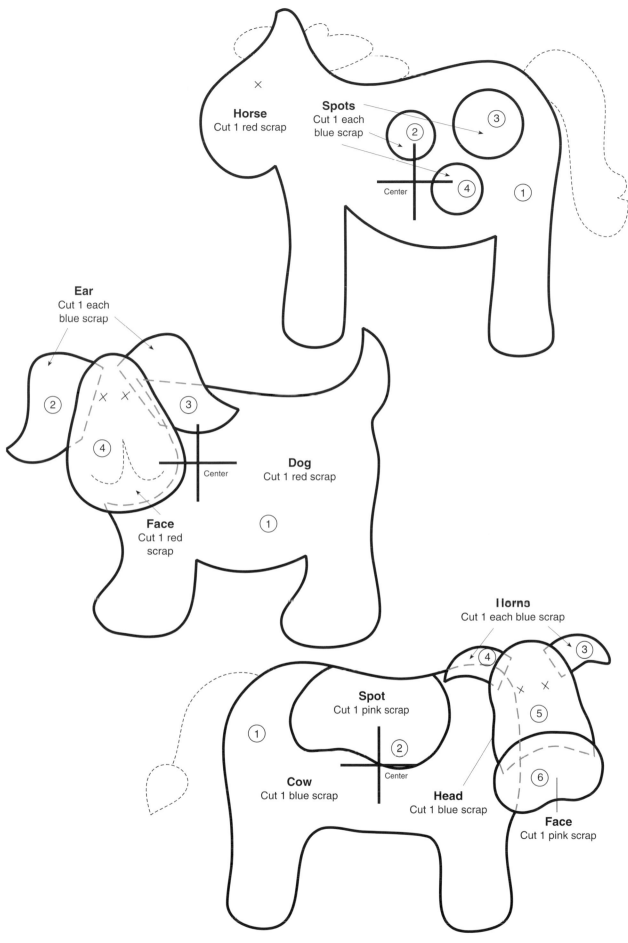

Horse
Cut 1 red scrap

Spots
Cut 1 each
blue scrap

2

3

4

Center

1

Ear
Cut 1 each
blue scrap

2

3

4

Center

Dog
Cut 1 red scrap

1

Face
Cut 1 red
scrap

Horns
Cut 1 each blue scrap

4

3

5

1

Spot
Cut 1 pink scrap

2

Center

Cow
Cut 1 blue scrap

Head
Cut 1 blue scrap

6

Face
Cut 1 pink scrap

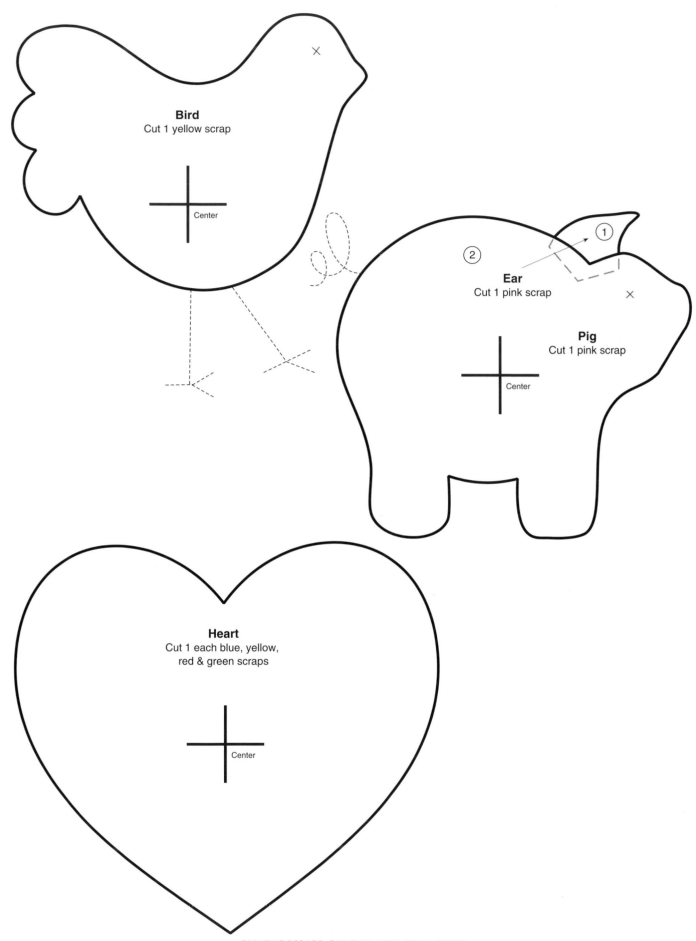

Bird
Cut 1 yellow scrap

Center

Pig
Cut 1 pink scrap

Ear
Cut 1 pink scrap

① ②

Center

Heart
Cut 1 each blue, yellow,
red & green scraps

Center

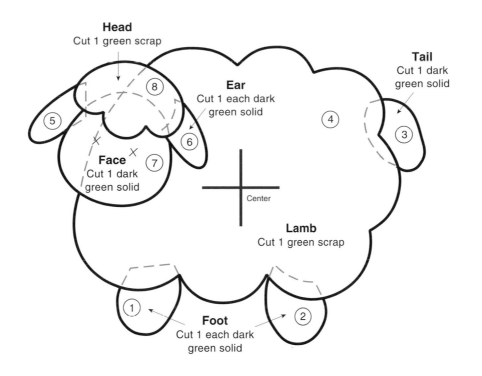

Head
Cut 1 green scrap

⑧

Ear
Cut 1 each dark
green solid

⑤

⑥

Tail
Cut 1 dark
green solid

④

③

Face
Cut 1 dark
green solid

⑦

Center

Lamb
Cut 1 green scrap

①

Foot
Cut 1 each dark
green solid

②

HERE A CHICK, THERE A CHICK

A juvenile print combines with bright scraps and an appliquéd chick in this cute child's quilt.

DESIGN BY JILL REBER

Project Specifications
Skill Level: Intermediate
Quilt Size: 47" x 59"
Block Size: 6" x 6"
Number of Blocks: 39

Materials
- Scraps gold and light blue fabrics
- 18 (4" x 10") rectangles different bright fabrics for pieced blocks
- ⅓ yard blue print for borders
- ⅓ yard yellow mottled for chicks
- ⅝ yard blue mottled for pieced blocks and binding
- 1¼ yards white solid for background
- 1⅞ yards juvenile print for borders
- Backing 53" x 65"
- Batting 53" x 65"
- Neutral color all-purpose thread
- Quilting thread
- Black and orange 6-strand embroidery floss for beaks and eyes
- Basic sewing tools and supplies

Cutting
Step 1. Cut three 6½" by fabric width strips white solid; subcut into (17) 6½" A squares.

Step 2. Prepare template for chick; cut as directed on pattern, adding a ¼" seam allowance all around for hand appliqué.

Step 3. From each of the 18 bright fabric rectangles, cut one 3½" x 3½" B square and four 2" x 2" C squares.

Step 4. Cut four 3½" by fabric width strips white solid; subcut into (72) 2" D rectangles.

Step 5. Cut four 2" x 2" E squares white solid.

Step 6. Cut two 2" x 30½" F strips and two 2" x 42½" G strips blue print.

Step 7. Cut one 2⅞" by fabric width strip white solid; subcut strip into eight 2⅞" H squares. Draw a diagonal line on the wrong side of each H square.

Step 8. Cut eight 2⅞" x 2⅞" I squares each light blue scrap and blue mottled.

Step 9. Cut eight 2⅞" x 2⅞" J squares gold scrap; draw a

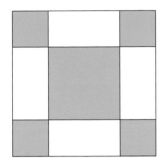

Nine Patch
6" x 6" Block

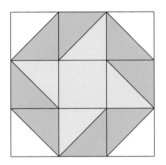

Spinning Stars
6" x 6" Block

Chick
6" x 6" Block

diagonal line on the wrong side of each J square.

Step 10. Cut four 2½" x 2½" K squares gold scrap.

Step 11. Cut four 1½" x 6½" L strips and four 1½" x 7½" M strips juvenile print.

Step 12. Cut two 7½" x 33½" O strips across the width and two 7½" x 45½" N strips along the remaining length of the juvenile print.

Step 13. Cut six 2¼" by fabric width strips blue mottled for binding.

Completing Chick Blocks

Step 1. Fold and crease each A square to find the centers.

Step 2. Turn under edges of each chick shape ¼"; baste to hold.

Step 3. To complete one Chick block, center a fabric chick on an A square using creased lines and center mark on chick pattern as guides referring to Figure 1; baste to hold in place.

Figure 1

Step 4. Hand-stitch chick shapes in place using matching all-purpose thread.

Step 5. Transfer wing, eye, beak and feet details to stitched block using water-erasable marker or pencil.

Step 6. Satin-stitch beak using 3 strands orange embroidery floss. Straight-stitch feet, eye and wing details using 3 strands black embroidery floss to complete one block; repeat for 17 Chick blocks.

Completing Nine-Patch Blocks

Step 1. To complete one Nine-Patch block, select one color set of B and C pieces.

Step 2. Sew D to opposite sides of B; press seams toward B.

Step 3. Sew C to opposite ends of two D pieces; press seams toward C.

Step 4. Join the pieced units as shown in Figure 2 to complete one Nine-Patch block; press seams toward B-D units. Repeat for 18 Nine-Patch blocks.

Figure 2

Completing Spinning Stars Blocks

Step 1. Referring to Figure 3, place an H square right sides together with an I square; stitch ¼" on each side of the marked line. Cut apart on marked line; press open to complete two blue mottled H-I units. Repeat to make eight each light blue scrap and blue mottled H-I units.

Figure 3

Step 2. Repeat Step 1 with remaining I squares and J to complete eight each light blue scrap and blue mottled I-J units.

Step 3. Arrange the H-I and I-J units in rows with K as shown in Figure 4; join units in rows. Press seams in top and bottom rows toward H-I units and toward

K in the center row; stitch to complete one Spinning Star block; repeat for four blocks (two each light blue scrap and blue mottled).

Figure 4

Completing the Top

Step 1. Join three Nine-Patch blocks and two Chick blocks to make a row referring to Figure 5; press seams toward Chick blocks. Repeat for four rows.

Step 2. Join three Chick blocks with two Nine-Patch blocks to make a row, again referring to Figure 5; press seams toward Chick blocks. Repeat for three rows.

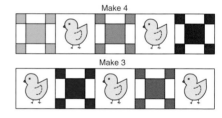

Make 4

Make 3

Figure 5

Step 3. Join the rows referring to the Placement Diagram for positioning; press seams in one direction.

Step 4. Sew a G strip to opposite long sides; press seams toward G. Sew an E square to each end of each F strip; press seams toward F. Sew an E-F strip to the top and bottom of the pieced center; press seams toward strips.

Step 5. Sew L to the bottom and M to one side of each Spinning

Star block as shown in Figure 6; press seams toward L and M.

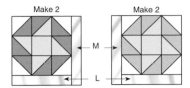

Figure 6

Step 6. Sew an N strip to opposite long sides of the pieced center; press seams toward N.

Step 7. Sew a bordered Spinning Star block to each end of each O strip as shown in Figure 7; press seams toward O. Sew a block/O strip to the top and bottom of the pieced center to complete the top; press seams toward block/O strips.

Figure 7

Finishing the Quilt

Step 1. Sandwich the batting between the completed top and prepared backing; pin or baste layers together to hold.

Step 2. Hand- or machine-quilt as desired. When quilting is complete, trim batting and backing even with top; remove pins or basting.

Step 3. Join the previously cut binding strips on short ends to make one long strip. Fold the strip in half along length with wrong sides together; press.

Step 4. Sew binding to quilt edges, mitering corners and overlapping ends. Fold binding to the back side and stitch in place. ✦

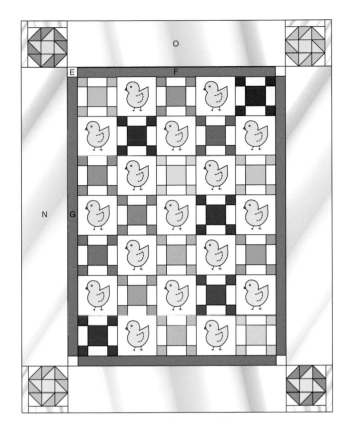

Here a Chick, There a Chick
Placement Diagram
47" x 59"

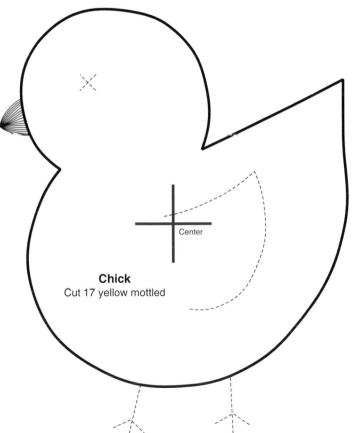

Chick
Cut 17 yellow mottled

Center

Add a ¼" seam allowance all around when cutting for hand appliqué.

CARTWHEEL CLOWNS

Bright-colored clowns are tumbling all over this quilt top.

Cartwheel Clown
9" x 9" Block

DESIGN BY JUDITH SANDSTROM

Project Specifications

Skill Level: Intermediate
Quilt Size: 43½" x 54"
Block Size: 9" x 9"
Number of Blocks: 20

Materials

- ⅛ yard each black and peach solids
- ⅜ yard each 12 bright prints
- ½ yard blue print for sashing squares and binding
- 1½ yards white-on-white print
- Thin batting 49" x 60"
- Backing 49" x 60"
- All-purpose thread to match bright prints and black and peach
- White machine-quilting thread
- 2¼ yards fusible web
- 1½ yards ½"-wide white lace
- Black, blue, red and brown fine-point marking pens or fabric pens
- Basic sewing tools and supplies

Making Clown Blocks

Step 1. Prewash and iron all fabrics before cutting.
Step 2. Cut two 2" by fabric width strips from each of the 12 bright prints; set aside.

Step 3. Prepare templates for clown shapes using the full-size pattern given; transfer details to templates. Referring to patterns for number to cut, trace all face, hand and shoe shapes in one area on the paper side of the fusible web, reversing half of the shoe pieces. Cut out the entire area and fuse the traced face and hand sections to the wrong side of the peach solid and the traced shoe section to the black solid.

Step 4. Cut out shapes on traced lines; remove paper backing. Place each face piece on pattern and add eyes with blue and black marking pens and mouth with red marking pen.

Step 5. Trace clown suit and hat shapes on the paper side of the fusible web as directed on patterns for number to cut. Cut out each shape, leaving a margin around each one.

Step 6. Fuse clown suit and hat shapes to the wrong side of the bright prints, making one of some fabrics and two of others. Cut hats to match each clown suit; remove paper backing.

Step 7. Cut 20 squares white-on-white print 9½" x 9½" for background. Fold and crease to mark center.

Step 8. Cut (20) 2" pieces of 1½"-wide white lace for clown collars.

Step 9. Arrange one clown motif in the center of each square in numerical order; tuck the raw edge of one piece of lace under the head piece. Fuse shapes in place with lace under head referring to manufacturer's instructions.

Step 10. Using the brown marking pen, draw curly hair on the sides of the face and along bottom edge of hat of each fused clown motif; press to set.

Quilt Top Construction

Step 1. Randomly stitch the 2"-wide bright print strips in groups of three with right sides together along length, using different color combinations for strips in each group; press seams open.

Step 2. Subcut each strip set into 2" segments for A as shown in Figure 1. Join two A segments on

the short ends to make an A strip as shown in Figure 2; you will need 49 A strips. Set aside remaining segments for another project.

Figure 1

Figure 2

Step 3. Arrange the blocks in five rows of four blocks each referring to the Placement Diagram for positioning of blocks. Join the blocks in rows with five A strips as shown in Figure 3; press seams away from blocks. Repeat for five rows.

Figure 3

Step 4. Cut two 2" by fabric width strips blue print; subcut into 2" square segments for B. You will need 30 B squares.

Step 5. Join four A strips with five B squares to make a sashing row as shown in Figure 4; repeat for six sashing rows. Press seams toward B.

Figure 4

Step 6. Join the block rows with the sashing rows referring to the Placement Diagram for

positioning; press seams away from blocks.

Finishing the Quilt
Step 1. Sandwich batting between the completed top and prepared backing piece; pin or baste layers together to hold flat for quilting.
Step 2. Using all-purpose thread to match fabric in the top of the machine and white-all-purpose thread in the bobbin, machine-appliqué clown pieces in place with a medium-width zig-zag stitch.
Step 3. Quilt as desired by hand

or machine. *Note: The quilt shown was machine-quilted in the ditch of block seams using white machine-quilting thread.*
Step 4. When quilting is complete, trim batting and backing even with quilted top; remove pins or basting.
Step 5. Cut five 2¼" by fabric width strips blue print. Join strips on short ends to make one long strip for binding.
Step 6. Fold the binding strip in half along length with wrong sides together; press.
Step 7. Bind edges to finish. ✦

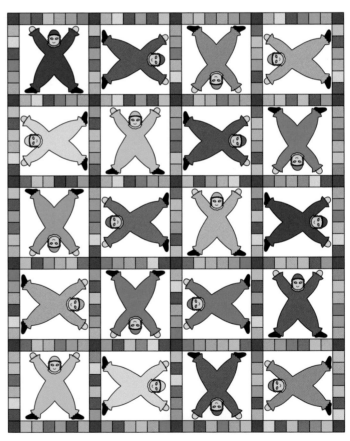

Cartwheel Clowns
Placement Diagram
43½" x 54"

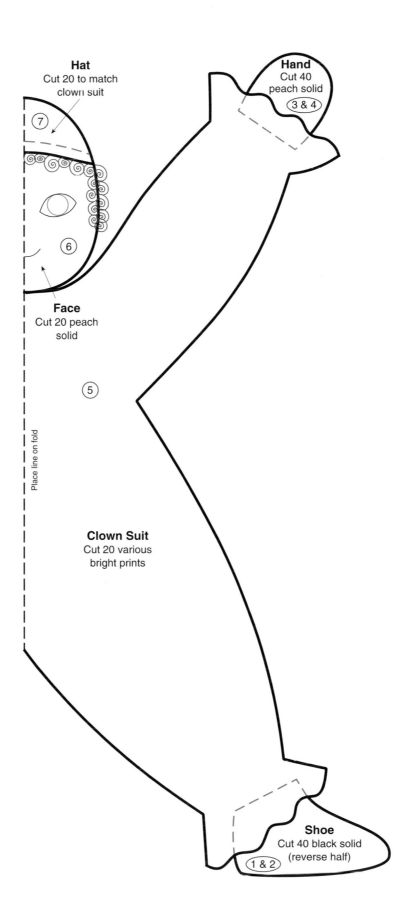

Hat
Cut 20 to match
clown suit

⑦

Hand
Cut 40
peach solid

3 & 4

Face
Cut 20 peach
solid

⑥

Place line on fold

⑤

Clown Suit
Cut 20 various
bright prints

Shoe
Cut 40 black solid
(reverse half)

1 & 2

PYRAMID & STARS CRIB QUILT

Lots of hand quilting fills the open spaces in this star-design quilt.

DESIGN BY JODI G. WARNER

Pyramid Hexagon
8" x 7" Block

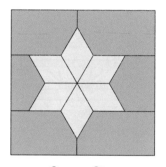

Corner Star
6" x 6" Block

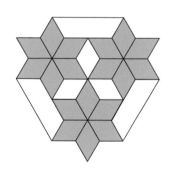

Star Cluster
8" x 8¹⁄₁₆" Block

Project Specifications
Skill Level: Intermediate
Quilt Size: 43" x 49"
Block Size: 8" x 7", 8" x 8¹⁄₁₆" and 6" x 6"
Number of Blocks: 6, 6 and 4

Materials
- 1 yard total scraps as follows: red/burgundy, pink, navy, medium blue, tan and ecru prints, solids or plaids for hexagons and border stars
- ½ yard medium blue print for stars
- ½ yard red print for border and binding
- 1 yard light tan print for background
- 1 yard dark tan print for border
- Backing 49" x 55"
- Batting 49" x 55"
- Neutral color all-purpose thread
- Red hand-quilting thread
- Basic sewing tools and supplies and water-erasable marker or pencil

Cutting Instructions
Step 1. Prepare finished-size templates for hand piecing using pattern pieces given. Cut as directed on each piece; transfer alignment markings to templates and to fabric patches.

Step 2. Cut two 1" x 37" strips red print for Q and two strips 1" x 31½" for R.

Step 3. Cut two strips 6½" x 37" dark tan print for S and two strips 6½" x 31½" for T.

Star Cluster Blocks & Units
Step 1. Join three medium blue print A diamonds as shown in Figure 1; repeat for two A units; press seams in one direction. Join two A units to form a star cluster as shown in Figure 2.

Figure 1

Figure 2

Step 2. To complete one Star Cluster block, join three star clusters with three light tan print A and three B pieces as shown in Figure 3; repeat for six blocks.

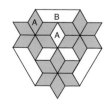

Figure 3

Step 3. To complete one double-star unit, join two star clusters with one light tan print A and two B pieces as shown in Figure 4; repeat for two double-star units for bottom edge of quilt.

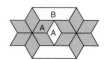

Figure 4

Step 4. To complete one single-star unit, sew H, HR and G to one side of one star cluster as shown in Figure 5 for left edge, bottom corner of quilt.

Figure 5

Step 5. To complete one left half-star unit, join two medium blue print G pieces with two medium blue print A pieces as shown in Figure 6. Join the half-star unit with one star cluster and light tan print A, B, G and HR pieces to complete one left half-star unit as shown in Figure 7.

Figure 6

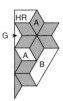

Figure 7

Step 6. To complete one right half-star unit, repeat Step 5 using H and referring to Figure 8; repeat for two units.

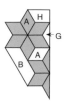

Figure 8

Pyramid Hexagon Blocks & Units

Step 1. Arrange 24 C triangles into a hexagon shape as shown in Figure 9.

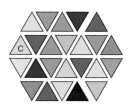

Figure 9

Step 2. Join C triangles into five-unit and seven-unit horizontal rows; press seams to right or left in alternating order.

Step 3. Join rows, aligning points to complete one block; press seams in one direction. Repeat for six blocks.

Step 4. Arrange 10 C triangles with four I triangles to make a half-hexagon unit as shown in Figure 10. Join triangles in rows; join rows to complete a half-hexagon unit. Press seams in one direction. Repeat for three half-hexagon units.

Background Units

Step 1. Sew D to each side of E; press seams toward D to complete one background unit

as shown in Figure 11; repeat for six background units.

Figure 10

Figure 11

Step 2. Sew D to K and add J to complete one right background unit as shown in Figure 12; press seams toward D or J. Repeat for two right background units.

Step 3. Sew D to KR and add J to complete one left background unit, again referring to Figure 12; press seams toward D or J.

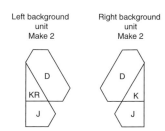

Figure 12

Center Panel Assembly

Step 1. Beginning at top edge, lay out one L and one J piece, two Star Cluster blocks, two F and two D pieces and one right half-star unit referring to Figure 13. Join adjacent edges of all pieces; press seams toward star unit and blocks.

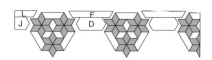

Figure 13

Step 2. Position one half-hexagon unit with two Pyramid Hexagon blocks in spaces below previously pieced unit as shown in Figure 14. Join adjacent edges of all pieces; press seams toward hexagons.

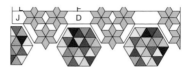

Figure 14

Step 3. Position two background units and one right background unit in spaces below previously pieced unit as shown in Figure 15. Join adjacent edges of all pieces; press seams toward hexagons or star units.

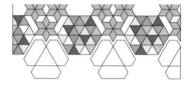

Figure 15

Step 4. Continue in a similar manner, positioning and then joining rows of star units and blocks, Pyramid Hexagon blocks and background units for three rows each of Star Cluster and Pyramid Hexagon blocks and background units referring to Figure 16.

Step 5. For final star cluster row, position and join the single-star unit at panel left corner with two double-star units. Complete lower straight edge by positioning and joining one L and two F pieces as shown in Figure 17; press seams toward star units.

Figure 16

Figure 17

Borders

Step 1. Sew Q border strips to opposite long sides and R border strips to the top and bottom of the pieced center, mitering corners; press seams toward strips.

Step 2. Join six same-scrap A pieces to make a star cluster referring to Step 1 of Star Cluster Blocks & Units; repeat for four scrap star clusters.

Step 3. Sew N, NR, M, MR, O and P to a star cluster to complete one Corner Star block as shown in Figure 18; repeat for four blocks.

Figure 18

Step 4. Sew a Corner Star block to each end of the T border strips with M pieces toward inside. Sew S border strips to opposite long sides and T strips to the top and bottom of the center panel; press seams toward strips. Round corners on the N or NR pieces referring to pattern.

Finishing

Step 1. Using the water-erasable marker or pencil, transfer the hexagon quilting design to the center of each star cluster and the heart quilting design over the background sections referring to Figure 19. Add vertical lines in the remaining background sections at ¾" intervals, again referring to Figure 19. Mark two ½" echo lines around corner star shapes with border cable quilting design in the S and T borders between star echo lines as shown in Figure 20.

Figure 19

Figure 20

Step 2. Sandwich batting between the completed top and prepared backing; pin or baste layers together to hold flat. Hand-quilt on all marked lines and in the ditch next to all seams (except miters) using red hand-quilting thread.

Step 3. When quilting is complete, remove pins or basting; trim edges even.

Step 4. Prepare 5¼ yards of double-fold bias binding from red print as shown in the General Instructions. Apply to edge, making miter folds at outside corners to finish. ✦

Pyramids & Stars Crib Quilt
Placement Diagram
43" x 49"

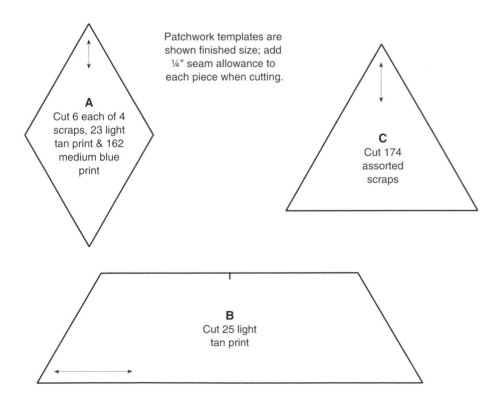

Patchwork templates are shown finished size; add ¼" seam allowance to each piece when cutting.

A
Cut 6 each of 4 scraps, 23 light tan print & 162 medium blue print

C
Cut 174 assorted scraps

B
Cut 25 light tan print

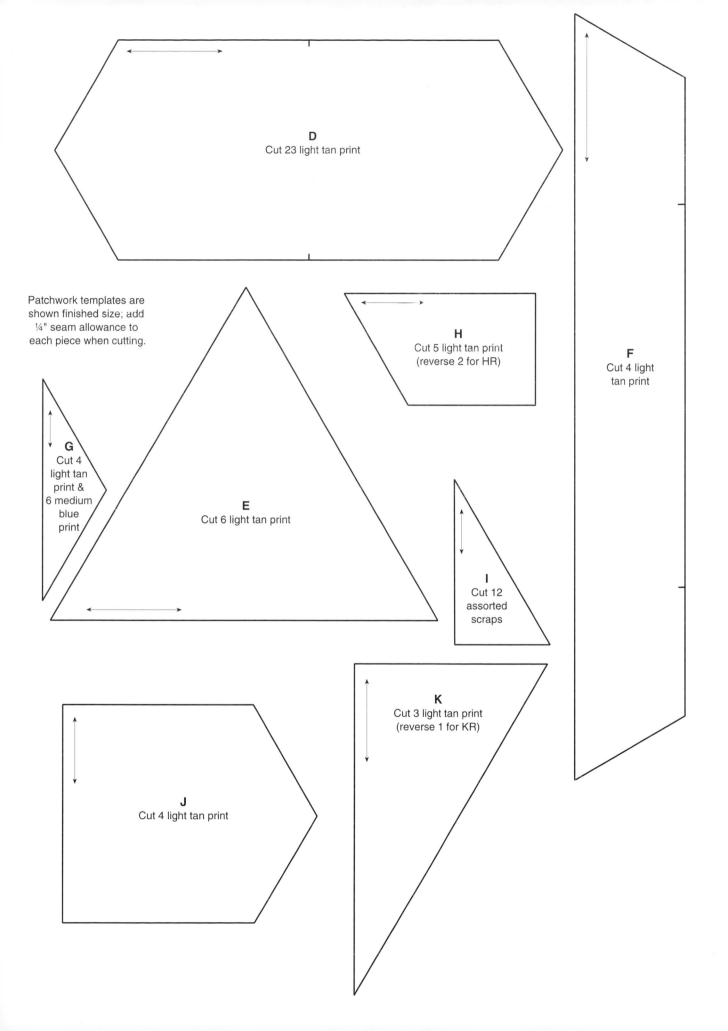

D
Cut 23 light tan print

Patchwork templates are shown finished size; add ¼" seam allowance to each piece when cutting.

H
Cut 5 light tan print
(reverse 2 for HR)

F
Cut 4 light
tan print

G
Cut 4
light tan
print &
6 medium
blue
print

E
Cut 6 light tan print

I
Cut 12
assorted
scraps

K
Cut 3 light tan print
(reverse 1 for KR)

J
Cut 4 light tan print

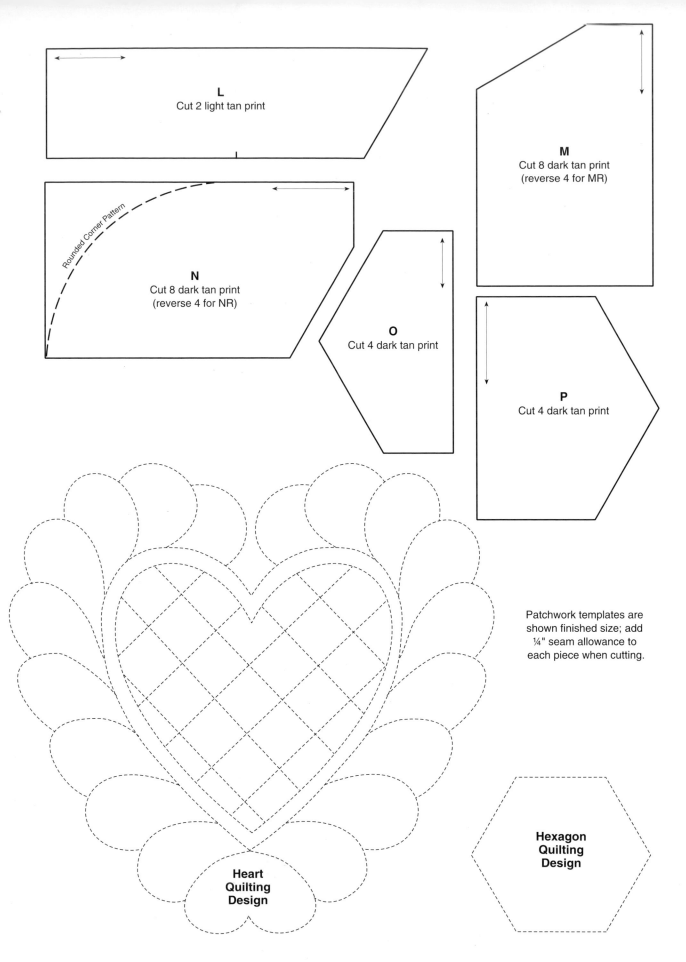

L
Cut 2 light tan print

M
Cut 8 dark tan print
(reverse 4 for MR)

Rounded Corner Pattern

N
Cut 8 dark tan print
(reverse 4 for NR)

O
Cut 4 dark tan print

P
Cut 4 dark tan print

Patchwork templates are
shown finished size; add
¼" seam allowance to
each piece when cutting.

**Heart
Quilting
Design**

**Hexagon
Quilting
Design**

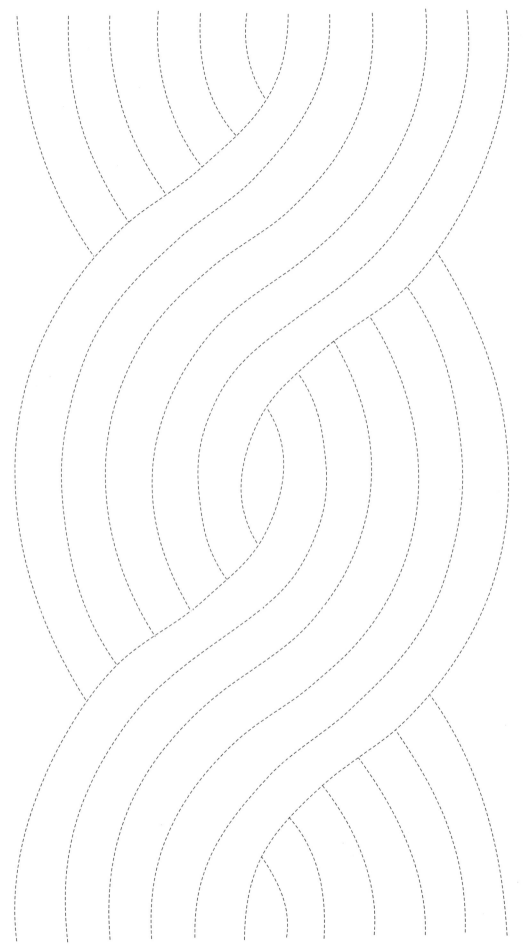

Border Cable Quilting Design

MOSAIC MEMORIES

The quilting lines create the appearance of seams where there are none in this easy lap-size quilt.

DESIGN BY JILL REBER

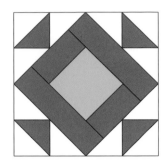

Mosaic Memories
8" x 8" Block

Project Specifications
Skill Level: Beginner
Quilt Size: 44" x 60"
Block Size: 8" x 8"
Number of Blocks: 24

Materials
- 24 different novelty print A squares 3⅜" x 3⅜"
- 12 different 6" by fabric width strips bright fabrics for B and C pieces
- ½ yard binding fabric
- ¾ yard border print
- 1⅜ yards white solid
- Backing 50" x 66"
- Batting 50" x 66"
- Neutral color all-purpose thread
- Quilting thread
- Basic sewing tools and supplies

Cutting
Step 1. Cut (11) 2⅞" by fabric width strips white solid; subcut into (144) 2⅞" D squares. Cut each square in half on one diagonal to make 288 D triangles.

Step 2. Referring to Figure 1, cut the following from each of the 12 different 6" by fabric width strip bright fabrics: four 1⅞" x 3⅜" B rectangles, four 1⅞" x 6⅛" C rectangles and two 2⅞" x 2⅞" E squares. Cut each E square in half on one diagonal to make four E triangles.

Figure 1

Step 3. Cut five 2½" by fabric width strips white solid for F and G strips.

Step 4. Cut five 4½" by fabric width strips border print for H and I strips.

Step 5. Cut six 2¼" by fabric width strips binding fabric.

Piecing the Blocks
Step 1. To piece one block, select one set of bright color pieces

and, referring to Figure 2, sew B to opposite sides of A; press seams toward B. Add C to remaining sides of A; press seams toward C.

Figure 2   **Figure 3**

Step 2. Join three D triangles with an E triangle to make a D-E unit as shown in Figure 3; press seams toward D pieces. Repeat for four D-E units.

Step 3. Join the D-E units with the A-B-C unit to complete one block; press seams toward the A-B-C unit. Repeat to make two blocks of each of the 12 fabrics to total 24 blocks.

Completing the Top

Step 1. Select three sets of same-fabric blocks; arrange in a vertical row as shown in Figure 4; repeat for four rows. Join the blocks to make rows; press seams of two rows in one direction and two rows in the opposite direction.

Step 2. Join the rows to complete the pieced center; press seams in one direction.

Step 3. Join the F and G strips on short ends to make one long strip; subcut into two 32½" F strips and two 52½" G strips.

Step 4. Sew F to the top and bottom and G to opposite sides of the pieced center; press seams toward strips.

Step 5. Join the H and I strips on

Figure 4

short ends to make one long strip; subcut strip into two 36½" H strips and two 60½" I strips.

Step 6. Sew H to the top and bottom and I to opposite sides of the pieced center; press seams toward strips to complete the pieced top.

Finishing the Quilt

Step 1. Sandwich the batting between the completed top and prepared backing; pin or baste layers together to hold.

Step 2. Hand- or machine-quilt as desired. When quilting is complete, trim batting and backing even with top; remove pins or basting. ***Note:*** *The quilt shown was machine-quilted using variegated quilting thread in the*

blocks as shown in Figure 5 to create an illusion of seams where there are none. The remainder of the background was machine-quilted with white thread in a meandering design.

Figure 5

Step 3. Join the previously cut binding strips on short ends to make one long strip. Fold the strip in half along length with wrong sides together; press.

Step 4. Sew binding to quilt edges, mitering corners and overlapping ends. Fold binding to the back side and stitch in place. ◆

Mosaic Memories
Placement Diagram
44" x 60"

GENERAL INSTRUCTIONS

Quiltmaking Basics

Fabrics

Fabric Choices. Quilts and quilted projects combine fabrics of many types. Use same-fiber-content fabrics when making quilted items, if possible.

Buying Fabrics. One hundred percent cotton fabrics are recommended for making quilts. Choose colors similar to those used in the quilts shown or colors of your own preference. Most quilt designs depend more on contrast of values than on the colors used to create the design.

Preparing the Fabric for Use. Fabrics may be prewashed depending on your preference. Whether you prewash or not, be sure your fabrics are colorfast and won't run onto each other when washed after use.

Fabric Grain. Fabrics are woven with threads going in a crosswise and lengthwise direction. The threads cross at right angles—the more threads per inch, the stronger the fabric.

The crosswise threads will stretch a little. The lengthwise threads will not stretch at all. Cutting the fabric at a 45-degree angle to the crosswise and lengthwise threads produces a bias edge which stretches a great deal when pulled (Figure 1).

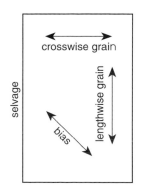

Figure 1

If templates are given with patterns in this book, pay careful attention to the grain lines marked with arrows. These arrows indicate that the piece should be placed on the lengthwise grain with the arrow running on one thread. Although it is not necessary to examine the fabric and find a thread to match to, it is important to try to place the arrow with the lengthwise grain of the fabric (Figure 2).

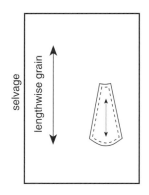

Figure 2

Thread

For most piecing, good-quality cotton or cotton-covered polyester is the thread of choice. Inexpensive polyester threads are not recommended because they can cut the fibers of cotton fabrics.

Choose a color thread that will match or blend with the fabrics in your quilt. For projects pieced with dark and light color fabrics, choose a neutral thread color, such as a medium gray, as a compromise between colors. Test by pulling a sample seam.

Batting

Batting is the material used to give a quilt loft or thickness. It also adds warmth.

Batting size is listed in inches for each pattern to reflect the size needed to complete the quilt according to the instructions. Purchase the size large enough to cut the size you need for the quilt of your choice.

Some qualities to look for in batting are drapability, resistance to fiber migration, loft and softness.

Tools & Equipment

There are few truly essential tools and little equipment required for quiltmaking. Basics include needles (hand-sewing and quilting), pins (long, thin, sharp pins are best), sharp scissors or shears, a thimble, template materials (plastic or cardboard), marking tools (chalk marker, water-erasable pen and a No. 2 pencil are a few) and a quilting frame or hoop. For piecing and/or quilting by machine, add a sewing machine to the list.

Other sewing basics such as a seam ripper, pincushion, measuring tape and an iron are also necessary. For choosing colors or quilting designs for your quilt, or for designing your own quilt, it is helpful to have on hand graph paper, tracing paper, colored pencils or markers, and a ruler.

For making strip-pieced quilts, a rotary cutter, mat and specialty rulers are often used. We recommend an ergonomic rotary cutter, a large self-healing mat and several rulers. If you can choose only one size, a 6" x 24" marked in ⅛" or ¼" increments is recommended.

Construction Methods

Traditional Templates. While some quilt instructions in this book use rotary-cut strips and quick sewing methods, many patterns require a template. Templates are like the pattern pieces used to sew a garment. They are used to cut the fabric pieces that make up the quilt top. There are two types—templates that include a ¼" seam allowance and templates that don't.

Choose the template material and the pattern. Transfer the pattern shapes to the template material with a sharp No. 2 lead pencil. Write the pattern name, piece letter or number, grain line, and number to cut for one block or whole quilt on each piece as shown in Figure 3.

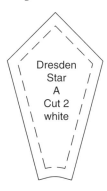

Figure 3

Some patterns require a reversed piece as shown in Figure 4. These patterns are labeled with an R after the piece letter; for example, B and BR. To reverse a template, first cut it with the labeled side up and then with the labeled side down. Compare these to the right and left fronts of a blouse. When making a garment,

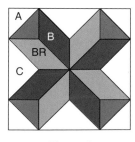

Figure 4

you accomplish reversed pieces when cutting the pattern on two layers of fabric placed with right sides together. This can be done when cutting templates as well.

If cutting one layer of fabric at a time, first trace the template onto the back side of the fabric with the marked side down; turn the template over with the marked side up to make reverse pieces.

Hand-Piecing Basics. When hand-piecing, it is easier to begin with templates that do not include the ¼" seam allowance. Place the template on the wrong side of the fabric, lining up the marked grain line with lengthwise or crosswise fabric grain. If the piece does not have to be reversed, place with labeled side up. Trace around shape; move, leaving ½" between the shapes, and mark again.

When you have marked the appropriate number of pieces, cut out pieces, leaving ¼" beyond marked line all around each piece.

To join two units, place the patches with right sides together. Stick a pin in at the beginning of the seam through both fabric patches, matching the beginning points (Figure 5); for hand-piecing, the seam begins on the traced line, not at the edge of the fabric (see Figure 6).

Figure 5

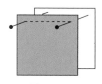

Figure 6

Thread a sharp needle; knot one strand of the thread at the end. Remove the pin and insert the needle in the hole; make a short stitch and then a backstitch right over the first stitch. Continue making short stitches with several stitches on the needle at one time. As you stitch, check the back piece often to assure accurate stitching on the seam line. Take a stitch at the end of the seam; backstitch and knot at the same time as shown in Figure 7. Seams on hand-pieced fabric patches may be finger-pressed toward the darker fabric.

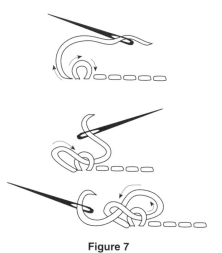

Figure 7

To sew units together, pin fabric patches together, matching seams. Sew as above except where seams meet; at these intersections, backstitch, go through seam to next piece and backstitch again to secure seam joint.

Not all pieced blocks can be stitched with straight seams or in rows. Some patterns, such as star designs, require set-in pieces. To begin a set-in seam, pin one side of the square to the proper side of the star point with right sides together, matching corners. Start stitching at the seam line on the outside point; stitch on the marked seam line to the end of the seam line at the center referring to Figure 8.

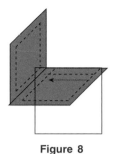

Figure 8

Bring around the adjacent side and pin to the next star point, matching seams. Continue the stitching line from the adjacent seam through corners and to the outside edge of the square as shown in Figure 9.

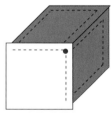

Figure 9

Machine-Piecing. If making templates, include the ¼" seam allowance on the template for machine-piecing. Place template on the wrong side of the fabric as for hand-piecing except butt pieces against one another when tracing.

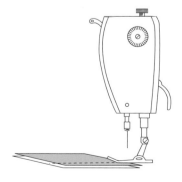

Figure 10

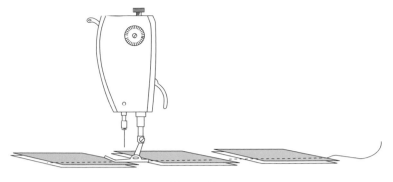

Figure 11

Set machine on 2.5 or 12–15 stitches per inch. Join pieces as for hand-piecing for set-in seams; but for other straight seams, begin and end sewing at the end of the fabric patch sewn as shown in Figure 10. No backstitching is necessary when machine-stitching.

Join units as for hand-piecing referring to the piecing diagrams where needed. Chain piecing (Figure 11— sewing several like units before sewing other units) saves time by eliminating beginning and ending stitches.

When joining machine-pieced units, match seams against each other with seam allowances pressed in opposite directions to reduce bulk and make perfect matching of seams possible (Figure 12).

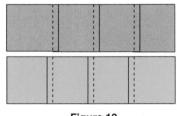

Figure 12

Quick-Cutting. Templates can be completely eliminated when using a rotary cutter with a plastic ruler and mat to cut fabric strips.

When rotary-cutting strips, straighten raw edges of fabric by folding fabric in fourths across the width as shown in Figure 13. Press down flat; place ruler on fabric square with edge of fabric and make one cut from the folded edge to the outside edge. If strips are not straightened, a wavy strip will result as shown in Figure 14.

Always cut away from your body, holding the ruler firmly with the non-cutting hand. Keep fingers away

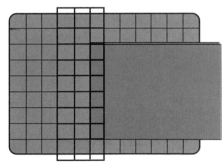

Figure 13

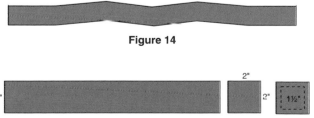

Figure 14

Figure 15

from the edge of the ruler because it is easy for the rotary cutter to slip and jump over the edge of the ruler if cutting is not properly done.

If a square is required for the pattern, it can be subcut from a strip as shown in Figure 15.

If you need right triangles with the straight grain on the short sides, you can use the same method, but you need to figure out how wide to cut the strip. Measure the finished size of one short side of the triangle. Add ⅞" to this size for seam allowance. Cut fabric strips this width; cut the strips into the same increment to create squares. Cut the squares on the diagonal to produce triangles. For example, if you need a triangle with a 2" finished height, cut the strips 2⅞" by the width of the fabric. Cut the strips into 2⅞" squares. Cut each square on the diagonal to produce the correct-size triangle with the grain on the short sides (Figure 16).

Triangles sewn together to make squares are called half-square triangles or triangle/squares. When joined, the triangle/square unit has the straight of grain on all outside edges of the block.

Another method of making triangle/squares is shown in Figure 17. Layer two squares with right sides together; draw a diagonal line through the center. Stitch ¼" on both sides of the line. Cut apart on the drawn line to reveal two stitched triangle/squares.

If you need triangles with the straight of grain on the diagonal, such as for fill-in triangles on the outside edges of a diagonal-set quilt, the procedure is a bit different.

To make these triangles, a square is cut on both diagonals; thus, the straight of grain is on the longest or diagonal side (Figure 18). To figure out the size to cut the square, add 1¼" to the needed finished size of the longest side of the triangle. For example, if you need a triangle with a 12" finished diagonal, cut a 13¼" square.

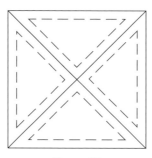

Figure 18

If templates are given, use their measurements to cut fabric strips to correspond with that measurement. The template may be used on the strip to cut pieces quickly. Strip cutting works best for squares, triangles, rectangles and diamonds. Odd-shaped templates are difficult to cut in multiple layers or using a rotary cutter.

Quick-Piecing Method. Lay pieces to be joined under the presser foot of the sewing machine right sides together. Sew an exact ¼" seam allowance to the end of the piece; place another unit right next to the first one and continue sewing, adding a piece after every stitched piece, until all of the pieces are used up (Figure 19).

Figure 19

When sewing is finished, cut threads joining the pieces apart. Press seam toward the darker fabric.

Appliqué

Appliqué is the process of applying one piece of fabric on top of another for decorative or functional purposes.

Making Templates. Most appliqué designs given here are shown as full-size drawings for the completed designs. The drawings show dotted lines to indicate where one piece overlaps another. Other marks indicate placement of embroidery stitches for decorative purposes such as eyes, lips, flowers, etc.

For hand appliqué, trace each template onto the right side of the fabric with template right side up. Cut around shape, adding a ⅛"–¼" seam allowance.

Before the actual appliqué

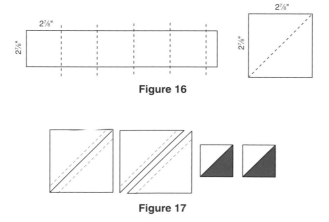

Figure 16

Figure 17

process begins, cut the background block. If you have a full-size drawing of the design, it might help you to transfer it to the background block to help with placement.

Transfer the design to a large piece of tracing paper. Place the paper on top of the design; use masking tape to hold in place. Trace design onto paper.

If you don't have a light box, tape the pattern on a window; center the background block on top and tape in place. Trace the design onto the background block with a water-erasable marker or light lead or chalk pencil. This drawing will mark exactly where the fabric pieces should be placed on the background block.

Hand Appliqué. Traditional hand appliqué uses a template made from the desired finished shape without seam allowance added.

After fabric is prepared, trace the desired shape onto the right side of the fabric with a water-erasable marker or light lead or chalk pencil. Leave at least ½" between design motifs when tracing to allow for the seam allowance when cutting out the shapes.

When the desired number of shapes needed has been drawn on the fabric pieces, cut out shapes leaving ⅛"–¼" all around drawn line for turning under.

Turn the shape's edges over on the drawn or stitched line. When turning in concave curves, clip to seams and baste the seam allowance over as shown in Figure 20.

Figure 20

During the actual appliqué process, you may be layering one shape on top of another. Where two fabrics overlap, the underneath piece does not have to be turned under or stitched down.

If possible, trim away the underneath fabric when the block is finished by carefully cutting away the background from underneath and then cutting away unnecessary layers to reduce bulk and avoid shadows from darker fabrics showing through on light fabrics.

For hand appliqué, position the fabric shapes on the background block and pin or baste them in place. Using a blind stitch or appliqué stitch, sew pieces in place with matching thread and small stitches. Start with background pieces first and work up to foreground pieces. Appliqué the pieces in place on the background in numerical order, if given, layering as necessary.

Machine Appliqué. There are several products available to help make the machine-appliqué process easier and faster.

Fusible web is a commercial product similar to iron-on interfacings except it has two sticky sides. It is used to adhere appliqué shapes to the background with heat. Paper is adhered to one side of the web.

To use, reverse pattern and draw shapes onto the paper side of the web; cut, leaving a margin around each shape. Place on the wrong side of the chosen fabric; fuse in place referring to the manufacturer's instructions. Cut out shapes on the drawn line. Peel off the paper and fuse in place on the background fabric. Transfer any detail lines to the fabric shapes. This process adds a little bulk or stiffness to the

appliquéed shape and makes hand-quilting through the layers difficult.

For successful machine appliqué, a tear-off stabilizer is recommended. This product is placed under the background fabric while machine appliqué is being done. It is torn away when the work is finished. This kind of stabilizer keeps the background fabric from pulling during the machine-appliqué process.

During the actual machine-appliqué process, you will be layering one shape on top of another. Where two fabrics overlap, the underneath piece does not have to be turned under or stitched down.

Thread the top of the machine with thread to match the fabric patches or with threads that coordinate or contrast with fabrics. Rayon thread is a good choice when a sheen is desired on the finished appliqué stitches. Do not use rayon thread in the bobbin; use all-purpose thread.

When all machine work is complete, remove stabilizer from the back referring to the manufacturer's instructions.

Putting It All Together
Finishing the Top

Settings. Most quilts are made by sewing individual blocks together in rows that, when joined, create a design. There are several other methods used to join blocks. Sometimes the setting choice is determined by the block's design. For example, a House block should be placed upright on a quilt, not sideways or upside down.

Plain blocks can be alternated with pieced or appliquéd blocks in a straight set. Making a quilt using plain blocks saves time; half the number of pieced or appliquéd blocks are

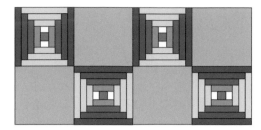

Figure 1

needed to make the same-size quilt as shown in Figure 1.

Adding Borders. Borders are an integral part of the quilt and should complement the colors and designs used in the quilt center. Borders frame a quilt just like a mat and frame do a picture.

If fabric strips are added for borders, they may be mitered or butted at the corners as shown in Figures 2 and 3. To determine the size for butted border strips, measure across the center of the completed quilt top from one side raw edge to the other side raw edge. This measurement will include a ¼" seam allowance.

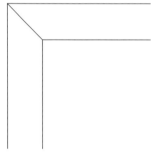

Figure 2

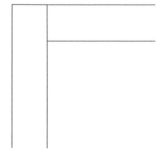

Figure 3

Cut two border strips that length by the chosen width of the border. Sew these strips to the top and bottom of the pieced center referring to Figure 4. Press the seam allowance toward the border strips.

Figure 4

Measure across the completed quilt top at the center, from top raw edge to bottom raw edge, including the two border strips already added. Cut two border strips that length by the chosen width of the border. Sew a strip to each of the two remaining sides as shown in Figure 4. Press the seams toward the border strips.

To make mitered corners, measure the quilt as before. To this add twice the width of the border and ½" for seam allowances to determine the length of the strips. Repeat for opposite sides. Sew on each strip, stopping stitching ¼" from corner, leaving the remainder of the strip dangling.

Press corners at a 45-degree angle to form a crease. Stitch from the inside quilt corner to the outside

on the creased line. Trim excess away after stitching and press mitered seams open (Figures 5–7).

Figure 5

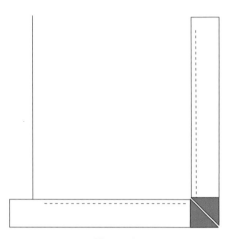

Figure 6

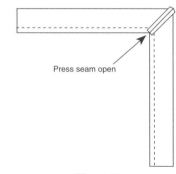

Press seam open

Figure 7

Carefully press the entire piece, including the pieced center. Avoid pulling and stretching while pressing, which would distort shapes.

Getting Ready to Quilt Choosing a Quilting Design.
If you choose to hand- or machine-quilt your finished top, you will need to select a design for quilting.

There are several types of quilting designs, some of which may not have to be marked. The easiest of the unmarked designs is in-the-ditch quilting. Here the quilting stitches are placed in the valley created by the seams joining two pieces together or next to the edge of an appliqué design. There is no need to mark a top for in-the-ditch quilting. Machine quilters choose this option because the stitches are not as obvious on the finished quilt. (Figure 8).

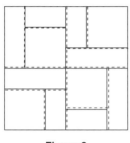

Figure 8

Outline-quilting ¼" or more away from seams or appliqué shapes is another no-mark alternative (Figure 9) that prevents having to sew through the layers made by seams, thus making stitching easier.

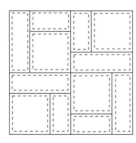

Figure 9

If you are not comfortable eyeballing the ¼" (or other distance), masking tape is available in different widths and is helpful to place on straight-edge designs to mark the quilting line. If using masking tape, place the tape right up against the seam and quilt close to the other edge.

Meander or free-motion quilting by machine fills in open spaces and doesn't require marking. It is fun and easy to stitch as shown in Figure 10.

Figure 10

Marking the Top for Quilting.
If you choose a fancy or allover design for quilting, you will need to transfer the design to your quilt top before layering with the backing and batting. You may use a sharp medium-lead or silver pencil on light background fabrics. Test the pencil marks to guarantee that they will wash out of your quilt top when quilting is complete; or be sure your quilting stitches cover the pencil marks. Mechanical pencils with very fine points may be used successfully to mark quilts.

Manufactured quilt-design templates are available in many designs and sizes and are cut out of a durable plastic template material that is easy to use.

To make a permanent quilt-design template, choose a template material on which to transfer the design. See-through plastic is the best because it will let you place the design while allowing you to see where it is in relation to your quilt design without moving it. Place the design on the quilt top where you want it and trace around it with your marking tool. Pick up the quilting template and place again; repeat marking.

No matter what marking method you use, remember—the marked lines should never show on the finished quilt. When the top is marked, it is ready for layering.
Preparing the Quilt Backing.
The quilt backing is a very important feature of your quilt. The materials listed for each quilt in this book includes the size requirements for the backing, not the yardage needed. Exceptions to this are when the backing fabric is also used on the quilt top and yardage is given for that fabric.

A backing is generally cut at least 6" larger than the quilt top or 2" larger on all sides. For a 64" x 78" finished quilt, the backing would need to be at least 70" x 84".

To avoid having the seam across the center of the quilt backing, cut or tear one of the right-length pieces in half, and sew half to each side of the second piece as shown in Figure 11.

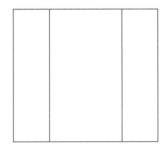

Figure 11

Figure 12

Quilts that need a backing more than 88" wide may be pieced in horizontal pieces as shown in Figure 12.

Layering the Quilt Sandwich. Layering the quilt top with the batting and backing is time-consuming. Open the batting several days before you need it and place over a bed or flat on the floor to help flatten the creases caused from its being folded up in the bag for so long.

Iron the backing piece, folding in half both vertically and horizontally and pressing to mark centers.

If you will not be quilting on a frame, place the backing right side down on a clean floor or table. Start in the center and push any wrinkles or bunches flat. Use masking tape to tape the edges to the floor or large clips to hold the backing to the edges of the table. The backing should be taut.

Place the batting on top of the backing, matching centers using fold lines as guides; flatten out any wrinkles. Trim the batting to the same size as the backing.

Fold the quilt top in half lengthwise and place on top of the batting, wrong side against the batting, matching centers. Unfold quilt and, working from the center to the outside edges, smooth out any wrinkles or lumps.

To hold the quilt layers together for quilting, baste by hand or use safety pins. If basting by hand, thread a long thin needle with a long piece of unknotted white or off-white thread. Starting in the center and leaving a long tail, make 4"–6" stitches toward the outside edge of the quilt top, smoothing as you baste. Start at the center again and work toward the outside as shown in Figure 13.

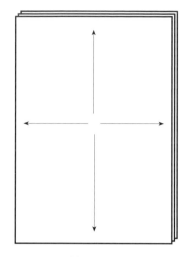

Figure 13

If quilting by machine, you may prefer to use safety pins for holding your fabric sandwich together. Start in the center of the quilt and pin to the outside, leaving pins open until all are placed. When you are satisfied that all layers are smooth, close the pins.

Quilting

Hand Quilting. Hand quilting is the process of placing stitches through the quilt top, batting and backing to hold them together. While it is a functional process, it also adds beauty and loft to the finished quilt.

To begin, thread a sharp between needle with an 18" piece of quilting thread. Tie a small knot in the end of the thread. Position the needle about ½"–1" away from the starting point on quilt top. Sink the needle through the top into the batting layer but not through the backing. Pull the

needle up at the starting point of the quilting design. Pull the needle and thread until the knot sinks through the top into the batting (Figure 14).

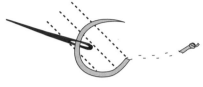

Figure 14

Some stitchers like to take a backstitch here at the beginning while others prefer to begin the first stitch here. Take small, even running stitches along the marked quilting line (Figure 15). Keep one hand positioned underneath to feel the needle go all the way through to the backing.

When you have nearly run out of thread, wind the thread around the needle several times to make a small knot and pull it close to the fabric. Insert the needle into the fabric on the quilting line and come out with the needle ½"–1" away, pulling the knot into the fabric layers the same as when you started. Pull and cut thread close to fabric. The end should disappear inside after cutting. Some quilters prefer to take a backstitch with a loop through it for a knot to end.

Machine Quilting. Successful machine quilting requires practice and a good relationship with your sewing machine.

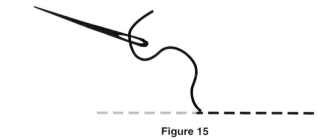

Figure 15

Prepare the quilt for machine quilting in the same way as for hand quilting. Use safety pins to hold the layers together instead of basting with thread.

Presser-foot quilting is best used for straight-line quilting because the presser bar lever does not need to be continually lifted.

Set the machine on a longer stitch length (3.0 or 8–10 stitches to the inch). Too tight a stitch causes puckering and fabric tucks, either on the quilt top or backing. An even-feed or walking foot helps to eliminate the tucks and puckering by feeding the upper and lower layers through the machine evenly. Before you begin, loosen the amount of pressure on the presser foot.

Special machine-quilting needles work best to penetrate the three layers in your quilt.

Decide on a design. Quilting in the ditch is not quite as visible, but if you quilt with the feed dogs engaged, it means turning the quilt frequently. It is not easy to fit a rolled-up quilt through the small opening on the sewing machine head.

Meander quilting is the easiest way to machine-quilt—and it is fun. Meander quilting is done using an appliqué or darning foot with the feed dogs dropped. It is sort of like scribbling. Simply move the quilt top around under the foot and make stitches in a random pattern to fill the space. The same method may be used to outline a quilt design. The trick is the same as in hand quilting; you are striving for stitches of uniform size. Your hands are in complete control of the design.

If machine quilting is of interest to you, there are several very good books available at quilt shops that will help you become a successful machine quilter.

Finishing the Edges

After your quilt is tied or quilted, the edges need to be finished. Decide how you want the edges of your quilt finished before layering the backing and batting with the quilt top.

Without Binding—Self-Finish.
There is one way to eliminate adding an edge finish. This is done before quilting. Place the batting on a flat surface. Place the pieced top right side up on the batting. Place the backing right sides together with the pieced top. Pin and/or baste the layers together to hold flat referring to Layering the Quilt Sandwich.

Begin stitching in the center of one side using a ¼" seam allowance, reversing at the beginning and end of the seam. Continue stitching all around and back to the beginning side. Leave a 12" or larger opening. Clip corners to reduce excess. Turn right side out through the opening. Slipstitch the opening closed by hand. The quilt may now be quilted by hand or machine.

The disadvantage to this method is that once the edges are sewn in, any creases or wrinkles that might form during the quilting process cannot be flattened out. Tying is the preferred method for finishing a quilt constructed using this method.

Bringing the backing fabric to the front is another way to finish the quilt's edge without binding. To accomplish this, complete the quilt as for hand or machine quilting. Trim the batting only even with the front. Trim the backing 1" larger than the completed top all around.

Turn the backing edge in ½" and then turn over to the front along edge of batting. The folded edge may be machine-stitched close to the edge through all layers or blind-stitched in place to finish.

The front may be turned to the back. If using this method, a wider front border is needed. The backing and batting are trimmed 1" smaller than the top, and the top edge is turned under ½" and then turned to the back and stitched in place.

One more method of self-finish may be used. The top and backing may be stitched together by hand at the edge. To accomplish this, all quilting must be stopped ½" from the quilt-top edge. The top and backing of the quilt are trimmed even and the batting is trimmed to ¼"–½" smaller. The edges of the top and backing are turned in ¼"–½" and blind-stitched together at the very edge.

These methods do not require the use of extra fabric and save time in preparation of binding strips; they are not as durable as an added binding.

Binding. The technique of adding extra fabric at the edges of the quilt is called binding. The binding encloses the edges and adds an extra layer of fabric for durability.

To prepare the quilt for the addition of the binding, trim the batting and backing layers flush with the top of the quilt using a rotary cutter and ruler or shears. Using a walking-foot attachment (sometimes called an even-feed foot attachment), machine-baste the three layers together all around approximately ⅛" from the cut edge.

Bias binding may be purchased in packages and in many colors. The advantage to self-made binding is that you can use fabrics from your quilt to coordinate colors. Double-fold, straight-grain binding and double-fold, bias-grain binding are two of the most commonly used types of binding.

Double-fold, straight-grain binding is used on smaller projects with right-angle corners. Double-fold, bias-grain binding is best suited for bed-size quilts or quilts with rounded corners.

To make double-fold, straight-grain binding, cut 2¼"-wide strips of fabric across the width or down the length of the fabric totaling the perimeter of the quilt plus 10". The strips are joined as shown in Figure 16 and pressed in half wrong sides together along the length using an iron on a cotton setting with no steam.

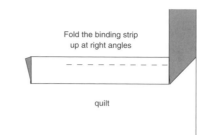

Figure 18

Fold the binding strip up at right angles

quilt

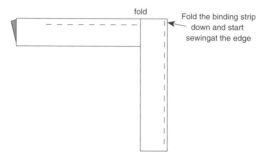

Figure 19

fold

Fold the binding strip down and start sewing at the edge

Figure 16

Lining up the raw edges, place the binding on the top of the quilt and begin sewing (again using the walking foot) approximately 6" from the beginning of the binding strip. Stop sewing ¼" from the first corner, leave the needle in the quilt, turn and sew diagonally to the corner as shown in Figure 17.

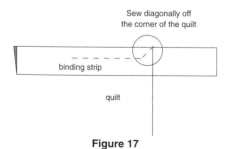

Sew diagonally off the corner of the quilt

binding strip

quilt

Figure 17

Fold the binding at a 45-degree angle up and away from the quilt as shown in Figure 18 and back down flush with the raw edges. Starting at the

top raw edge of the quilt, begin sewing the next side as shown in Figure 19. Repeat at the next three corners.

As you approach the beginning of the binding strip, stop stitching and overlap the binding ½" from the edge; trim. Join the two ends with a ¼" seam allowance and press the seam open. Reposition the joined binding along the edge of the quilt and resume stitching to the beginning.

To finish, bring the folded edge of the binding over the raw edges and blind-stitch the binding in place over the machine-stitching line on the back side. Hand-miter the corners on the back as shown in Figure 20.

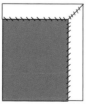

Figure 20
Miter and stitch the corners as shown.

If you are making a quilt to be used on a bed, you may want to use double-fold, bias-grain bindings because the many threads that cross each other along the fold at the edge of the quilt make it a more durable binding.

Cut 2¼"-wide bias strips from a large square of fabric. Join the strips as illustrated in Figure 16 and press the seams open. Fold the beginning end of the bias strip ¼" from the raw edge and press. Fold the joined strips in half along the long side, wrong sides together, and press with no steam (Figure 21).

Follow the same procedures as previously described for preparing the quilt top and sewing the binding to the quilt top. Treat the corners just as you treated them with straight-grain binding.

Figure 21

Since you are using bias-grain binding, you do have the option to just eliminate the corners if this option doesn't interfere with the patchwork in the quilt. Round the corners off by placing one of your dinner plates at the corner and rotary-cutting the gentle curve (Figure 22).

Figure 22

As you approach the beginning of the binding strip, stop stitching and lay the end across the beginning so it will slip inside the fold. Cut the end at a 45-degree angle so the raw edges are contained inside the beginning of the strip (Figure 23). Resume stitching to the beginning. Bring the fold to the back of the quilt and hand-stitch as previously described.

Figure 23

Overlapped corners are not quite as easy as rounded ones, but they are a bit easier than mitering. To make overlapped corners, sew binding strips to opposite sides of the quilt top. Stitch edges down to finish. Trim ends even.

Sew a strip to each remaining side, leaving 1½"–2" excess at each end. Turn quilt over and fold binding down even with previous finished edge as shown in Figure 24.

Fold binding in toward quilt and stitch down as before, enclosing the previous bound edge in the seam as shown in Figure 25. It may be necessary to trim the folded-down section to reduce bulk.

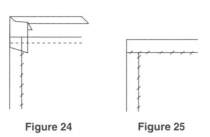

Figure 24   **Figure 25**

Instead of cutting individual bias strips and sewing them together, you may make continuous bias binding.

Cut a square 21" x 21" from chosen binding fabric. Cut the square once on the diagonal to make two triangles as shown in Figure 26. With right sides together, join the two triangles with a ¼" seam allowance as shown in Figure 27; press seam open to reduce bulk.

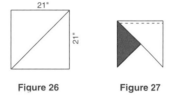

Figure 26   **Figure 27**

Mark lines every 2¼" on the wrong side of the fabric as shown in Figure 28. Bring the short ends together, right sides together, offsetting one line as shown in Figure 29; stitch to make a tube. This will seem awkward.

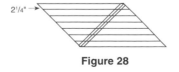

Figure 28

Begin cutting at point A as shown in Figure 30; continue cutting along marked line to make one continuous

Figure 29

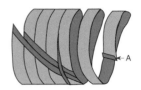

Figure 30

strip. Fold strip in half along length with wrong sides together; press. Sew to quilt edges as instructed previously for bias binding.

Final Touches

If your quilt will be hung on the wall, a hanging sleeve is required. Other options include purchased plastic rings or fabric tabs. The best choice is a fabric sleeve, which will evenly distribute the weight of the quilt across the top edge, rather than at selected spots where tabs or rings are stitched, keep the quilt hanging straight and not damage the batting.

To make a sleeve, measure across the top of the finished quilt. Cut an 8"-wide piece of muslin equal to that length—you may need to seam several muslin strips together to make the required length.

Fold in ¼" on each end of the muslin strip and press. Fold again and stitch to hold. Fold the muslin strip lengthwise with right sides together. Sew along the long side to make a tube. Turn the tube right side out; press with seam at bottom or centered on the back.

Hand-stitch the tube along the top of the quilt and the bottom of the tube to the quilt back, making sure the quilt lies flat. Stitches should not go through to the front of the quilt and don't need to be too close together as shown in Figure 31.

Slip a wooden dowel or long curtain rod through the sleeve to hang.

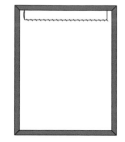

Figure 31

When the quilt is finally complete, it should be signed and dated. Use a permanent pen on the back of the quilt. Other methods include cross-stitching your name and date on the front or back or making a permanent label which may be stitched to the back. ◆

SPECIAL THANKS

We would like to thank the talented quilting designers
whose work is featured in this collection.

Betty Alderman
T Is for Tulips, 97
Peekaboo Yo-Yo Quilt, 120

Dana Bard
Bountiful Baskets, 159

Ann Boyce
Lazy Log Cabin, 74

Eunice Brower
Tipsy Trail, 60

Norma Compagna
Chimneys & Cornerstones, 43

Barbara Clayton
Winter Snowflake, 123

Nancy Brenan Daniel
Kansas Dugout, 80

Holly Daniels
By the Seashore, 175
Stained Glass Diamonds, 117
Stars & Swirls Toddler Quilt, 264

Mary Edwards
Log Cabin Stars at Midnight, 91

Lucy Fazely
Bear Paw Jewels, 180
Have a Happy Scrappy Christmas, 228
Patchwork Fun, 261

Lucy Fazely & Michael L. Burns
Garden of Eden, 184

Sue Harvey
Lollipop Flowers, 238
Posy Patch, 234
Summer's Dream, 155

Sandra L. Hatch
Broken Wheel, 51

Checkerboard Four-Patch, 220
Connecting Star, 35
Eight-Pointed Star, 17
Fruit Basket, 11
Grandmother's Flower Garden, 38
Job's Troubles Antique Quilt, 24
Scrappy Prairie Queen, 114

Connie Kauffman
Crazy Logs Kid's Quilt, 245
Plaid Lap Robe, 137
Polka-Dot Party, 249

Mary Jo Kurten
Sunflower Star, 69

Kate Laucomer
Nine-Patch & Four-Patch Stars, 83

Pauline Lehman
Antique Nine-Patch, 30

Toby Lischko
An Autumn Evening, 146
Red & White Frustration, 193

Chris Malone
Farm Animal Baby Quilt, 268

Janice McKee
Stars & Diamonds, 110

Marty Michell
Winding Ways, 129

Dorothy Milligan
Stars & Stripes, 164

Shirley Palmer
Tulips Around the Cabin, 132

Jill Reber
Here a Chick, There a Chick, 275
Mosaic Memories, 290

Judith Sandstrom
Cartwheel Clowns, 278
Love of Patchwork Friendship Quilt, 107

Carol Scherer
Rainbow of Rings, 46
Snowball, 20

Christine Schultz
Butterfly Dance Duo, 255

Karla Schulz
Christmas Puzzle, 209
Christmas Wreaths, 212
Teaberry Twist, 188

Barb Sprunger
Delectable Mountains Variations, 65

Ruth M. Swasey
Christmas Log Cabin, 231
Scrappy Stars, 56
Squares & Triangles, 89

Cate Tallman-Evans
Sunbonnet Sue, 6
Zoi's Violets, 101

Jodi G. Warner
Christmas Counter-Change, 224
Pomegranate Four-Patch, 196
Prairie Lily Wall Quilt, 151
Pyramids & Stars Crib Quilt, 282

Julie Weaver
Holly, Wood & Vine, 203
Oh, Christmas Tree, 206
Tic-Tac-Toe, 216
Turning Leaves, 141
Scrap-Patch Hearts, 252

Janet Jones Worley
Harvest Four-Patch Quilt, 77
Scrapwork Diamonds, 172